CHINA

Including Beijing, Guangzhou, Shanghai, and Shenzhen

Navjot Singh

503-968-6777
www.firstbooks.com

TABLE OF CONTENTS

INTRODUCTION

The initial conceptions that many people have of China are of people dressed in traditional Chinese costumes, busy streets filled with bicycles, men wearing pointy straw hats while pulling tricycles with their hands, men with shaved foreheads and long ponytails, and women with long silky hair wearing beautiful dresses. In reality it's not quite as you would have imagined! These days, a first-time visitor to China would be somewhat disappointed to know that most of these ancient stereotypical traditions of Chinese culture are to be seen in museums, Hollywood movies, or Chinese soap operas shown on state-owned television channels.

New arrivals into the country will also be taken aback at how surprisingly modern China has become. Though still miles behind other Asian developing countries such as Singapore or South Korea in terms of infrastructure and economy, it is, however, catching up rapidly with Western economies.

A developing country that is no longer just the most populous in the world, twenty-first century China is firmly placed on a fast track to being the largest trading power on the globe and among the top three economies. Many economic pundits are predicting that China's economy is set to overtake that of the USA by around 2050 and will continue to dominate the global economic scene. Above all else, moving away from the economic and political topics, China is also a very beautiful and romantic country.

Whatever differences China has had with its rivals in the past, these days no country wants to make enemies with her because the whole world is now enmeshed with China, politically and economically, as never before. Proof of this exists through the country's major cities, where foreign investment thrives on a massive scale. Two things strike a first-time visitor to China, the first being the massive population density and the other the amount of construction going on. "It looks like a huge building site" was what I thought when I first came, and at one time it was reported that roughly sixty percent of the world's cranes were in Shanghai alone!

Before the early 1980s there was no advertising on the streets or in other forms of media, there were very few cars on the roads (if you had a car you were considered a millionaire or even a billionaire!), and everyone wore navy blue Mao suits with Mao caps (including children and women).

1

A traditional Chinese girl in the Summer Palace in Beijing, 2006

So what do we have now? A country that has an endless hunger for modern cars, planes, trains, advertising, and fashion.

There are too many cars on the streets, too many planes (and too many airlines), people are wearing the latest designer clothes, an increasing number of Chinese people go on holiday abroad, and there is an abundance of advertising everywhere, marketing everything ranging from the latest electronic goods to the latest coffee being offered at Starbucks (yes, coffee being sold in China—no longer mission impossible!). Modernism and traditionalism, communism and capitalism—all seem to be living comfortably side by side. It's amazing how the Chinese have achieved this as it certainly is not an easy mix to deal with. The Chinese people are proud to be making history by contributing to the economic growth, and this emerging market has become a role model and a prime example for other developing nations to look up to.

And the run-up to the Beijing Olympics 2008 made the future for this country look even better. No country in history has seen such rapid economic growth in its culture, infrastructure, and environment in such a short period of time as China has. The objective of this book is not to be a tourist guide but instead to provide an insight into Chinese life and a guide for expats who are planning on relocating to China for a job, for marriage, or for whatever other purposes that they may have. For me it has been a privilege to witness the immense beauty and growth of this country at first hand and I hope that anyone who is coming to China for the first time to start a new life as an expat (for business or pleasure) would get contentment from the benefits of living in this stunning nation, as I have done. I wish you a very pleasant stay in China and hope this book provides you with a smooth welcome.

Quick Facts About China (中国, Zhong Guo)

Official Name	Zhōnghuá Rénmín Gònghéguó (People's Republic of China, 中国人民共和国)
	Not to be confused with the "Republic of China," as this is the official name of Taiwan.
Capital City	Beijing (北京)
Largest City	Shanghai (上海) (also China's financial capital)
Government	Socialist Republic. Communist Party members choose the leader and other think tanks. No general elections. The country operates on a one-government, two-systems policy where Hong Kong and Macau are designated as the Special Administrative Regions (S.A.R.), each one having a governor to oversee the day-to-day running, while all the important decisions are made by Beijing.
Leader of the P.R.C.	Hu Jintao (AKA Chairman Hu) is the party general secretary and President of the People's Republic of China.
Second Official in Charge	Premier Wen Jiabao
Establishment	People's Republic declared on October 1st, 1949
Area	9,598,086 km²
	3,704,427 sq mi
	China is officially the third largest country in the world by area.

Population	1,321,851,888 Officially the world's largest population. Although the figures vary slightly, some 20–25% of the world's population consists of Chinese people.
Special Economic Trade Zones	Shenzhen, Dalian, Xiamen, Hainan Island and Shantou.
Nationalities	Han (Approx 94%). The rest are minority groups made up of: Yao, Zhuang, Hui, Manchu, and She. There are officially 56 ethnic minorities listed in China, plus smaller tribal minorities within the rural areas.
Density	140/km² (72nd), 363/sq mi
GDP (PPP)	Total: $10 trillion, second in the world. Per Capita: $7,700, 84th in the world as of 2007
GDP (nominal)	2007 estimate Total: $2.68 trillion (4th in the world) Per capita: $2,040 (108th in the world)
Growth Rate (Overall)	For the past few years, China has seen a healthy growth rate of around ten percent annually. At present, this is higher than any other country in the world.
Currency	Renminbi, 人民币 (RMB, ¥) Symbol: CNY Approx 15.15 RMB is equal to £1 GBP Approx 8 RMB is equal to 1US$ Approx 10 RMB is equal to 1 Euro
Average Salary	Average salaries used to be very low in China, normally as little as 4000 RMB per annum for some professions. The last ten years have seen a steady rise in salaries for both farmers and city professionals. The current average salary for a degree-holding professional with 5 years' experience is around 6000 RMB per month.
Major Ports	Tianjin, Shanghai, Guangzhou, Hong Kong (S.A.R) and Qiangdao (Tsingtao).
Official Languages	Chinese Pǔtônghuà- 普通话, also known as Mandarin, 中文. There are seven main Chinese languages and at least another 56 minority languages.

Official Airline	Air China (IATA Code: CA) HQ: Beijing Capital Airport
Official Airport	Beijing Capital International Airport
Official Bank	People's Bank of China (Zhong guo ren min yin hang, 中国人民银行)
Time Zone	Beijing time is officially used, +8 Hours GMT (+7 Hours GMT during the summer). The country extends over five time zones; however the Beijing time is used exclusively.
Border Countries	(From East to West, anti-clockwise): North Korea (DPRK), Mongolia, Russia, Kazakhstan, Kyrgyzstan, Turkmenistan, Uzbekistan, Pakistan, India, Nepal, Bhutan, Burma, Laos, and Vietnam.
International Internet Domain	.cn (In 2006 there were just over a staggering 120 million internet users and this number is estimated to double every two years.)
International Calling Code	00 86
Water Coverage	2.85% of the Earth's supply
Rivers	China's major rivers are the Yangtze, Yellow River, Heilongjiang River, Pearl River, and the Huaihe River. The Yangtze River is the third longest in the world, and the longest river in China, with a total length of approximately 6,350 kilometers. The river snakes its way across major cities such as Shanghai, Nanjing, Wuhan, and Chongqing.
Food & Agriculture	Rice and noodles are the staple foods, while soya, cow's milk and various lentils are available throughout in abundance. China has become a country that can support its own people and be able to support people in the poorest of nations around the world. Remarkably only 15–20% of the land is arable. Self-sufficient food.
Top 10 Trade Partners	Australia, Britain, Russia, India, France, Germany, Italy, Japan, United States, South Korea
Electricity	China uses 220v/50Hz. Wall sockets have two or three pin connectors. It would be useful to have a travel voltage adaptor.

Age Structure	0–15 Years: 27.1% 15–65 Years: 68.5% 65 Years and above: 4.4% (2007 Figures)
Life Expectancy	69 (Male); 72 (Female)
Religion	Majority of Chinese people do not believe in god (Atheist). Taoism, Confucianism, and Buddhism are practiced by many, while there are minorities consisting of Muslims, Jews, Catholics and Protestants.
Products	Rice, potatoes, corn, sorghum, millet, wheat, sugar cane, peanuts, soybeans, sesame, tea; silk cocoons, ambary hemp, jute; sun-cured tobacco; bananas, oranges, lychees, pineapples, longans, and other tropical and subtropical fruits; rubber, oil palm, sisal hemp; coffee, cocoa, lemongrass, pepper; oyster, abalone, pearl, sea horse, and other sea products; timber; wolfram, tin, antimony, bismuth, molybdenum, copper, lead, zinc, oil shale, salt, sulphur.

CHAPTER 1:
CHINA: A BRIEF HISTORY

Ancient China	Neolithic 12000–2000 B.C.	
	Xia 2100–1800 B.C.	
	Shang 1700–1027 B.C.	
	Western Zhou 1027–771 B.C.	
	Eastern Zhou 770–221 B.C.	770–476 B.C.—Spring and Autumn period 475–221 B.C.—Warring States period
Early Imperial China	Qin 221–207 B.C.	
	Western Han 206 B.C.–A.D. 9	
	Hsing (Wang Mang interregnum) A.D. 9–25	
	Eastern Han A.D. 25–220	
	Three Kingdoms A.D. 220–265	
	Western Chin A.D. 265–316	
	Eastern Chin A.D. 317–420	
	Southern and Northern Dynasties A.D. 420–588	Southern Dynasties 420–478—Song 479–501—Qi 502–556—Liang 557–588—Chen
		Northern Dynasties 386–533—Northern Wei 534–549—Eastern Wei 535–557—Western Wei 550–577—Northern Qi 557–588—Northern Zhou

	Sui A.D. 580–618	
Classical Imperial China	T'ang A.D. 618–907	
	Five Dynasties A.D. 907–960	907–923—Later Liang 923–936—Later Tang 936–946—Later Jin 947–950—Later Han 951–960—Later Zhou
	Ten Kingdoms A.D. 907–979	
	Song A.D. 960–1279	960–1125—Northern Song 1127–1279—Southern Song
	Liao A.D. 916–1125	
	Western Xia A.D. 1038–1227	
	Jin A.D. 1115–1234	
Later Imperial China	Yuan A.D. 1279–1368	
	Ming A.D. 1368–1644	
	Qing A.D. 1644–1911	

History

Given China's history of over five thousand years, it's no surprise that there is a lot of culture and heritage waiting to be absorbed in this vast land. It's not easy to describe the rich history of China in just a few pages, and so instead I will provide a brief outline. "**Zhōnghuá Rénmín Gònghéguó**" is the official Chinese name of the People's Republic of China (not to be confused with the Republic of China, which is the official name of Taiwan). However, in everyday usage, it is referred to as "Zhong Guo" (meaning "Middle Kingdom"). This name is thought to have been invented by previous civilizations to describe the central importance of China.

One of the proudest and most industrious people I have ever met, the Chinese people strongly believe that China is the future and it's the place to be in. The roots of this hard-working culture and pride lie in the history of the Chinese. Many inventions and concepts originated in China. Chinese science, transmitted to Europe, Africa, and the Middle East in waves, laid the foundations for many of the constituents of the modern world. Indeed, the

Chinese are known worldwide for much that we in the West take for granted without noticing that they are in actual fact "Made in China."

Approximately 3500 years ago the Chinese were heavily involved in the trade of silk and carving jade (both silk and jade are of high importance to the culture even today) as well as growing wheat and rice. Fireworks (namely gunpowder), paper, and the noodle (including pasta, spaghetti which, according to many historians, Marco Polo took back to Europe from China) were invented in China. The crossbow, used in Europe and the Middle East, was also invented in China.

The Chinese were also famous for recording events in a written language of thousands of characters. The first known dynasty was the Xia Dynasty (historians estimate that before the Xia was the Neolithic, from about 12000 to 2000 B.C.). The Xia ruled from about 2100 to 1800 B.C. By 1027 B.C. (during the reign of the Shang Dynasty) a full written language had been developed along with the first Chinese calendar being introduced. Next came the period of the Western and Eastern Zhou (pronounced Chou) Dynasty (1027–221 B.C.). This period saw the introduction of money, formal laws, metals (including iron) and the philosophy of Confucianism. The idea of Confucianism led to the idea of a "Mandate of Heaven" (known as Ti'en Ming), in which the Heavens tended to give the rulers a mandate to impose laws on the people. Ultimately this led to the Chinese addressing their Emperors as the "Son of Heaven." Since that period, this concept remained very much alive in Chinese culture, right up to the death of Chairman Mao Zedong in 1976. The "Mandate of Heaven" had various beliefs such as that natural disasters are caused by disapproval by the rulers of Heaven. Such was the superstition among the rulers that the "Mandate of Heaven" started to go hand in hand with the Daoist belief. This book won't delve any deeper into the concept of the Daoist belief because there is so much of it to write about and it goes beyond our scope.

During the period between 481 and 221 B.C. the Zhou Empire broke up into smaller kingdoms; this period was known as the "Warring States Period." Even today, historians refer to the Zhou Empire as the golden age in Chinese history and the Chinese are very much proud of this era as it established the firm foundations for the China that we witness today.

The Qin Dynasty (221–207 B.C., pronounced "Chin") had successfully defeated its enemies and united the empire in 221 B.C. The Qin Dynasty favored numerous construction projects instead of agriculture. These projects included the partial construction of the Great Wall, a monumental man-made structure, claimed to be visible from space by the naked eye, which has effectively become one of the iconic attractions of China. The consequent famine resulting from the lack of concentration in agriculture assisted in the upsurge of a farmer's revolt, which eventually ended with the fall of the Qin Dynasty.

Subsequent to the Qin's rule came the four-hundred-year reign of the Western and Eastern Han dynasties (206 B.C. until 220 A.D.) which orchestrated an increase in relationships with cultures in central Asia. This allowed China to exchange its silk for precious minerals such as gold, all along the famous Silk Road that runs through the Northwest of China and into some countries in Central Asia.

During this period, Buddhism from India was established for the first time in China. Despite the Han Dynasty only ruling for approximately four hundred years, its influence on the Chinese people was vital, and even today the native Chinese are known as the "Han," while the alternative word used for Mandarin is "Hanyu" (pronounced "Han U").

The Han Dynasty's demise put the country into almost four hundred years of civil war, brought on by an uprising and social divide that split the country into three territories. Not long after that, the Sui Dynasty (580–618 A.D.) came into power, which formed a new government by reuniting China. The Sui Dynasty gave way to the Tang Dynasty (618–907 A.D.). The Tang Dynasty had its government seat based in the capital of Shaanxi province, Xian (then known as Chang'An). The Tang Dynasty did not last long either, as it experienced war and an economic decline that led to a period of approximately fifty years of no rule until the arrival of the Song Dynasty in 960 A.D.

The introduction of the Song Dynasty paved the way for trade with most foreign countries, especially in Africa and the Middle East, to flourish. Towards the conclusion of the Song Dynasty's ruling years came an explorer from the west called Marco Polo. His travels in China lasted almost two decades and during that time, some historians claim that some trade secrets were taken back to Europe, such as noodles—hence the introduction of pasta in Italy! Despite all of this there was a considerable amount of instability and threat looming in northern China. Genghis Khan, emperor of the Mongol Empire, which had already taken control of Russia and Central Asia, took over China in 1279, therein ending the rule of the Song Dynasty.

The grandson of Genghis Khan, Kublai Khan, took control of Beijing and declared the city to be the capital of the Mongol Empire. The Mongols did not last long and were eventually succeeded by the Ming Dynasty in 1368. It was during the reign of the Ming Dynasty that the first foreigners to arrive by sea into China, the Portuguese, arrived into the southern city of Guangzhou in 1516. Around this time the Portuguese started making Macau a home away from home. The British, Spanish, and the Dutch followed in subsequent years. The Ming Dynasty, instead of focusing on all these foreign visitors that were coming into southern China, was deeply embedded in preventing any threats from other advances such as Mongolian highwaymen and Japanese pirates in northern China.

The Ming Dynasty was eventually succeeded by the Qing administration in 1644. Between this time and the early 1800s, there is a lot to write about; however the next interesting era in Chinese history didn't arrive until the early 1800s when the British started selling smuggled Indian-grown opium to the Chinese, in return for tea and silk. This smuggling of opium started to cause widespread addiction throughout the country, naturally disturbing the Qing government.

In return for the opium, the British demanded that the payment be made in silver. However with finances running short and the opium trade blossoming, the Qing emperors were not able to meet the demands of the British and therefore confiscated all the opium from Guangdong province. This provided a perfect setting for a conflict between the British and the Qing government and hence resulted in the commencement of the Opium Wars. There were two major Opium Wars, with the first one taking place between 1839 and 1842, in which the British attacked Guangzhou and Nanjing. During the course of these Opium Wars the Chinese were forced to open up six ports (including Hong Kong and Shanghai) for trade purposes with Europe. The second Opium War started in 1856 and was prosecuted by the British and the French against the Qing Dynasty for four years.

Towards the beginning of the 19th century, the powerhouses of Britain, Germany, Russia, and France made separate attempts to colonize China, with Shanghai bearing the brunt of the impact. None of these attempts was successful, and following an open door policy led by America, colonial partition was eventually vetoed. Because of this experience, the Chinese know what it is like to be under colonial rule, which may provide enough evidence to counter any suggestion from economic think tanks, who believe that the Communist party wants to colonize the African continent in this day and age.

During and after the Opium Wars, peasants were angered with the liberties that foreigners were taking at China's cost. The boxers or "Anti-western society of the harmonious fist" (direct translation from their Chinese name), as they were known, were formed by peasants, starting in Shandong province. They put into practice a principle called the "Boxer Rebellion," which cemented their nationalistic viewpoint that all foreigners should be expelled from China. The bloodbath that followed included the deaths of many foreigners and destruction of any infrastructure which they brought with them into China, such as churches, ships, train lines, and even their homes. This did not last long and eventually the Boxers were defeated by foreign armed forces. This brought further bad news for the Qing Dynasty, which became powerless overnight.

Dr. Sun Yat Sen (formally known as Sun Zhongshan) was the leader of the National People's Party (known as the Guomindang), who with his revolutionary leadership in 1911 tried to bring democracy to China. He was partly responsible for the overthrowing of the Qing Dynasty and the expulsion of foreigners from China. Victory was gained in 1912 for the revolutionists and Dr. Sun Yat Sen proudly declared the birth of the People's Republic of China. A new flag was introduced and Dr. Sun Yat Sen became an overnight hero throughout China, and was subsequently better known as the father of modern China. Even today, most cities have parks, roads, educational establishments, shopping centers, hospitals and lakes named after him. Even the city of his birth, Zhongshan in Guangdong province, bears the great man's name.

Meanwhile the Japanese had taken the German colonized port of Qingdao in the aftermath of World War One and were advancing further into Shandong province.

In 1921 the Chinese Communist Party was founded and in the same year Dr. Sun Yat Sen was elected the leader of the National People's Party, the Guomindang. In the years ahead, both the Communist party and the Guomindang party worked together on many issues ranging from agriculture, which won them the support from the peasants, to the economy. After Dr. Sun Yat Sen's death in 1925, his brother-in-law Chiang Kai-Shek (Jiang Jieshe) took over the nationalist party. Instead of working together with the communists, Chiang Kai-Shek fell out with them and there was a period of civil unrest from 1926 onwards.

Around the same time the Japanese took control of Shanghai in 1937, followed by Beijing and Nanjing (including the Nanjing massacre), and eventually made inroads into Guangzhou. These were understandably painful times for the Chinese, as they bore the aggression by the Japanese. According to many Chinese history books, bodies, some horribly mutilated by the Japanese samurai, lay scattered in major cities such as Shanghai or Nanjing, and people were starving to death, naturally engendering even until today strong feelings against the Japanese. With the most modern days, relations between the two nations are getting somewhat better given the fact that most Chinese people today drive Japanese-manufactured cars and indulge in Japanese food.

Led by Mao Zedong, almost 81,000 communists responded to the military campaign from the nationalists by taking part in the famous "Long March" that started off in southeast China and made its way to the northwest of the country, stretching a distance of just over three thousand miles. By the time the marchers reached its final point at Yan'an in Shaanxi province, only about eleven percent of the troops had survived the journey. Coming from an affluent farmer's family, Mao had belief and trust in peasants, miners, and laborers. He in return won their support, admiration, and trust.

While all of this was going on in the south, the Japanese were attacking major northern cities, especially Shanghai, where many foreigners became trapped in unfortunate events. Quite a number of movies have portrayed these events in China's history, the most famous of which is the Hollywood movie *Empire of the Sun*, directed by Stephen Spielberg, which illustrates to viewers how foreigners coped during the Japanese occupation of Shanghai.

After the Japanese finally surrendered in 1945, a civil war erupted between the nationalists and the communists the following year, and in 1949 the Red Army (later known as the People's Liberation Army or PLA as they are known today) led by Mao Zedong defeated the nationalists in Nanjing. Chiang Kai-Shek withdrew to Taiwan (then known as Formosa Island) along with two million other refugees.

This finally led to Chairman Mao Zedong to stand in Tiananmen Square in front of thousands of people and officially declare the 1st of October 1949 as a national day. The People's Republic of China was confirmed as a communist state and China was officially born!

Subsequent to the declaration, China enjoyed her first few years as a sovereign republic and the early 1950s seemed to be prosperous for her people. Then with the economy improving, Mao Zedong introduced the principle of the "Great Leap Forward" in 1958, a five-year ambitious plan to accelerate the Chinese economy to bring it to par with most developed countries. This did not materialize as the Communist party wanted it to; with natural disasters causing widespread damage to the economy in 1959, things did not go quite as planned. During this time China sadly bore the brunt of the world's worst famine, leading to the bereavement of almost nineteen million people.

China's economy went in a down spiral, bringing about massive protests in 1966 from students who denounced their educational establishment administrations; an era that Chairman Mao called the "Great Cultural Revolution" began. Under Mao's teachings, many of Beijing's students organized themselves into a political private army called the "Red Guards." The Red Guards were up in force against party opponents, at times almost taking the country to the brink of another civil war.

China was effectively separated from the world as all western philosophies were neglected. Mao consistently encouraged the Chinese people to take notice of the farmers and those not so well off. His famous slogan "the poorer the better" was something that people looked up to during the Cultural Revolution. China, in those days, was in a state of chaos that led to academics being publicly humiliated and tortured. The only books available to read were "The Quotations of Chairman Mao" or the "Little Red Book of Thoughts" as it was known, or other minor communist propaganda material. Many of the ideologies of the Chinese Communist party were taken from the Soviet Communist party.

It was observed as somewhat of an opportunity to rekindle relations with the west when President Nixon paid a visit to Beijing in 1972 and went on a diplomatic tour of the Great Wall with Chairman Mao. In a way this thawed the period in which political brutality loomed over China.

Chairman Mao died on September 9th 1976. His portrait was placed on the top of the main gateway of the Forbidden City facing Tiananmen Square in Beijing, where his body is on public display at the mausoleum.

Towards the end of the Cultural Revolution, Deng Xiao Ping took control of daily duties within the Communist party in 1977, and started leading the country a few years after Mao's death. With Deng Xiao Ping at the helm, the

Chairman Mao's portrait looms over Tiananmen Square, Beijing

future became brighter. Deng actively encouraged foreign trade and opened Special Economic Zones (SEZ) across the east coast of the country, such as Shenzhen and Dalian, where an open door policy was inaugurated. As opposed to Chairman Mao's slogan of "the poorer the better," Deng's slogan of "to get rich is glorious" is certainly being put to good practice in the current climate. Economic and political ties with the world started to improve; a prime example of this was the first China-Russia summit in Beijing since 1959, in May of 1989. Foreign investment increased and China's economy since 1979 has seen a doubling in figures every eight years.

Present Situation

The twenty-first century has already witnessed some remarkable events in China's history such as its entry into the World Trade Organization (WTO) in December 2001, which has enabled its economy to move forward at a rocketing pace. With rapid urbanization, a technological revolution could mean that manual jobs may be short lived. Thirty years ago the existence of foreign brands was unthinkable, along with the prospects for foreigners to open their private stores, as everything used to be state controlled. All of that is changing now, and for these reasons, an increasingly high number of expatriates are coming to live and work in China. The UK, USA, and many European countries are investing heavily in China's experiment with capitalism.

People are no longer starving, general standards of living are improving along with an increase in life expectancy, electric power cuts are rare, people have clean water in almost all of the major cities, infrastructure is one of the best in the Asia Pacific region, and Chinese people have an abundance of food and minerals. You might be amazed at how much rice people throw away these days and how they take things for granted, just as people do in the developed world. Mao would have been shocked to see all of this!

Higher standards of living in China are driving inflation high in Europe and the USA. It's having a direct impact on things such as food and fuel prices that have been steadily increasing. This is especially true in the western world, where there is a huge demand for cereals and dairy products.

Making Friends Around the World

In recent years the current Chinese government has made a number of attempts to sustain friendships with neighboring countries as well as with countries which in the past China may have had some differences with. There has been interest in building a stronger partnership with developing countries

*CHINA THE BEAUTIFUL (View of the Lake and Bridge
in Yuan Ming Yuan)*

such as India, Korea, and many countries in the African continent. Ever since
the foundations of the Communist party in 1921, there have been continuous
relationships with Russia as well as with all the major European countries.
Germany, France, Italy, Australia, Pakistan, and the USA are among some of
China's many trading partners. China continues to enjoy being a member of
the UN Security Council since November 1971.

China and the African Continent

An African friend told me that there is a saying along the lines of "Without
Chairman Mao there would be no China," "Without Deng Xiao Ping there
would be no modern China," and "Without modern China, there would be no
twenty-first century Africa." Cities such as Guangzhou and Shanghai have a
large number of expats from the African continent. China is the third largest
investor in Africa, with annual trade reaching over $29 billion in the 2006
financial year. There has been an increase in both passenger and cargo flights
between Chinese cities and such important African hubs as Nairobi (Kenya),
Addis Ababa (Ethiopia), Johannesburg (South Africa), and Lagos (Nigeria).
It sounds like a weird combination, but the China-Africa bonding is in actual

fact working quite well, even better than expected, as pointed out by some think tanks in the west. And the west is taking notice of this.

Although China has been open to traders from the African continent for thousands of years, China's presence and relationship with Africa has become stronger only since the late twentieth century. During a China-Africa co-operation summit in Beijing in the winter of 2006, leaders from all African countries were invited to sign numerous trade agreements and discuss vital roadmaps for the future of their solid relationship. One of the highlights of the summit was the announcement by President Hu Jintao of a $5 billion China-Africa development fund, described by Beijing as economic aid which will be used to invest entirely in Chinese business enterprises.

Such generous offerings of aid to the African continent by China have been greeted with open arms by some African governments because infrastructure, construction, and other aid come with hardly any of the governance and human rights strings that usually accompany western contributors.

China is providing tremendous assistance in the building of a modern twenty-first century Africa. China has by far the largest number of professionals based on the African continent compared with any other country, from Chinese doctors helping to treat AIDS victims to engineers building the much-needed infrastructure in some of the poorer regions. Amazingly, food (rice, wheat, and fruit) is provided to many African countries through international charities by China, a country that was classed as part of the third world only thirty years ago. In return Africa offers vast reserves of coal, oil, and gas to China and many African nationals who speak fluent Mandarin are attending Chinese universities or working for Chinese companies.

The relationship is so cemented that some economic analysts have also commented that perhaps China wants to colonize Africa, a rumor consistently denied by the communist government. Whatever the facts, it may well be that China could be the nation that assists in bringing most countries in Africa in line with other newly industrialized countries in the developing world. Clearly, for the moment, wooed by Beijing's hands-on approach, African countries are willing to fill whatever needs China may have.

China and India

Prior to the latter parts of the twentieth century, Asia's two largest neighbors, India and China, were, with all due respect, not close in any economic or political ways. Relations have been improving since the early twenty-first century following four decades of hostility over a border dispute that resulted in a short war in 1962. India still claims that China occupies 14670 square miles (38,000 hectares) of territory, while Beijing claims the entire North Eastern state of Arunachal Pradesh. Thankfully, with the change of the times, these two giants of Asia have established friendship years (2006 and 2007), joint military exercises, and exchange visits by political figures as well as captains of industry. Economic and political ties have been boosted since the 2006 visit by President Hu to India, when promising trade agreements were signed, including an annual forecasted trade figure of $12 billion by 2010 between the two countries.

The word "expat" was normally associated with people from Britain, America, or Western Europe who would get a tax-free western salary and live a life of luxury, similar to the colonial times in many ways. However all of this is slowly changing with the growing trend of globalization.

With the increasing exchanges of manpower between India and China, many of the software engineers and Indian businessmen working in China nowadays are classed as "expats" from India, and in exchange, a large number of Chinese businesses have started opening in India's major cities.

There has also been a steady increase in the number of mixed marriages between Chinese and Indian couples—in both countries—as well as a general interest in all things "Chindian" between the two cultures, such as clothes and food. For example, in Beijing I was very surprised to see a Chinese woman wearing a traditional Indian Salwar Kameez, and walking with her Indian husband.

Other positive signs of bonding between the two cultures have included Chinese state television CCTV airing a popular Indian soap opera called "Koshish Ek Asha" (dubbed in Mandarin) as well as occasional airing of popular Hindi cinema songs. Indian cinema megastar Shah Rukh Khan seems to be popular among the Chinese girls.

In 2006 Air China commenced services to India with a direct flight from Beijing to New Delhi (with a stop in Kathmandu), while Air India, India's flag carrier, started operations from both Beijing and Shanghai for the first time in history.

Another area in which these two Asian powerhouses are burgeoning is technology. Both China and India are major players in the international consumer marketplace, and the transition of both countries to all-digital information and entertainment networks is now fueling significant domestic demand for the latest electronic products, such as set-top boxes, which can bring the luxuries of satellite TV to the heart of even a rural village. With the world's attention firmly focused on India and China, the future can only get better and more interesting for these two nations. An enchanting insight into the importance of both India and China's entry as emerging economies is beautifully explained in the book *The World Is Flat* by Thomas L. Friedman.

China and Japan

Despite great efforts by both the Chinese and Japanese governments in recent years to put their past troubles behind and look forward to the future with confidence, some Chinese still have negative feelings towards the Japanese. On a positive note, there is a large amount of trade between the two nations, especially in the food and automotive manufacturing industries. When I asked one friend why there are Japanese restaurants everywhere in China and why Chinese people drive Japanese manufactured cars, all this despite the fact that most Chinese have uncomfortable feelings towards the people from the land of the rising sun, his reply was, to my surprise: "In China we have a saying: Will you drop a stone into the well when someone is drowning?" or "do you try to provide them with a rope to pull them?" He went on to confirm that the "Chinese don't think at times of difficulty that you should wash your hands and walk away in an old friendship, and in China friendship is a tradition." It goes without saying that this is very much true in all aspects of Chinese culture.

Tibet

Since the commencement of the Qinghai to Lhasa train route in the summer of 2006, Tibet has become economically open to the world and there is a feeling in the air that finally some of the restrictions seen in the past, such as traveling to/from the autonomous region and trading with Tibet, may well fade away in time. A celebratory mood was not only felt in Lhasa, but also in neighboring Nepal and India as well other parts of China, which are now more open for trade than ever.

It is feasible to make travel arrangements to Tibet from outside of China. Once in China, individuals or groups wishing to visit Tibet must join a group, which can be arranged by any Chinese travel agency. The travel agency will arrange for the necessary permits and collect any fees. The Chinese government requires all foreigners wishing to visit Tibet to apply in advance for approval from the tourist administration of the Tibetan Autonomous Region. More information is available from the Chinese Embassy or one of the Chinese consulates in your country, or, while in China, from your embassy or the nearest consulate general. Recently, some foreigners with long-term Chinese visas have experienced difficulty obtaining permits to visit Tibet.

The Future for China?

After the revolution in 1949, the Taiwanese government announced that mainland China would withdraw as a GATT (General Agreement on Tariffs and Trade) member, even though the Beijing central government never officially accepted this decision in public and in 1986, to the surprise of the international community, China rejoined GATT. During that time, China was one of the original members of the GATT. In 1994 the GATT was transformed into the WTO (World Trade Organization) and the entry of China into the WTO has been extremely significant in the country's modern economic history.

The advantages the WTO has brought to China include the direct decision-making based on straightforward cost considerations by foreign investors and businesses as well as factors such as tax, land use fees, labor and insurance. It's not just the "cheaper operative" and "distributive costs" that have contributed to the attractiveness of setting up businesses on the mainland; the logistics of distribution in China also mean that companies find it easier to set up production manufacturing plants in the major cities.

With the inaugural manned space flight in October 2003, captained by China's first astronaut Yang Liwei, and the future manufacturing of world-class semiconductor technology taking place in China, the next fifteen to twenty years definitely belong to this country. It is effectively an exciting time to be in this country and a privilege for those who are able to witness its immense growth. For example in the four years that I have lived in China, I have seen more changes than I have seen in twenty-seven years in the UK. Most expats comment that whenever they return to Europe or the States, the skyline and infrastructure does not change much, while in China the skyline and even your local road will most likely change in a very short period of time.

In the Chinese government's roadmap for the next ten years, a large proportion of the funds are for the improvement of newer cities (such as Shenzhen, Dalian, and Zhuhai) as well as the financial and infrastructural improvement of the country's agricultural industry. It will be interesting to see how long this economic boom is going to continue.

CHAPTER 2:
THE MAJOR CITIES

China is the world's third largest country by land area, and topographically the country is 35% mountains, 27% high plateau, 17% basin or desert, 8% hilly areas and 13% plains. Surprisingly, only 11% of the country is agriculturally useful. China is officially the world's most populous country, with approximately 1.3 billion people (2007 figures). It goes without saying that unlike in the past, when almost everyone lived under strict communist standards of living, nowadays there is a widening gap between the extremely rich and the poor, and they live side-by-side in the major cities. This chapter will describe some of the largest and well-known cities in greater China: Beijing, Guangzhou, Hong Kong, Macau, Shanghai, and Shenzhen. Although Shenzhen is not as large or well-known as the other cities, I have included it because of its vital economic importance as an emerging city where foreigners are coming to live and work in (especially those expats working in the oil, gas, and telecom industries).

Beijing （北京）

Beijing (or "Peking" as foreigners used to pronounce it) is the capital city of the People's Republic of China. History tells us that before Beijing was made a capital city by the Mongol Emperor Kublai Khan in the early thirteenth century, Xian and Nanjing were also capital cities of China at one time or another. In 1421 the third Ming Emperor moved his government from Nanjing to Beijing and he became the city's main architect, establishing Beijing as we know it today.

Geography

The city, with a population of almost thirteen million people, lies in northern China surrounded by the provinces of Hebei and Tianjin. The most striking thing any first-time visitor notices about Beijing is how symmetrical the city is, laid out in an east-west and north-south design. It must be one of the world's most carefully planned and laid-out cities. Everything from parks and roads to buildings is laid out as mirror images on either side. Unlike the other cities in China, it is a city that is becoming modern at a dizzying pace

Tian Tan, Beijing

while keeping intact its ancient historical features—there are areas of Beijing where people still live as they would have done hundreds if not thousands of years. For example the ancient way of traveling in China using bicycles is still largely practiced throughout the metropolis; however, these days the cycle lanes run side by side with multiple-lane carriageways that are flooded with vehicles of all shapes and sizes. Then there are the historic buildings lying side by side with large concrete blocks that have high shining glass, making Beijing look similar to any western metropolis.

Beijing's "Silicon Valley" is located in the northeastern areas of Shangdi and Qi Er Xi, where the likes of IBM/Lenovo, P&G, and many others have their China HQ offices. China's most prestigious seat of learning is also located around here, including Beijing and Qinghua universities (around the Wu Dao Kou area).

Climate

Winters are freezing with temperatures well below zero Celsius, while the summers are very hot and dry. Beijing's climate is defined as one of "continental monsoon." The four seasons are distinctly recognizable with a temperate spring, rainy summer, clear autumn, and a cold, snowy winter. The best time to be in Beijing is during the spring and autumn, especially during the months of April, May, September, and October. Unfortunately Beijing is also exposed to occasional sandstorms during the spring period, and sometimes in the autumn as well. These are propelled in from the Gobi desert and the outer Mongolian region, accompanied by rather windy conditions. The government has invested heavily to protect the city by improving the ecosystems in the suburbs to the north and north-west to prevent serious damage being done. It is generally considered that autumn is the best time to visit Beijing because the skies are clear and the weather is comfortable. The average temperature throughout the year is approximately fifteen degrees Celsius. The coldest month is January, with an average temperature of approximately minus five degrees Celsius and the hottest month is July at an average temperature of approximately twenty-eight degrees Celsius. Unfortunately, spring and autumn are shorter than summer and winter. Although winter is quite cold, indoor heating is widely available so the temperatures should not prevent you from traveling to Beijing.

Transportation

Buses

Beijing has a numbered bus system, from which you can distinguish the type of bus operating. Buses that are numbered in the 200s are used for night service. Buses that are numbered in the 800s are air conditioned and comfortable to travel in while the rest of Beijing's buses are older, more crowded, and shabbier than public transport in other cities. It is not uncommon to see a bus jam-packed at, say, 6 a.m. on a Sunday. There are four well-established bus terminals in the capital.

1. **Deshengmen bus station** is located within walking distance from either Gulou or Jishuitan subway stations. Deshengmen serves routes to the north of the capital, including (at the time of writing) an express service running every 15 minutes to the Badaling Great Wall.
2. **Dongzhimen bus station** is located close to the subway station that bears the same name. It is close to the expat area and Sanlitun, where most of the embassies are to be found.
3. **Majuan bus station** is located on Guanqumenwei Dajie in the southeast of the city and serves for most long-distance destinations to the east and south of the city.
4. **Yongdongmen bus station** is located in the south of the city next to the train station that bears the same name. There are plenty of long-distance

A crowded bus in Sanlitun district, Beijing

buses available to various destinations within Hebei province and to Tianjin and connections by rail to other cities in China.

Air Travel

The capital's only passenger airport, Beijing Capital International Airport, is located approximately 28 km to the northeast of the city center. The airport underwent some refurbishment with new runways and terminal buildings, all in preparation for the Beijing 2008 Summer Olympics. On average every year, over sixty international and domestic airlines use the airport. In 2007 Beijing airport handled more than twenty-nine million passengers.

Taxies

Taxies are ubiquitous, metered and available twenty-four hours a day. The base rate at the time of writing is ten Yuan (approx $1.50) between 6:00 a.m. and 11:00 p.m. for the first mile. Bear in mind that taxies are not allowed to drop off or pick up passengers on the roads surrounding Tiananmen Square.

Metro

Beijing has two metro (called subway in Beijing) lines in operation and an above-ground train line (line thirteen). Line two runs in a circular pattern around the city. It has connections with line thirteen at XiZhimen (to the northwest of the city) and DongZhimen (to the northeast of the city). Line one runs in an east-west direction across the city center between Pingyuoyuan and Sihui Dong station. The subway operates between 5.30 a.m. and 11 p.m. seven days a week. Tickets for using the metro are priced at three Yuan per single journey, irrespective of how many stops you make and can be used if you change lines. If your journey to the city center starts on line thirteen, then the price is five Yuan per single trip.

Three more lines should have been added to the Beijing metro system by the time of the Beijing Olympics. By 2020, Beijing's metro system will extend to 561 kilometers, surpassing London's Underground as the longest subway system in the world, according to a construction plan for the capital city's public transportation offerings. According to the plan, the 561 kilometers will be laid out along 19 lines knit together beneath the capital.

Unlike metro lines 1 and 2 (the loop lines), which encircle the Tiananmen Square area, the traditional city center, the new lines are expected to reach all the major corners of the capital.

In contrast with the other subway systems in China, where tickets are obtainable in coin-operated machines, the Beijing subway system requires you to purchase small paper slips from the ticket office. These need to be shown to a station attendant before you enter the platform.

Train Travel

There are two main stations in Beijing: Beijing Zhan and Beijing Xi Zhan (Beijing West Station). The former is located in the city center while the latter is located just south of the Junshi Gowuguan subway. Beijing Xi Zhan was opened in 1996. It's more modern and larger in size than Beijing Zhan and sends trains to the north and west of the city. Beijing Zhan is used for destinations to the south and east of the city (such as Shanghai for example). Currently Beijing Xi Zhan is classed as Asia's largest railway station, covering an area of over 510,000 square metres. However it will only enjoy this title for a short period as by 2010, Shanghai Hongqiao railway will overtake it as Asia's largest railway station.

Food and Shopping

Beijing has plenty of cuisines to cater to all kinds of tastes. In 2006 there were just over 8370 restaurants registered in the capital! The most famous foods are roasted duck, Beijing hot pot (boiled meat balls, slices of meat, and various vegetables) and dried fruit. Some of the tours operated by local

Squid and Scorpions are just some of the exotic treats
on offer in Wangfujing, Beijing

companies to the Great Wall and the thirteen Ming Tombs may also include a visit to a duck factory (normally on the outskirts of the city), where you can purchase all kinds of duck meat products, such as freshly made roasted ducks, sweets made from duck meat, duck pies, preserved duck meat, and medicine derived from the organs of ducks.

These factories also have a "live" exhibition where you can see the end–to-end production of roasted ducks from behind a reinforced glass wall. On one side of the shop floor you have the ducks quacking away, while on the other side you will see the roasted end product! A famous Peking duck restaurant, and also one of the oldest, established in 1864, is the "Quanjude Roast Duck Restaurant" on 32 Qienmen Avenue (Qienmen Dajie). The huge, luxurious dining hall is filled with diners eager to try the dishes on offer in their most authentic setting.

The two major areas for shopping are Xidan and Wangfujing. Xidan is located to the west of Tiananmen Square and Wangfujing is located to the east of the square. Both have a myriad of shops and restaurants, some offering the usual gifts and tags, while others offer more unusual items such as a cushion that contains self-heating crystals (once a button is pressed a chemical reaction causes the crystals to heat up and turn the hard bag of crystals into a soft hot cushion that can be used to keep warm at night), or you might like to try fried scorpions or freshly boiled beetles and worms in Wangfujing.

China's biggest indoor shopping mall, known as the Lufthansa Shopping Center, is located in Beijing. As well as shops and restaurants, the mall houses corporate and government offices (including airlines) as well as a large multi-story car park.

Places of Interest

Beijing's rich history and presence as the seat of government and education in China makes it a natural destination that is also full of great tourist attractions.

One of the largest open squares in the world, Tiananmen Square can accommodate up to a million people (although this has never been officially confirmed on record). The square has borne witness to many historical events, the most famous of which was the declaration of the founding of the People's Republic of China by Chairman Mao on October 1st 1949. From the spot where he made that speech, today Chairman Mao's portrait lies facing towards the south of the square.

Towards the west of the square is the Peoples Hall (Renmin Da Hiutang) and on the east are the Museum of Chinese History and the Museum of Revolution. Mao's Mausoleum lies in the south of the square, where his body lies in state and open to public view every day for a short while.

Towards the north of the Forbidden City is Beihai Park (Beihai Gong Yuan), home to the famous wall of nine dragons and the former palace of the Mongol Emperor Kublai Khan. To the south of the Forbidden City is the remarkable Tian Tan (Temple of Heaven), which dates back to the Ming Dynasty and lies splendidly in the middle of a park that, in harmony with most of the architecture of the capital, is symmetrical in all aspects, ranging from the lining of pathways to the trees. Inside the park are two marvelous structures, Qiniandian (Hall of Prayer for Good Harvests) and Hianqiutan (Altar of Heaven). The former is a wooden building, amazingly constructed without the use of a single nail, while the latter is a circular terrace.

Two historical palaces are located in the west of the city, Yi He Yuan (Garden of Cultivated Harmony) and Yuan Ming Yuan (Garden of Perfect Purity). Yi He Yuan (more commonly known in English as the "Summer Palace") is a wonderful landscape of small parks, gardens, romantic pathways and temples. On a lake there, called the Kunming He, which covers approximately twenty-four square kilometers, visitors can take a ride on a "dragon boat" or smaller paddling boats for love-struck couples. The landmark of the Summer Palace is the "Pagoda of the Incense of Buddha" (Foxiange) on top of Wanshou Shan, which overlooks Lake Kunming.

Yong He Gong, the famous Tibetan temple in Beijing,
which gives one a sense of peace and tranquility

Outside the city are a countless number of beautiful parks. In the west of the city there is Xiang Shan (Lotus Mountain) and the Beijing Botanical Gardens. Both of these attractions can take a whole day to experience in full. The best time to visit Xiang Shan is in the autumn when the leaves are red and the scenery from the peak is breathtaking.

Less historic yet an exciting adventurous place is the Beijing Zoo (located near the XiZhiMen station), which houses young and cute pandas as well as other exotic animals.

Accommodations

Rental accommodations in Beijing are generally more costly than other Chinese cities, especially in view of the 2008 Olympics. For example a one-bedroom fully furnished apartment near Beijing University (near Wu Dao Kou area—towards the northwest of the city center) would cost anything between 1500 RMB (Renminbi, or Yuan) a month and 3500 RMB a month. Of course if you are an expat who wants to live in luxury then why not experience renting (or even purchasing) an apartment for approximately 20,000 RMB a month in one of the exclusive apartments near the city center. In winter, most homes are supplied with a heater that can be purchased in advance, usually about 1000 RMB for a six-month lease.

Major Universities

Beijing is the ancient seat of learning in China, with famous "red brick" world class universities such as Tsinghua University and Beijing University. Here are listed website addresses of some of the leading universities in Beijing. Because there are so many (over fifty universities and colleges, mostly state owned), only the oldest and most famous ones are listed here:

www.pku.edu.cn Beijing University (Established 1898)
www.tsinghua.edu.cn Tsinghua University (Established 1911)
www.bnu.edu.cn/eng Beijing Normal University

Useful Beijing Links

www.ebeijing.gov.cn Official government website for Beijing
www.thatsbj.com Monthly expat magazine for Beijing
www.beijingpage.com Official directory of all things in Beijing
www.beijingimpression.com Website for Beijing tours—in and around
    Beijing
www.bjreview.com.cn Weekly news—online edition
www.beijingtrip.com Tour operator—with tours in and around Beijing
www.bjsubway.com The corporate website of Beijing subway
www.bcia.com.cn Official website of Beijing Airport

Guangzhou （广州）

Guangzhou, the capital of Guangdong province, is the industrial hub of southern China. It is sometimes referred to as Canton by westerners. For many travelers Guangzhou is still the first real taste of China once they cross the border in from Hong Kong. (Shenzhen is a modern city with no real history and does not feel like China because of its close proximity to Hong Kong and high-rise glass buildings everywhere). First impressions of Guangzhou are that it is teeming, noisy, and polluted. The last is obvious with the smell of overflowing drains in most neighborhoods.

Guangzhou is famous for its great food and its biannual (April and October) trade fair, known as the Canton fair. Among many other trade fairs that take place in China, the Canton fair is by far the biggest and most popular. It's just a huge market where traders from around the world come to Guangzhou to find a good deal for all kinds of "Made in China" goods. Imagine a city where it feels like you are living in the ancient past with night-time bazaars and trade markets, where you can buy almost anything that tickles your fancy; and at the same time that city tries to keep pace with life in twenty-first century China; that's Guangzhou.

Geography and History

Guangzhou is located on the Pearl River (Zhu Jiang) Delta and lies 45 km upriver from Humen (also called Bocca Tigris on older maps). The city has a magnificent history dating back to approximately 214 B.C., when, according to historians, the city may have been founded. The original name of the metropolis was Panyu (named by the Qin Emperor, Qin Shi Huangdi), and Guangzhou first appeared sometime between the years 222 and 280. Towards the conclusion of the Han Dynasty, the city's name was changed to Jiaozhou. In 226, the eastern part of Jiaozhou became the part of Guangzhou, and ever since then Panyu has been called Guangzhou. Guangzhou has been a trade center ever since the Tang Dynasty (618–906).

In the period of the five Dynasties, Guangzhou was firmly placed as the capital city of southern China (or Han as it was known), and it was still the biggest foreign trade port and commercial city in China. This was especially true from 1757 to 1842, when Guangzhou was used as a major center for trading in China, as in those days it was the only port opened for foreigners for trade. The initial securing of the trade monopoly by the Portuguese in the fifteenth century was later broken by the British in the latter part of the seventeenth century, while in the eighteenth century the French and Dutch followed suit into the city. However it was only during the reign of the Tang Dynasty that Guangzhou became a world-famous port.

French and British forces occupied Guangzhou during 1856 following a political uproar. Later the island of Shameen (now known as the expat area of Shamian) was acquired for business and residential purposes rather than colonial quarters (much of the architecture can still be seen today).

During the nationalist uprising, Guangzhou was the residence of many revolutionaries, including the popular Dr. Sun Yat Sen in 1911. From Guangzhou the Nationalist armies of Chiang Kai-shek marched northwards in the 1920s to establish a government in Nanjing. In 1927, Guangzhou was briefly the seat of one of the earliest Communist movements in China. The fall of Guangzhou to the Communist armies in late October of 1949 signaled the Communist takeover of the whole country.

Since then, Guangzhou has been built up as an industrial center and a modern port for Southern China. Amongst the locals, Guangzhou's famous nickname is "Yangcheng," which means "City of the Ram," and this name comes from an enchanting myth. It is said that over two thousand years ago, five immortals rode five rams with rice stalks in their mouths and they literally flew to Guangzhou. These immortals gave the rice to peasants and prayed that they would be blessed with harvests. The immortals flew away and left the five rams behind, now turned into stones. The stone structure of the Five Rams is one of the symbolic attractions of the city, and can be seen in Yuexiu Park.

Climate

For the majority of the year Guangzhou has a tropical climate with a relative humidity between seventy to ninety percent—very unpleasant if you don't enjoy getting sweaty all the time! One key cause of this is that the Tropic of Cancer runs not many miles to the north of the city, making life very uncomfortable even at night time during the summer months. For a short period of time in July the sun is straight over the city—making life incredibly hot and hard in the congested and polluted streets. The year is made up of a subtropical-tropical, humid monsoonal climate, with the rainy season from April to September and occasional typhoons from May to November. Thankfully the majority of offices and homes have air conditioning.

Transportation

Buses

Guangzhou has numerous bus connections operating all around the city during the day and a few at night time. Bus fares are one Yuan for buses that have no air conditioning (i.e., those that are noisy and have crackling/open windows, uncomfortable seats that look like wooden park benches, and no PA system to inform you which stop is approaching) and two Yuan for those with air conditioning (i.e., those that have TVs showing adverts or music videos, have plastic seats, and have a automated PA system that informs you which stop is approaching next). The majority of buses in Guangzhou are clean but normally overcrowded.

Guangzhou has quite a number of bus stations. There is a bus station located at Guangzhou Dong Zhan (Guangzhou East Station), with buses operating to almost all destinations around the city as well as surrounding towns and villages.

The city's main bus station for long-distance travel is located near the Guangzhou Train Station on Huanshi Xi Lu at the Provincial Bus Station.

Not far across the road is the Liuhua Bus Station, which also caters to long-distance buses.

The third main coach station for medium- to long-distance coach operations is located in Tianhe (opposite the Tianhe Stadium and adjacent to the tallest building in Guangzhou—the CITIC Plaza). Buses within Guangdong province also operate from here (to Shenzhen, Zhongshan, Dongguan, and Foshan).

Air Travel

Guangzhou has one major international airport. Stuated 32 km northwest of the city center, near the Pearl Delta, Guangzhou Baiyun International Airport offers connections to major Asian, African, and European cities as well as many domestic flights. China Southern Airlines has its HQ and base at Baiyun airport with flights within China and internationally. With its opening in 2004, the airport is one of the most contemporary in Asia. The airport is large enough to accommodate wide-bodied jets such as the latest Boeing 777-200LR, Airbus A340-500 and the Boeing 747-400, and even the super jumbo Airbus A380.

Taxies

Taxies are ubiquitous, metered, and available 24 hours a day. The base rate at the time of writing is seven Yuan (approx. $1) 24 hours a day, plus a fuel charge of one Yuan that is added to the final bill.

Trains

Guangzhou has two main train stations, Guangzhou Train Station (Guangzhou Zhen) and Guangzhou East Train Station (Guangzhou Dong Zhan). The former is extremely chaotic and is the focal point for connecting Guangzhou with the rest of China, whereas the latter is used for more local routes. The most frequently operated route out from Guangzhou East Train station is the Guangzhou to Shenzhen line. Trains run every 20/25 minutes with some trains stopping in Dongguan or Shi Long; the trip takes just over one hour. The one-way fare at the time of writing is seventy Yuan.

Metro

Guangzhou has an extensive metro system with four lines operating at the time of writing. Line one operates from Guangzhou East Station in Tianhe District through to the ferry terminal at Nanhai (Pingzhou). Line two operates from north of Guangzhou (Baiyun Airport) to the south via the interchange with line one at Gong Yuan Qian. Two additional lines are operational, although not complete, and more lines are planned and under construction.

Metro stations can be identified by a large logo consisting of a Red "Y" made up of two lines on a yellow or white background. Costs for single trips range from one Yuan up to six Yuan depending on the length of the journey.

Sea Travel

Guangzhou has a small ferry terminal located in the southwest of the city. The Nanhai port (Pingzhou) has twice daily service to Hong Kong Central. It takes about two hours and costs approximately 170 RMB for a single trip. To get to the ferry terminal you can either take a taxi or the Metro (Line one). The latter is a preferred option because it is cheap and quick.

Food

Guangzhou offers a considerable amount of choice when it comes to trying local and international restaurants. Being the capital of Canton, it is no surprise that the food is one of the strengths of this fantastic city. Because of the presence of various consulates and international companies, Guangzhou has a myriad of choice for international cuisines including Turkish, Ethiopian, Middle Eastern (Egyptian tea house!), and European. As an expat you will be spoiled for choices as new food may be enjoyed every day and for a very reasonable price too.

Shopping

Having been China's trading center for centuries, Guangzhou has naturally attracted shoppers for all kind of products. Most of these are "Made in China" goods or more specifically "Made in Guangzhou," although shoppers should be cautious because many of these products may not match the quality of, say, your local genuine Nike store. There is plenty of choice for both the trading businessman and individual street consumers alike as well as bargaining (although not encouraged in past years); achieving a good deal can be an art you will have to get used to while in China. Usually after maintaining your persistence on a certain price for the product that tickles your fancy, you are bound to triumph on a deal on most occasions. Here is a list of some of the main shopping malls in Guangzhou:

Grand View Mall—a bustling and vibrant shopping area located in Tianhe district, opposite the CITIC Plaza. It is perceived by many Guangzhouners to be the biggest shopping mall in Southeast Asia, although this is not officially confirmed by any data.

The five rams located in Yuexiu Park

Beijing Road (Beijing Lu)—Guangzhou's busiest street, which houses many interesting shops and restaurants including a "Greenery Café" that uses the refurbished fuselage and cockpit (without wings/engines) of a China Southern Airlines De Havilland Aircraft as seating area.

Friendship stores are common in many of the large cities and most of these friendship stores house banks, designer fashion outlets, and chic restaurants. In Guangzhou there is a friendship store located inside the Guangzhou World Trade Center, next to the Baiyun Hotel on Huanshi don Lu.

In China, don't be fooled by the term "World Trade Center," as it's not the kind of World Trade Center that you would have found in New York City. In China, the term "WTC" is a loose one, which can be used to refer to a building that accommodates a large shopping mall or a collection of banks. In China every major city has a WTC.

Places of Interest

Yuexiu Park (Yuexiu Gong Yuan)—A typical Chinese landscaped park located in downtown Guangzhou with entrances on all four roads that surround the park. The main entrance is located on Jiefeng Lu and leads the visitor, through an uphill walk, to the Five Rams Statue. The five rams are the symbol of Guangzhou because according to local myths as mentioned earlier, the city of Guangzhou was founded by five immortals riding five rams. There is also the attractive "tower looking at the sea" (Zhen Hai Lou), which is a museum about the history of Guangzhou.

White Cloud Mountain Park (Baiyun Shan Gong Yuan)—A beautiful and romantic park that is located in the north of Guangzhou. This park provides an oasis for weekends and national holidays. There are some stunning views of downtown Guangzhou from the peak, along with lots of beautiful temples and even a cable car that runs to the top of the mountain.

Sun Yat-Sen Memorial Hall (Sun Zhongshan Jiniantang)—A grand theatre located in a large square park between Dongfeng Zhong Lu and Qingyun Lu (facing Yuexiu Park). It is host to quite a number of foreign orchestras and opera shows (normally from Russia, the former Soviet states, and eastern European countries).

Six Banyan Trees Temple (Liurong Si)— Located on Liurong Lu to the south of Yuexiu Park, this is a very beautiful and old temple (dates back to the fifth century and is considered even older than the city itself). You can climb to the top of the pagoda in the middle of the courtyard; however, the views are somewhat restricted due to the numerous buildings surrounding the temple. Located behind the pagoda is an exhibition illustrating the history of Buddhism from its beginnings in India.

As in the rest of China, there are many small and beautiful parks around the city. Parks in China have an entrance charge, normally approximately three Yuan, and it is worth it.

Major Universities in Guangzhou

www.gdufs.edu.cn Guangdong University of Foreign Studies (GDUFS)
www.gdut.edu.cn Guangdong University of Technology
www.gzhu.edu.cn Guangzhou University
www.jnu.edu.cn Jinan University
www.sysu.edu.cn Sun Yat-Sen University Guangzhou
www.scut.edu.cn South China University of Technology

Useful Links

www.gzmtr.com Guangzhou metro official website
www.guangzhou.gov.cn Guangzhou official website
www.gz.gov.cn Guangzhou (Government) official website
www.destinationprd.com Information about some cities around the Pearl River Delta
www.baiyunairport.com Official website of Guangzhou Baiyun Airport
www.gz2010asiangames.org Official website for the 2010 Asian Games in Guangzhou
www.thatsgz.com That's Guangzhou Magazine (published monthly)

China Foreign Trade Center

China Foreign Trade Center (Group)
117 Liuhua Road
Guangzhou, P. R. China
Tel: +86 (0)20 2608 8888
Website: www.cftc.org.cn
Website: www.cantonfair.org.cn

View of the Pearl TV Tower and Pudong Distract across the Huang Pu River

Shanghai （上海）

In the era before the Second World War, Shanghai was known as the "Paris of the East" and was a bustling place for foreigners from Britain, France, and the United States. These days, although no longer the holder of that exquisite title, Shanghai still attracts the world's attention—although not quite in the same way it used to do. All around the city reminders of Shanghai's colonial past mingle side by side with western-styled Chinese architectures, ranging from hotels to ancestral homes that hold some historical significance.

Twenty-first century Shanghai has developed into the financial capital of China and has in recent years also become a trademark city as well as a branding image for this country. With a population of over eighteen million, Shanghai can also be seen as a city which has paths leading towards China's future, as this beautiful city will be hosting the International Expo in 2010. Native Shanghainese people are very proud of themselves, as well as their city. Despite Shanghai being a bustling modern city with neon lights, crazy bars, and restaurants, one has to always bear in mind that it is still a Communist country.

Just taking a walk around many of the smaller streets of Shanghai gives a feeling of the romance that is attached to the city. One can imagine what it

Nighttime view of the building in Shanghai

must have been like in the pre–Second World War era when the city was a bustling beehive for westerners in search of a life full of luxury. They would have expected life to be similar to what they would have had back in their homelands, but instead, in China, and so Shanghai was one city in Asia which could offer those luxuries to them. These include theatres, expat bars, and large colonial mansions in the expat areas, then known as the International settlement and the French concession.

Since the early twenty-first century, the city has hosted major international sports events such as the Shanghai Grand Masters (Tennis), the annual Shanghai Formula One Grand Prix (since October 2005), annual Snooker world championships, and major international Golf tournaments held annually—all of these firmly putting Shanghai on the map.

View of a Shanghai street with the Pearl TV Tower
across the river in Pudong

Geography

The name Shanghai stands for "over the sea" and is classed as a province itself, known as Shanghai Shi Province. It's flanked by Jiangsu province to the west/northwest and Zhejiang province to the west/southwest. The eastern side of Shanghai is surrounded by Hangzhou Bay to the south and by the mouth of the Yangtze River (which flows into the East China Sea) to the northeast.

Central Shanghai is densely populated despite covering an area of only approximately 15 km². It is amazing to observe just how much of the Pudong area has grown in the few years since the beginning of the twenty-first century.

Climate

Winters are bitterly cold, but not as cold as up in the northern cities such as Beijing or Dalian, while the summers are hot and humid. The best time to visit Shanghai is either around April and May when the weather is neither too cold nor too hot, or between August and September when again the weather is mildly cold as it creeps towards the bitterly freezing Shanghai winter. During this "midly cold" weather, it is neither as hot as mid-summer or exactly cool, but just appropriate for late summer/early autumn. Which means you can still wear your shorts and T-shirt on some days!

Transportation

Buses and Coaches

Shanghai has numerous bus connections operating all around the city during the day and a few at night time. Most buses run from early in the morning (around 5 a.m.) to 11 p.m. For long-distance travel there is a bus station located on Heinan Bei Lu about 1.5 km north of Suzhou Creek. The bus station is within walking distance of the "Baoshan Jie" Metro stop. The Shanghai Tour Bus Lines depart from Shanghai Stadium to destinations mostly in the suburban districts.

Air Travel

Shanghai has two major international airports, HongQiao and Pudong. Pudong is the new international airport located 45 km to the east of the city beside the East China Sea, while HongQiao, located 15 km west of the city, is much smaller and older. HongQiao is mostly used for domestic flights. Pudong is also the base and HQ of China Eastern Airlines. Over forty world-wide airlines use the airport, with an annual average passenger capacity of over eighteen million (2007 figures).

Downtown Shanghai—taxies galore!

Taxies

The minimum fare is eleven Yuan (US$1.38), which covers the first three kilometers, and then two Yuan is charged for every additional kilometer. After ten kilometers, the fare jumps fifty percent— to three Yuan for every additional kilometer.

Trains

Shanghai has two train stations; Shanghai station is north of the Suzhou Creek. The station has several routes connecting with other Chinese cities. The other is Shanghai west station, which is situated remotely to the northwest of the city.

Metro

Shanghai has one of China's largest metro systems with five metro lines running across the city. Line one operates from Xinzhuang to Gongfu Xincun,

Line two from Zhongshan Park to Zhangjiang High-Tech District, Line three from Jiangwan Town to Shanghai South Railway Station, Line five from Xinzhuang to Minhang Development District. The section of Line four from Damuqiao Road Station to Lancun Road Station is still under construction at the time of writing.

Ticket prices range between 3 RMB to 5 RMB depending on the length of your journey. The metro starts operation at 5:30 a.m. or 6:30, depending on which line, with last trains from each terminus leaving between 10:20 p.m. and 11:00 p.m.

Plans are in place for ten new metro lines to be built between 2005 and 2012, stretching almost 389 kilometers. The entire length of the Shanghai metro system is expected to reach around five hundred kilometers by 2012, among which four hundred kilometers is expected to be put in use before the 2010 Expo.

The World's Fastest Train—The Maglev

An air-conditioned and high-tech transrapid link, known as the Maglev, operates between downtown Shanghai (Longyang Road metro station) and Pudong Airport. The Maglev is the fastest train in the world, capable of accommodating speeds of up to 400 km/h. Because of the relatively short distance, however, it travels at approximately 320 km/h for the seven-minute journey. It uses the technology of a raised magnetic track that allows the trains to effectively "hover" at high speeds. Inside the train it feels no different to sitting inside a plane and is considerably more comfortable.

A one-way ticket costs fifty Yuan. If you show your flight ticket for that day, you will benefit from a ten-Yuan discount. However, you can buy only one discounted train ticket per flight ticket.

Operation from Longyang Road Station starts at 7 a.m. and ends at 9 p.m. at intervals of fifteen minutes. The operation from Pudong lasts from 7:02 a.m. to 9:02 p.m. at the same intervals.

Shopping

Most shopping areas in China's big cities are similar in style and in terms of what they have to offer (compare Beijing's Wangfujing and Xidan with Guangzhou's Beijing Lu and Shenzhen's Hua Qiang Bei and Dongmen). Shanghai is a consumer's paradise for locals and foreigners.

Nothing quite matches the sheer magnitude of Shanghai's Nanjing Xi Lu (Nanjing West Road), which is one of China's busiest streets. The Chinese used to consider Nanjing Xi Lu the busiest street in the world, with its multitude of people, cars, and bicycles. However that title disappeared when the government closed off a large section to cars during the 1980s. Between Henan Lu and Xizang Lu, it is now a pedestrian walkway, full of myriad shops and restaurants.

Huaihai Road, Xu JiaHui, and the ZhongZhan Park area also offer shopping. The "electronic/IT city" is based around the Huaihai Road area.

Be aware of ticket touts who can speak English to some degree and will use all kinds of ways to persuade you to purchase the latest counterfeit "Rolex" watch and so on. Conversation typically starts on the lines of "Hello, where are you from? Would you like Chinese food/Shanghai lady?" and so on. Of course the best response is to just ignore the chit-chat and move along.

Places of Interest

Despite the perception that most foreigners have about Shanghai with regard to its beauty and history, the city itself isn't really classed as a tourist destination. It is, after all, China's financial capital so its presence is regarded more for working purposes. Nevertheless, just the buzz of the city makes it a wonderful place to be in and the breathtaking sights from the Bund towards Pudong are also worth visiting.

The Shanghainese consider the **Oriental Pearl Television Tower (Dongfang Minzhu)** to be equivalent to the Eiffel Tower. It is made up of eleven steel spheres of different sizes that are supposed to represent pearls (as in Shanghai, Pearl of the Orient), with the top "pearl" offering a 360-degree view of the surroundings. It is best to go to the top on a nice clear day, which can be a challenge itself considering the muggy atmosphere for majority of the year. Shanghai runs a tourist bus, "The Shanghai sight-seeing bus," with a free hotline for information—800-820-1585 in both English and Mandarin.

The Pearl River Promenade—The waterfront avenue, more formally known as the Bund (Waitan), is Shanghai's symbolic landmark. During the pre–Second World War era, Europeans and other foreigners built their banks, clubs, hotels and consulates here. The Bund is now a busy place for both tourists and residents, at all times of the day and much more so in the evenings. The historical buildings have been beautifully renovated to restore the glory of their original architecture. Some of the notable landmarks that are worthwhile visiting are the Peace Hotel and the former HSBC Building (now the Pudong Development Bank).

There are two museums, the **Shanghai Museum,** opened in 1996, and the **Shanghai Art Museum.** The former is home to some famous house paintings, sculptures, ceramics, calligraphy, jade, and Ming and Qing Dynasty furniture and coins. The collection of bronzes is among the best in the world, echoing the architecture of the museum, which looks like a large bronze urn. The Shanghai Art Museum is a place where exhibitions of varying interest and quality rotate through the museum, year round. It's a nice place to while away your time in case you have a few hours to spare before moving on your travels or if you just need to relax in the air-conditioned chambers on a hot summer's day.

If you are a first-time visitor to this part of China and are after the marvels of the exquisite beauty that China has to offer, then Shanghai's satellite cities, such as Suzhou and Hangzhou (West Lake) may be the ideal destinations for you. Both Suzhou and Hangzhou are within a few hours' ride by train or coach. Hangzhou is famous for the west lake scenery and original high-quality Chinese silk, especially silk pajamas and scarves that are offered at a fraction of the cost you would most likely to pay in the west.

Major Universities in Shanghai

www.dhu.edu.cn Donghua University
www.fudan.edu.cn Fudan University
www.sjtu.edu.cn Shanghai Jiao Tong University
www.shu.edu.cn Shanghai University

Shanghai Theatre

www.tongji.edu.cn Tong Ji University
www.shufe.edu.cn Shanghai University of Finance and Economics

Useful Links

www.thatssh.com Monthly guide of Shanghai for expats.
www.shanghai-ed.com Website for expats
www.shanghaiexpat.com Website for expats in Shanghai
www.shanghaidaily.com Online edition of the Shanghai English news
    paper
www.shanghai.gov.cn Official Government portal of Shanghai
www.portshanghai.com.cn Official website for the sea ports in Shanghai
www.f1china.com.cn The official website for the Shanghai Formula One
    Grand Prix
www.expo2010china.com The official website for the World Expo in
    Shanghai in 2010.
www.smtdc.com The official website for the Shanghai Maglev train
www.shtmetro.com The official website for the Shanghai metro (is in
    Chinese)
www.shanghaiairport.com Both Pudong and Hongqiao airports have one
    common website

Shenzhen (深圳)

Formally established in November 1979, Shenzhen, nicknamed "China's Garden City," is considered to be China's youngest, cleanest, and most modern city. Shenzhen used to be just a fishing village until Deng Xiao Ping declared the city as a Special Economic Zone (SEZ), along with four other Chinese cities on the east coast. It is known as China's garden city because of its abundance of greenery and flower beds scattered on almost every roadside and infrastructure. Shenzhen will probably surprise you if this is the first city you come to on your inaugural trip to China. People from the west have usually never heard of it. Hong Kong media tell you that it's the most dangerous place in China and the Taiwanese and Japanese think it's some poor cousin of Shanghai. Shenzhen is actually a city of some eleven million people, with the majority of them migrants from other parts of China as well as overseas. It is also the wealthiest city in China, paying the highest average salaries to its inhabitants.

To a first-time visitor, Shenzhen would seem a brash and vibrant place to be in. Indeed Shenzhen is China's migrant city where people from other parts of China have come to seek an opportunity, and it provides a sense of freedom for the younger population. With the close proximity to Hong Kong, it provides an excellent weekend break for people to stay and enjoy their time in Shenzhen. The majority of the expatriate community lives approximately 30 km west of the city center in the port area known as Shekou, with most of the expats working in the oil, gas, or electronics industries.

For many Hong Kong citizens, Shenzhen is increasingly becoming a cheaper alternative to live in rather than commute to on a daily basis. So many people are working in Hong Kong, but choose to live in Shenzhen.

Geography

Shenzhen is located in Guangdong province, SE China, on the border of Hong Kong. Shenzhen covers an area of approx. 2020 sq km and is made up of five main districts, Luhou, Longgang, Futian, Nanshan, and Baoan. Luhou and Futian share borders with Hong Kong and there are three main border entry points with Hong Kong, the main one being at Luhou Train Station and the other two being Huanggang and Shekou seaport. Plans are being made to open two more border crossings (one at Liantang in Luhou and the other with the opening of the new bridge between Hong Kong and Shekou in time for the 2008 Olympics).

Climate

Shenzhen's climate has the transitional characteristics of subtropical and tropical zones. The overall characteristics of the climate can be generalized as long summers often stretching out for the majority of the year. This often makes it difficult to distinguish between the other seasons, namely autumn and spring. A high percentage of the year's precipitation falls between November and January and between April and September. Winter is short and surprisingly very cold (normally experienced for about one or two months in December and January).

Transportation

Buses

Shenzhen has numerous bus connections operating all around the city during the day and a few during night times as well. Long-distance coaches operate from the main train station at Luhou and also from Futian Bus Station.

Air Travel

Shenzhen has one major international airport. Bao-an International Airport is located 32 km northwest of the city center, near the Pearl Delta, with connections to major Asian cities as well as many domestic flights. Shenzhen has its own airline, Shenzhen Airlines, with numerous daily flights to destinations within China and several Asian cities.

Although Shenzhen airport is an international airport, most of the flights outside China are destined around the Asia Pacific region. For the majority of international flights, connections are made either via Beijing or Shanghai, or the other alternative is to go from Hong Kong or Guangzhou airports.

Bao-an airport is large enough to accommodate wide-bodied jets such as the latest Boeing 777-200LR, A340-500, and the Boeing 747-400. At the time of writing, there were plans to either expand the current runway or construct another runway. This option would enable Shenzhen Airport to accommodate the "Super Jumbo" Airbus A380 aircraft when it comes into service in 2008. There is a regular daily helicopter service to Macau operated from the airport.

There is a heliport in the Nanshan District, quite close to the Shekou port; however this is used mainly by the Shenzhen Police Force and the oil & gas companies to transport workers to/from the offshore oil platforms in the South China Sea.

Taxies

Metered taxis are available 24 hours a day. The base rate at the time of writing is 12.50 RMB (Approx $1.50) between 6:00 a.m. and 11:00 p.m. for the first mile. Between 11:00 p.m. and 6:00 a.m. the base rate is 16.50 RMB (just over $2). Inside the city center (Special Economic Zone) the taxis are colored red, while those operating outside the city are colored green. So be aware that if you take a green-colored taxi from outside the city center, that taxi won't be allowed to enter the city center. The red taxis are allowed to go out of the city only to a certain distance, and you will have to pay the toll gate fare if you are traveling between two cities (e.g., from Shenzhen to Guangzhou, and vice versa).

Ferry Travel

The main port for traveling by ferry is Shekou. Destinations include Hong Kong (Central and Kowloon), Macau, Hong Kong Airport, Guangzhou, and Zhuhai. At the time of writing the standard fare for going to Hong Kong airport (should take approx. thirty minutes) is 250 HKD (you will get about a 150 HKD refund if you show your flight ticket at check-in), and to go to either Hong Kong (Central or Kowloon and takes approx. forty-five minutes) or Macau (takes approx. one hour) will cost 100 HKD one way. Services to these destinations operate every forty minutes at the time of writing.

You can also check in at the Shekou port for some airlines, including Cathay Pacific and Dragonair.

Trains

Shenzhen has many routes connecting to other Chinese cities. The most frequently operated route is the Guangzhou to Shenzhen route. Trains run every twenty to twenty-five minutes with some trains stopping in Dongguan, and it takes approximately one hour. The one-way fare at the time of writing is 70 RMB.

A word of caution: When you leave Hong Kong and enter Chinese soil, immediately you will notice the remarkable difference—of how much Shenzhen still has to improve (even though it is improving). It feels like entering a different country, or on occasions, even going back in time. At Luhou station you will most likely be met by a large number of beggars, ticket touts shouting "Fa Piao! Fa Piao!" (tickets to sell), and, annoyingly, a number of pimps/prostitutes saying things such as "Hello, you want miss massage?" (Mostly around the Shangri La Hotel, this is situated right next to the station and cannot be missed.) The best response is to ignore this.

Even though it has a crime rate similar to other cities in China, Shenzhen, because of the large influx of visitors each day, has seemingly been the scene of unlawful acts, mostly petty but infrequently serious, aimed at visitors and residents. The border crossings tend to attract the attention of pickpockets and other criminals. There have been reported cases of daytime muggings and individuals being abducted and forced to withdraw cash from ATMs.

Metro

Shenzhen Metro opened in December 2005 and is very clean, fast, and new. Trains are not as crowded as one would experience in other Chinese cities. At the time of writing there are two lines (line one and line four) open, with three additional lines set to be in full operation by 2010.

Construction on line three commenced towards the end of 2005. Line three will be approximately 33 km long, running from Hung Ling Road Station to Long Hing Road Station in Longgang. Line three is scheduled for completion in the summer of 2009. Line two has been under construction since late 2004. It will run from Shekou west to Window of the World and is scheduled to

open in the winter of 2010. Finally, line eleven will run from Shenzhen West
Station to Tongkeng. By the time it is opened in 2010 it will be Shenzhen's
longest metro line with over 38 km of track.

The symbol for the Shenzhen metro consists of a Green Y logo in a green
circle. Fares range from one Yuan to five Yuan depending on the length of the
journey.

Food

Although Shenzhen may not have as large a variety of restaurants featuring
international cuisine as do Guangzhou, Shanghai, and Beijing, there is a
sound selection of restaurants available (for a list see the Shenzhen party
website link given towards at the end of this section). A number of western-
style restaurants (mainly Indian and Italian) are available in the Luhou area,
while the MixC center (opposite The Diwang building on Shen Nan Zhong
Lu) has an abundance of Chinese, Japanese, and western style restaurants
including "Taco Bell" (Mexican style) and "Spaghetti House." It could be
considered, however, a waste of precious time in China if you don't try one
of the many local eateries in town. For example there are a myriad of Chinese
restaurants that offer some scrumptious provincial Chinese cuisine (food
from Guizhou, Sichuan, Xinjiang, etc.) for as little as 8 RMB per person. The
major setback you are likely to encounter is language problems, as the menu
is almost always in Chinese; therefore knowing a few essential characters or
words in Chinese is useful. Some of the words that may be required are listed
at the end of this book.

Shopping

The following is a list of the main shopping areas:

Dongmen in Luhou district—a bustling and vibrant shopping area in the
heart of Shenzhen's most happening place.

Hua Qiang Bei in Futian district—similar to Dongmen but specializes in
selling electronic "Made in Shenzhen" goods.

King Glory Plaza in Luhou district—a classy and upmarket shopping area
where you can find just about every western designer shop (including CK,
Gucci etc) and even a BMW Store selling chic leather jackets, baseball caps
and so on.

The MixC is a new shopping center, located opposite the Diwang Building
(Shenzhen's tallest building in the heart of the city) on Shennan Road. The
MixC is a modern shopping mall with all kinds of restaurants including

Modern shopping malls are not a uncommon sight in 21st-century China

Mexican (Taco Bell) and a supermarket catering for the expat community with imported goods (Ole). The MixC also has many other familiar stores, a huge indoor ice rink, and a cinema.

Another supermarket that is used by both locals and expats is Jusco. It's located in the basement of the CITIC Plaza (Zhong Xin Da Sha) on Shennen Road. Apart from food, Jusco also has housewares, clothing, and sporting goods, but for housewares it's best to go to Wal-Mart (and it tends to be cheaper because it is made under local license rather than imported). There are a few Wal-Mart stores in Shenzhen. There is one on Fuxing Road and this is probably the best. There is also a Sam's Club to the west on Shennan Road that sells western goods. It's a members-only club but anyone can join and the process is easy.

If you want to buy clothes, City Plaza and the MixC have all the expensive brand names but Dongmen and Luhou offer cheap fakes.

For coffee there are plenty of Starbucks available in Shenzhen. The Starbucks at City Plaza, The MixC, Shekou, and Nanshan are very popular and always packed. Kosmo is a nice alternative offering healthy options. There are also a couple of Illy cafés (one in the MixC and the other one on the ground level of the Diwang Building).

KFC, McDonald's, Pizza Hut, and Häagen-Dazs are in abundance. In Shekou there is one Subway sandwiches outlet at the time of writing.

Further information regarding restaurants can be obtained from the Shenzhen party website listed below.

Places of Interest

There are three major must-see places of interest in Shenzhen:

1. Window of the World

Shenzhen's star attraction, it features the world's wonders, historic sites, scenic spots, natural landscapes, folk customs, and world-renowned sculptures. Occupying an area of almost forty-eight hectares, it is composed of 118 attractions set up on different scales from 1:1 to 1:100 including the Eiffel Tower, The Taj Mahal, Niagara Falls, and the Egyptian Pyramids.

2. Happy Valley

An amusement park that is especially appealing to the Chinese people because amusement parks are part of the experiment of all things "western" that China is engaged with. It is Shenzhen's answer to UK's Thorpe Park or Alton Towers. Consisting of a water park and a dry park, it features attractions for both adults and children. The park also has a 4D cinema, the fist of its kind in Asia. On a smaller scale than other international attractions, it is a family theme park and quite impressive.

3. Splendid China and the China Folk Cultural Village

Splendid China and the China Folk cultural village are located adjacent to the Window of the World. "Splendid China" features theatrical cultural shows based on China's five-thousand-year history and life in the rural areas. The world-famous open air evening show known as the "Dancing with the Dragon and the Phoenix" made its debut in 2003.

There are also other areas such as the **Shekou Sea World**—this is the main restaurant and bar area catering to the expat community; it feels like Hong Kong or Europe with lots of Irish, American, and British expat bars. The magic of this area is that the expats are the ones who make this area feel rather like Europe in China! Inside the bars (including the famous Macawleys Irish pub), you feel as if you are suddenly sitting in Dublin or Manchester; watching a game of footie on Sky TV and drinking the black stuff! Guinness anyone?

In addition, the **Diwang Building (Diwang Da Sha)** is one of the 10 tallest buildings in Asia. You can go to the top for a small charge and take in some impressive views of Shenzhen and on a clear day, it's possible to see Hong Kong.

Leisure

Shenzhen has a number of golf courses with many people from Hong Kong coming over for the weekend to play golf here. The most popular and famous venue is the Mission Hills Golf Course, expensive even for China, but it does cater to the affluent market.

Beach Resorts

There are two main beach resorts in Shenzhen, both approx 15 km east of the city center. They are clean, not busy, and safe to swim in:

- Da Mei Sha (free of charge at the time of writing) – a 1.8-km long beach.
- Xiao Mei Sha (20 RMB entrance ticket at the time of writing).

Accommodations

Rental accommodations in Shenzhen (as well as in other parts of China) include the good, the bad, and the ugly.

The majority of foreigners live in either Shekou or Nanshan (Haiwang Da Sha near HaiYa Bai Hu, or near the Overseas Chinese Town in Shi-Jie-Zhi-Chuang).

The first years of the twenty-first century have seen the establishment of a number of new high class International hotels including Sheraton, Pavilion, and Kemplinski. Plus there are two western five-star International hotels in the Luhou area: the Hilton and the Shangri-La Hotel. A full list of hotels in Shenzhen is available on the Shenzhen party website.

Major Universities in Shenzhen

www.szu.edu.cn Shenzhen University

Useful Links

www.sznews.com/szdaily Shenzhen Daily is the main English daily tabloid
www.shenzhenparty.com The "What's happening" guide for expats in
    Shenzhen
www.shenzhenwindow.net
www.szftz.gov.cn/sze/index.htm Shenzhen Administrative Bureau of Free
    Trade Zones
http://english.sz.gov.cn/lis/ Shenzhen Government Online

www.destinationprd.com Website detailing some of the cities around the
    Pearl River Delta
www.missionhillsgroup.com Official website of the Mission Hills Golf Club
www.szwwco.com Window of the World attraction, official website
www.szmc.net Shenzhen Metro Website
www.heliexpress.com The website for Heli Express, based at Shenzhen
    Airport.
www.szairport.com The official website of Shenzhen airport
www.sz2011.org Shenzhen Universiade 2011 official website

Shenzhen High-Tech Industrial Park
3F Virtual University
P.R.C 518057
www.ship.gov.cn/en/index.htm

Hong Kong

Hong Kong (Xiang Gang is the Chinese name) was a British colony until
1997, and the official name now is Hong Kong Special Administrative Region
(HK SAR). It's known as an SAR because it operates on a one government, two
systems (the other one being Macau) scheme where the central government

Hong Kong skyline at night

is based in Beijing, and a Chief Executive Officer is in charge of affairs in the day-to-day running of life in Hong Kong.

Because Hong Kong is on the border of China, it is convenient to visit for a one- or two-day excursion. Hong Kong's slogan is "Asia's World City" and this statement is most certainly true considering the multicultural environment, which offers a good mix of the east and the west. Immediately as you cross the border from Shenzhen into Hong Kong, the environmental change is so dramatic that it really does feel as if you have stepped thirty years into China's future. Since independence from the British in 1997, Hong Kong has still managed to retain many of the traditions that are forbidden in mainland China. Amazingly it is doing well economically too. Speaking English in Hong Kong is not a problem because of its history as a British colony. Cantonese (Guangdonghua) is the national language of Hong Kong and not many people understand Mandarin.

In Hong Kong, apart from the multiculturalism, you will notice the free press (there are myriad publications that would be prohibited in the mainland), fashion, the twenty-four hour hustle and bustle, and food (even the Chinese food tastes different than in the mainland). The general lifestyle of Hong Kong is very appealing, not just to mainland Chinese but also to Asians from other parts of the region. The main drawback is the air pollution, much of which is blown inwards from the industrialized Pearl River delta area.

Hong Kong is a must for shopping and sight-seeing. Don't miss the many beautiful exotic islands scattered around the main Hong Kong Island that you can visit on one- or two-day excursions.

The majority of British expats left after the handover in 1997; however, a considerable number have decided to keep Hong Kong their second home. Most British subjects tend to be employed in the financial and insurance sectors (many investment banks have their Asia Pacific headquarters in Hong Kong). A considerable number also work in the airline industry (Cathay Pacific Airways is the national flag carrier of Hong Kong and many of its British staff members, including pilots and cabin crew, are based in Hong Kong).

Useful Websites

www.discoverhongkong.com Official tourist website for Hong Kong
www.gov.hk Official government website of the SAR Hong Kong
www.tdctrade.com Hong Kong Trade Development Council
www.yp.com.hk Hong Kong Yellow Pages
www.hongkongairport.com Official website of Hong Kong Airport

Macau

Macau (Aomen is the Chinese name), a Portuguese colony until 1999, is on the border of Zhuhai to the south of Guangdong province. The Portuguese heritage is evident everywhere as all the signs are in two languages—Mandarin and Portuguese—and the operational currency is "Patacas."

Smaller than Hong Kong (only 26 sq km in size), Macau is now beginning to attract a large number of tourists. However, it is still considered the younger brother to Hong Kong. Macau is famous for gambling and homemade almond butter cookies. The former has been around since licensed gambling was first introduced during the 1850s, and these days Macau is being classed as the Las Vegas of Asia. Macau's casinos are scattered across the region, a peninsula connected to mainland China and two outlying islands by a reclaimed land called Cotai. In August 2007, the world's largest casino, Venetian Casino, managed by the Las Vegas Sands Corporation, officially opened on the island of Cotai. Valued at over $2.4 billion, the Cotai resort contains a hotel with 3,000 rooms, a 15,000-seat sports arena, 1.2 million square feet of convention

Macau Church

space, fine dining and room to accommodate 6,000 slot machines as well as 800 gambling tables. Without a doubt that there is a lot of money here and everyday a considerable number of Chinese from the mainland and Hong Kong come to fill its many casinos in search of fortune. Surprisingly you won't find many James Bond type characters with tuxedos in these casinos, as the majority of gamblers seem to be retired pensioners who are just whiling away time and enjoying the company of fellow senior citizens. Nevertheless they do seem to be minted.

A sizable number of expats from Canada, America, and some European countries are investing in the casino business and have therefore effectively made Macau their second home.

Apart from gambling and almond cookies, Macau is also famous for the Grand Prix (both motorbike and racing car), which is held annually.

Useful Websites

www.macautourism.gov.mo Official Macau Government website
www.macau-airport.gov.mo Macau International Airport website
www.wtc-macau.com Macau World Trade Center
www.macaunews.net Macau News
www.cityguide.gov.mo Macau City Guide
www.umac.mo University of Macau
www.yp.com.mo/en/ Macau Yellow Pages

CHAPTER 3:
HOUSING/ACCOMMODATIONS

It should not pose many problems if you want to rent accommodations in China. For the majority of expats, their employer would arrange some sort of relocation assistance, such as helping to find accommodation close to the office. If your employer is unable to assist you with this, an alternative option would be to ask other expats or any Chinese friend who speaks good English, and go with them to the estate agent. It should be borne in mind that not many estate agents can converse in English.

Along with the growing economy, high-rise apartment buildings are being constructed all the time, offering plenty of choice for price, location, and space. Renting or buying a home in China is not as complex as in Europe or America; however, for the Chinese, the rocketing pace at which house prices are rising is a major issue. Most developments will have a management office situated on location. It's usually just a matter of finding a complex that suits your daily needs and then you can ask to be shown around all the apartments that are up for rent (or those that are of interest to you). Most apartments have an average living space of approximately 400 sq ft (approx 37 square meters) with one or two bedrooms or a studio apartment.

The Chinese taste in furniture and furnished housing is usually different from European or Western tastes, so you can specify that you want to have a western style kitchen or bathroom and also a western style toilet, unless you prefer a Chinese style toilet. You should also specify that you want air conditioning in your apartment as it will get exceedingly uncomfortable in the summer months. Normally most homes only have one air conditioning unit placed in their bedroom, leaving the rest of the home feeling like a sauna.

On the whole, China does have a problem with housing, simply because of the high population. Homes are generally very simple and seem cramped. The toilet and the kitchen are usually built side by side. One Chinese friend told me the reason behind this is that it saves trouble having to go to the other side of the house if someone needs to go to the toilet or wash their hands while they are in the kitchen. Chinese kitchens and bathrooms tend to be much smaller than those in the west. There are two reasons for this, one being the lack of space and the other being the convenience of having everything within arms' reach in the kitchen, rather than wandering around the kitchen to get your cooking ingredients. Homes don't have a carpet as they do in the west, even in northern China, where it can get bitterly cold. This does create the problem of having to clean floors filled with dust and small amounts of black soot that piles up due to the polluted atmosphere, especially in cities such as Guangzhou and Xian.

In some homes people prefer to have a sofa bed in the living room, which can double as extra seating if relatives or visitors arrive and an extra bed for them if they stay overnight. Sometimes it is common for more than two families to live in cramped conditions in one home. In the main cities this is becoming increasingly less common as people are rewarded with higher salaries. Washing machines are smaller in size than in the west and even though they do the job properly, during spinning clothes are vulnerable to being either shrunk or torn.

There may be hidden issues that you won't be exposed to when you initially rent your apartment, such as noise at night time or early in the morning. Some Chinese people like to play cards or Mah-Jong well into the night while under the influence of alcohol; often with their windows and apartment doors open; this is the case in some hotels as well. And if you are living near a Chinese school, then most likely you will be awakened at about six thirty in the morning, during schooldays of course, by children arriving in school and singing the national anthem or playing loud instrumental music that is often terribly out of tune!

Most developments consist of high-rise flats. Choosing a high floor is probably the best option to avoid street noise and mosquitoes. It's common that you may get some bad smell through the drainage pipe. The best remedy for this is to use liquid bleach, which can be purchased from any supermarket or convenience store. Most landlords will push you to sign for at least six months, although it is possible to rent a room for three months in some areas—it purely depends on the landlord and the area where the house is up for rent. It's a buyers' market so if you really like a place, even if there are slight flaws such a new paint job being required or a tacky piece of furniture being present, then inform the landlord and he or she may change it for you at no charge.

Foreigners who rent apartments with gas appliances should be aware that in some areas, natural gas is not scented to warn occupants of gas leaks or concentrations. In addition, heaters may perhaps not constantly be vented, thus allowing surplus carbon monoxide to build up in living spaces. Due to some fatal accidents relating to foreigners, individuals are advised to make sure that all gas appliances are suitably vented or install gas and carbon monoxide detectors in their residences. These devices are not extensively obtainable in China, and they should be purchased, if possible, prior to arrival.

Bathrooms and Toilets

A Chinese home is most likely to have a shower fitted with access to hot water. Bathtubs are rare, only to be seen in western-style hotels and maybe the more affluent apartments.

Usually the shower and toilet are in the same room. Modern homes have a western-style toilet, whereas the majority of homes are fitted with a Chinese-style toilet, which is basically an open drain in the ground where people can sit by putting their feet on each side. Public toilets are much the same except that there is no tissue available, so it would be advisable to take some with you when out and about. This provides an explanation as to why the tissue paper is perfumed.

As a foreigner you will find it strange and unhygienic that the Chinese prefer to throw the used toilet paper into the bin rather than flush it down the toilet. This is very much the case in any home, office, or hotel, simply because the quality of the sewage system is poor. From my unfortunate experience I discovered that my toilet got blocked in the five-star hotel in Guangzhou where I was staying—and on my first trip to China! The hotel staff politely advised me to put the tissue into the bin in the bathroom—at first I thought the guy was joking.

Maids (Baomu)

The country's rush to prosperity, and rules that make it easier for rural residents to move to the cities, mixed in with the middle class who are too busy to look after their daily housing needs, has meant an increase in the number of young people from the rural areas (mostly women) taking up employment as maids in affluent households in the big cities.

If you are going to lead a busy working life and seldom have time to cook for your family, then perhaps it's more convenient for you to hire a house maid. It's common in China to employ a house maid who would do the cleaning and cooking. The average costs vary between 400 RMB and 1500 RMB per month depending on the area where you live and the amount of hours he or she would work.

The advantage of employing a house maid is that he or she will cook the food just like you want it to be, and also the type of food that you want. With prior notice, the maid will go and buy the required food, cook it, and have it ready for you to eat when you come back from work.

House maids are, of course, Chinese and speak limited amounts of English. In some expat areas in the major cities, in recent times Filipino and Indonesian maids have started being employed. The main advantages of hiring Filipinos are that they can speak English as well as cook western food if you prefer. The hiring costs may be a little higher than hiring Chinese maids, but it will be worthwhile. For further information on hiring maids, the best source would be to get in touch with your friends or colleagues at work or try any of the local English literature such as the "That's" series of magazines (e.g., That's Guangzhou, see p. 36).

Electricity and Water

China has an efficient power supply throughout the country, with electricity shortages and blackouts a rare occurrence. In case of an emergency it would be wise to stock up with some candles (Lazhu) and a working torch (shoudiantong). Bills can be paid using a direct debit scheme with your associated bank, or a monthly deposit can be made from the dedicated bank account. Your landlord or employer (if the accommodation is provided by your company) would be first point of contact for any assistance.

It would not be wise to drink straight from the tap (even in five-star hotels or restaurants). Tap water should be boiled before drinking. Don't be surprised to see some yellow/slightly muddy water pouring through the taps, even in some five-star hotels (although the latter is rare). Bottled water is available in most shops.

People seldom use tap water for drinking and only use boiled tap water for cooking. For drinking water, most households (and offices) in China have a five-liter capacity water tank in their living rooms. This is operated by the main electricity and has hot and cold water taps.

Dry Cleaners (Gan Xi)

You can get all your laundry washed, dried, and ironed at a small price at most dry cleaners. The service is excellent and professional and at a set price—don't worry about being charged extra because you are a foreigner, because you won't. If you are not provided with a washing machine in your accommodation, then the dry cleaners may be the best option for you.

DIY (Ziji Dongshou)

China's middle class and expats alike have IKEA, B&Q and Dulux Paint shops that cater for those who want to have a go at DIY. Something that started off as an experiment, for foreign investors, has actually proved to be quite successful so far, aiming at the younger generation with high level incomes and who are potentially first-time buyers in China's booming property market. B&Q has over fifty stores on the mainland and has proved popular with the Chinese consumers.

If you are planning on carrying out your own DIY then be assured that you should have no problem buying that much missed BBQ that you wish you had in China—well, now you can!

Noise

Unlike in other countries, where workmen only work during the weekdays and business hours on construction sites, in China, construction goes on twenty-four hours a day and seven days a week. It's astonishing to observe that when a project is commissioned for construction to start, the workmen first build their own homes, usually with timber and corrugated iron, and then they start building the actual assigned project.

The Chinese have grown accustomed to such noise in their neighborhoods that many people don't even bother complaining. Therefore there is not much you can do to stop the noise, say for example, of a drill in the middle of the night, except maybe complain to the accommodation management office. Even if the staff in the management office take the complaint into account, especially if it's made by a foreigner, it is most likely that the workers won't stop just because one person is complaining. Or they may stop for a while, and then start again by ignoring the plea made by the sleepless residents!

Security Guards

Expats will be relieved to know that every apartment building has security guards on duty twenty-four hours a day and seven days a week, except the very low end of the housing market where foreigners are highly unlikely to stay. Your landlord should be able to provide you with details of emergency numbers, for which guards can come to assist with any problem, ranging from your water supply not running to any other neighborhood problems. Most homes have a small watch glass in the front door that allows you to see who's outside but doesn't allow them to see you.

Foreigners should not open the door without looking through the watch glass in their door first. The security staff usually don't allow a non-resident into the neighborhood; however, sometimes people posing as "mailers" get through, and this can be dangerous if intruders or trespassers find their way in. There have been some cases of foreigners being targeted by prostitutes, thieves, and robbers in expat areas because somehow they know where a foreigner lives.

Registering as a Foreigner in China

As a foreigner you will need to register your residential address and contact details with your local Public Security Bureau (PSB). It is best that you register as soon as you are aware of your residential address. This is mandatory as infrequently the PSB will carry out random checks, and a fine is most likely to be given if they have no record of you. Also if you want to extend your visa, and you haven't registered, problems are sure to occur. Because not many police officers can converse in English, it's best if you can either take one of your Chinese-speaking colleagues or an English-speaking Chinese friend with you. The procedure is simple and takes only a few minutes. All you need is your original passport, visa, and your original rental contract/agreement. The PSB will take copies of all documents and then issue you with two copies of the resident certificate. One copy is kept on file by the PSB while the other you will need to provide when you apply for

Private housing estates in Guangzhou

a work permit. If you are residing in a hotel, then the staff will take care of all procedures when you check in, and all you need to provide them with is a copy of your original passport.

Real Estate Boom

With the rising demand for luxury apartments by the middle class, China's real estate market is one of the fastest growing in the world. These real estates are being built on farmland that is either no longer in use or where the farmers are being asked to give up the land by Communist party–friendly "real estate moguls," in return for a small compensation. Communist party–friendly developers are investing heavily in building an array of real estate across the country as there is a big demand for luxury apartments from China's middle class. Usually the farmers are paid around the equivalent of $40-$50 per month. With nearly seventy million acres of farmland converted to real estate development and approximately 130 million people unemployed in 2006, the disadvantages of real estate development in china are clear. The farmers themselves have no choice.

Taking a look at this real estate does make one wonder where the future of China's middle class is heading. The majority of the estates are beautifully located in the suburbs of major cities, along with their own man-made lakes, sports fields, supermarkets, schools, and even their own small hospitals. The houses themselves are as impressive as their location, with some of the crème de la crème penthouses offering designer furniture, swimming pools, and gold-trimmed bath tiles. It's the kind of stuff that British footballers would love to have. Prices for some of the high-end market homes start from around $250,000. With increasing competition in the region (Japan, Korea, and India are all experiencing such property booms), it may be considered a good investment for the future.

In actual fact purchasing property in China is easier than renting it simply because you don't have to worry about bothering your landlord with monthly payments or any extra costs that may appear out of the ordinary. It's a very simple procedure and there is not much paperwork involved. All you need to do is to register the property with your local PSB (Public Security Bureau) and pay the money in full or as a mortgage to your Estate Agent.

If you are staying in China for a long period of time, or if you like China, then as an expat it may be tempting for you to buy property in one of the major cities such as Shanghai, Beijing, Shenzhen, and Guangzhou. With the Beijing Olympics in 2008, the Shanghai Expo 2010, the Guangzhou Asian Games 2010 and the Shenzhen Universiade in 2011 all around the corner, it could make economic sense to invest in China's boom now rather than later. The value of the property is set to rise and so some expats are looking at buying property in these tempting areas now and then perhaps selling it at a higher price when the above-mentioned events occur. The key to being successful in the property investment business is to decide carefully which property to invest in and where exactly within the city. Of course the stakes are high if you are investing near the CBD or near major ports—but it's more expensive too.

If you are unfamiliar with China, then buying property here would be awkward as you are not accustomed to the local practices and laws. It would also be helpful to have Chinese friends who can advise on such issues on the mainland. This can sometimes save you a mint because you are not spending much on getting similar advice from relocation consultants.

Hotels in China

Hotel costs in China vary depending on the quality. In China, hotels are generally much cheaper than western standards and if booked within China, then even internationally renowned five-star hotels can be reserved at a cheaper price. Beijing, for example, has several classes of hotels (these are just ballpark figures; please don't take them as actual prices):

1. Five-star hotels – Expensive, comparable with international standards – anything from 400 RMB upwards.
2. Middle-range western-style hotels – 300 RMB-500 RMB per night
3. Middle range Chinese hotels – 200 RMB-450 RMB per night
4. Inexpensive Chinese hotels (may contain just a simple room with a Chinese style toilet and bathroom) – Under 200 RMB per night.

Numerous middle-range western-style hotels have offered discount rates to those who book in advance through travel agencies on the high street or through the online travel companies (such as www.ctrip.com or www.elong. net). The discounts can be as much as seventy percent off the original price. Some hotels can give discounts if you show your business card or company ID card as some companies in China have partnerships with hotels. Consult the hotel reception upon checking in for this.

Inexpensive Chinese style hotels may not include amenities that a foreigner from a westernized country might consider essential, such as English black tea, international television stations, or a western style bathroom. Most hotels in China offer air conditioning and hot water as basic amenities, irrespective of their standards. The Chinese government started talks in 2006 for the country's first underground five-star hotel to be open in Shanghai's southeastern Songjiang district by 2010, in time for the Expo.

There are a number of things you may find different as a foreigner in any hotel in China, such as that the toilet may get blocked and that the water supply of the shower is either too hot or too cold and you cannot have anything warm in between! The "blocked toilet" problem is simply because the sewage system in China is not as good as that in developed countries. Noise may be a problem in some Chinese hotels because if traveling in groups, then Chinese people like to keep their doors open and talk loudly while playing cards or drinking. It creates a nice party atmosphere for them but in the excitement people tend to forget that some people need to get some sleep, especially after a long flight or a long day!

Other minor but important things such as toothpaste, razor blades, and shaving cream are not quite what you would expect in a developed country. Bring your own if you can. Most hotels provide a clean plastic comb, disposable slippers, and clean bathrobes (only in the western style hotels!). Sometimes there is a fridge provided in the room but it may be empty.

Other inexpensive housing accommodations may likewise be very different from what most foreigners from developed countries may be accustomed to, and therefore you may not find them suitable to your needs, especially with a new baby or toddler. In the major cities, universities are able to offer accommodations at a cheaper price and they are comfortable, clean and offer all the basic amenities that good western style hotels offer. For example in Beijing, both of the famous universities (Qinghua and Beijing universities) have rooms for rent to foreigners, and in Guangzhou, Jinan University offers very good quality rooms for under 200 RMB per person. It's always best to consult a Chinese friend about university accommodations as staff members seldom speak English and if your friend is a student then they might be able to get an extra discount for you.

Personal Experience

A Tunisian friend I met in a hotel in Foshan once told me that "All hotels in China are more or less the same!"; "it's not like in Europe or Tunisia where we can distinguish the quality of the hotel by the name or the number of stars." Not quite right, I thought to myself, but I think what he actually meant is that all hotels in China have the basic amenities that any human would expect in any part of the world such as a nice clean room with a working toilet and bathroom.

In amusement, I told him that I have had the "pleasure" of seeing the worst! I was on a business trip in Beijing when my Chinese manager decided that we should save the company some money and stay in a Chinese hotel close to the office. I remember arriving at the hotel on a typical hot and dry summer's day. The first impressions of the hotel (which was in the IT area of Beijing, Shangdi) were that it looked like something out of an American western movie with dust everywhere. Inside it was old, dark, and shabby. To my shock there was a pile of live toads and snails lurking in a large green net in the hotel reception, I assumed waiting to go to the kitchen for supper that evening!

After checking in at the reception, it took some time for me to first open the room, and then took the same amount of trouble to lock it once I was inside. The air conditioning was working but it sounded rather like an engine of a Spitfire aircraft about to take off, the water supply was a contrast of either being boiling hot or being freezing cold—so having a nice warm shower was out of the question, the bed sheets were smelly but amazingly still white and clean in appearance, and to top it all up there were mosquitoes to keep me company throughout the night (along with that roaring AC!). Oh and I forgot the nuisance calls I got at about two or three in the morning, which went something on the lines of: *"Hello, You like Chinese girl/massage?"* Taking the cable out of the telephone socket solved that problem!

The following morning my manager told me that someone entered his room twice at night thinking that they were booked into his room; clearly both the hotel management's booking system and his door lock didn't work. We decided to have breakfast in the company canteen instead of the hotel.

Without question we checked out in the morning and went to a four-star western style hotel that was a short taxi ride away in downtown Beijing. To our surprise the cost of the room in the western hotel was exactly the same as that of the Chinese hotel from hell in which we stayed the previous night. Hence we didn't really save anything by staying there! Plus there was cable television with CNN and the BBC world service, English tea, a daily dose of the *South China Morning Post* (SCMP) newspaper and English breakfast all included in the price! Let me reassure you that not all hotels in China are like this but I was just unlucky to have witnessed one of the worst.

CHAPTER 4:
TRANSPORT IN CHINA

Gone are the days when China was known as the land of bicycles. These days it's all about planes, trains, and automobiles, and there are plenty of all three here. Taxies, planes, and the general traffic on the road are susceptible to jams as soon as there is any sign of rain—so expect delays if it is raining—queues at airports (for passengers and for planes waiting to depart) and at train stations can be very long indeed.

The Pedestrian Is Not the King of the Road

Shocking as it may seem to any foreigner, in China the driver does not give way to the pedestrian, but the pedestrian has to give way to the driver first. The car driver here is the king of the road, so be careful when crossing the road as it is very easy to get in trouble. If you are crossing the road the driver will not stop to give way, instead they will just keep on driving slowly towards your direction until they either hit you or you move out of the way!

Air Travel

As in the global aviation industry, flying domestically in China has steadily become cheaper than before and there is plenty of choice in times and destinations. During off-peak seasons flights can usually be bought at the last minute and for a reasonable price. The cabin crews of airlines in China are professional, friendly, and speak good English. Unlike the "dress down code" that some airlines follow these days, Chinese cabin crew and pilots are immaculately dressed in airline uniform throughout the entire flight, complete with pointy hats, which are reminiscent of the 1960's era, the halcyon days for flying.

Flying in China as a westerner can be bit of an amusing affair to say the least. While even the smallest of the airports is to some extent clean and modern and the aircraft used by the large number of Chinese airline companies are the best in the industry, the manpower behind the operation of the airports and those magnificent flying machines is not so up to scratch with modern times.

While it may seem that China has too many airlines and too many airports, you will be glad to know that there are plans for further airports to be opened in rural and remote areas, as well as more private airlines, thus making it easier for everyone to fly around China at affordable rates. Tickets are available either at travel agents throughout the country, at airline offices (listed in this book), or at the airport. Another problem that you may encounter is that in most places airline tickets need to be paid for in cash only, although some travel agents are starting to accept credit cards.

One of the main problems experienced by foreigners includes flights being delayed or cancelled without explanation. As air traffic in China is on the increase, and will continue to be so for the next few decades, the logistic problems associated with this industry also continue to increase. Thankfully, however, gone are the days when hair-raising hard landings with aircraft being

An Air China Boeing 737-700 decorated in special Olympics livery parked at Zhuhai International Airport, October 2006

"kangaroos'" on the runway were the norm. Better airport infrastructure, more experienced maintenance staff, the latest western manufactured aircraft, and better trained pilots have contributed to the ongoing success and boom in the Chinese aviation industry. With domestic air travel increasing for the Beijing Olympics and air ticket prices falling, flying in China is becoming an affordable luxury for many.

One particular incident I have experienced occurred at Beijing airport in 2004. I had been in China for only about a month and was traveling back to Guangzhou after a holiday in the capital. There seemed to be a considerable number of foreigners on this flight, including Canadians and Americans, on vacation in China. We were due to catch the second from last flight of the day to Guangzhou and while waiting at the boarding gate that was assigned for this flight, suddenly there was confusion all around. It seemed that the gate number was changed at the last minute. Airport staff were clearly seen panicking and could not offer any explanation as to which gate number we had to go to.

Finally, after about an hour of walking up and down the three different gates that were assigned for our flight, we were, to our shock and anger, informed by the airport PA announcement that the flight had by now been cancelled. No explanation was given for this and no financial compensation offered except that the airline did book the passengers into a hotel for the night. Unlike at Hong Kong airport, where the ground staff are exceedingly efficient in getting planes to meet their departure slots, airports in China have quiet a way to go before those standards are matched.

Passengers themselves may also contribute to crashes as in China, some passengers ignore the safety warnings and use their mobile phones while the plane is accelerating down the runway for take-off, while it's in the initial climb, or while cruising at 35,000 ft! One time when I was flying on a business trip from Shenzhen to Beijing with a Chinese colleague, we must have been cruising about one hour into the three-hour short-haul flight when the passenger sitting in the front seat started shouting "Wei!, Wei Ni Hao!" ("Hello!"). As I turned to look, I was shocked to see her yelling on the mobile phone rather than talking to her fellow passengers. I did what any other human being would do and advised the cabin crew. Later I found out that this solution seemed to work temporarily; as sometime into the flight, as the plane was about to approach Beijing, she seemed to forget the earlier incident (or maybe ignored it!) and started using the phone again.

Airline food on Chinese airlines is another popular topic that crops up when expats are conversing while waiting in airport lounges because it seems that the catering management has no clue whatsoever as to how to make a decent airline meal. Airline catering companies have in recent times recruited expats who specialize in nothing but airline food to try and improve the standards. In the meantime, anyone fancy dry roasted peanuts that taste like rock salt? Or locally branded (copied) coca-cola and other fizzy drinks that I have only seen on domestic flights. Vegetarians have to take caution as it is difficult, if not impossible, to get vegetarian options on domestic flights.

There are very few, if any, in-flight magazines that are printed in English. The in-flight magazines for all the airlines in China are published by the state owned CAAC (Civil Aviation Authority of China), which operates the state-owned flag carrier, Air China.

As for the in-flight entertainment, Kenny G seems to be doing good business with the Chinese airline companies, as every time a domestic flight lands, the cabin crew play one of his tunes on the PA.

You need to pay airport tax when you depart from any city in China. Departure tax on all domestic flights is fifty Yuan at the time of writing (approx. US $6.00) and for international flights it is ninety Yuan (approx. US $12.00). You need to pay the airport tax at the booth near check-in.

Bicycles

Cycles are without a doubt still used vastly in rural areas and smaller cities. In the big cities there are separate lanes for cycles, and in view of the Beijing Olympics, steps are being taken to create more separate cyclist lanes, which are safer and much more efficient for moving the traffic along.

In any city, town, or tourist destination, you can hire a bike for a day. In places such as Yangshou, Guilin, Xian, and Beijing, hiring a bike is not a problem for foreigners and it's a highly recommended mode of transport, since you get to see more than you would just by sitting in a taxi. If you are going to be cycling in the cities, it would be wise to wear a mask to cover your nose and mouth to protect yourself from the ever-growing pollution. These masks are available in Watson's drug stores as well as any sports shop.

To own a bike, registration will need to be completed. Registration is normally done at the time of buying. Most embassies and consulates advise people not to buy second-hand bikes unless the owner has proof of receipt or registration, as otherwise these are likely to have been stolen. Cycles can be bought at any sports shop or foreign market such as Wal-Mart and Carrefour. When buying a cycle in China always make sure that the body structure, brakes, lights, and tires are working properly.

Punctures are common in the suburbs due to the dusty uneven tracks and therefore can also damage the brakes. Cycle repair shops, usually managed by young boys, can repair minor faults such as punctures and broken lights for a small charge while you wait.

Buses

The majority of public transport buses in China are air conditioned, clean, and have a non-smoking policy (except the ones with open windows). However, they normally tend to be overcrowded, hence pickpocketing and groping are common in the big cities. On the whole petty crime against foreigners on public transport is rare and China on the whole is safer than London or New York. Nevertheless like anywhere in the world, just be careful not to put your mobile phone or wallet in your breast pocket or somewhere thieves may find it an easy target: Pickpockets normally operate in groups of three or four people; usually one person steals as the bus comes to a stand, then the rest of the group scatter in different directions to deceive the victim.

Coach Travel

Coaches are clean and air conditioned with televisions that show Chinese movies or songs. Bottled water is provided free of charge on majority of the routes and coaches are equipped with toilets, although ironically, on long journeys these may be out of service. Apart from the normal coach, there is also the sleeper coach, which is slightly pricier than the former. The sleeper coach contains beds aligned in a dormitory style configuration with no privacy and with very little space to move around, making them less than comfortable to say the least. They are used for journeys involving more than seven hours and are normally meant to be operated during the night; however, they can be used for daytime travel if it's a long journey.

There is also the possibility that "unexpected" maintenance stops may be made, hence delaying the journey. For those who detest the smell of cigarettes, it may be delightful to know that smoking is not permitted on any sleeper coach. One thing you will have to bear with is passengers snoring loudly, which is common on packed trains, buses, and planes throughout China!

One thing that foreign travelers may find strange is that before every long-distance journey the driver or the coach staff normally take photos of every passenger; rest assured this is for your own good in case there is a crash, so that they have a record of all passengers abroad. This may, however, give you the uncomfortable feeling that coach operators are well aware that road crashes are common in China! The service on the coach is similar to flying as the coach hostesses are always dressed like 1960's-style air hostesses with pointy hats.

Driving Yourself

It goes without saying that driving in China is an erratic and nerve-racking experience. It also may seem dangerous to the newcomer. Even though car ownership has soared in recent years, the private car is still a very new thing in China and therefore driving is also a very new concept in China. Despite there being set rules in place it's fair to say that people tend not to think much when driving because they just drive without observing or considering the consequences of an accident. One Chinese friend told me that in China people like to drive the way they want to drive. People always have the thought at the back of their minds that "it will never happen to me."

Therefore don't be surprised to see a person driving a Ferrari at 30 mph in the fast lane on the highway or a car suddenly changing lanes without putting on the indicator. The driving and therefore the traffic in Shenzhen is somewhat better than most other cities in China; however, it is still considered very poor compared to international standards. On average, six people get killed on the roads of Shenzhen everyday, as compared to over 200 in the rest of China. In the many years that I have lived in China, almost every day to and from work, I witnessed at least one accident (normally it's a car with a large vehicle or a small bus).

Obtaining a Driver's License in China

The following is the information obtained from the Shanghai Vehicle Management Bureau. With their kind permission, this has been translated into English. This information gives you an idea of what is involved in the process of obtaining a driver's license in China. On the whole, it's strongly recommended that in case you do decide to embark on getting a driving license in China, then the best channel to go through would be the local Shanghai Vehicle Management Bureau in your city.

Foreigners should provide their passport along with the original script and copy of their Resident Permit or work visa (Z Type). Individuals are authorized to submit an application for a driver's license if their resident permit is for over one year. You are allowed to apply only for a temporary driver's license if your resident permit or work visa is for over three months but less than one year. As a holder of an international driver's license, you have to go to an authorized "Foreign Language Translation Company" to translate the driver's license into Chinese. This is important because your Chinese driver's license cannot be issued if it is not printed in both Chinese and English.

This is the procedure in all cases; even if you have an International driving license, then you still need to apply for a Chinese license. The steps required to obtain a Chinese driver's license:

1. Normally require two or three color passport-sized photographs.
2. A completed driver's license application form, available from the local Vehicle Management bureau.
3. Take the driving practical test and supply the medical check certificate issued by the hospital (normally this can also be a copy of the medical certificate which you took before applying for a work permit).
4. Finally you need to take the test that checks your communication regulation knowledge—this is a short theory test that is sometimes conducted verbally if the learner cannot read Chinese. Therefore expats would be asked questions verbally by the examiner instead of a paper test.

After the submission of all the above-required documents to the driving bureau, a payment of 20 RMB needs to be paid as the commission fee. Normally it takes approximately one week to get your Chinese driver's license.

Ferry Travel

Taking a boat ride on the river at night time in a city such as Shanghai or Guangzhou can be a very pleasant and romantic experience. Various types of tickets are available depending on if you want to sit on the upper deck to marvel at the scenery or enjoy a meal, which normally is a Chinese buffet accompanied with free-flowing Chinese tea and drinks.

For long-distance trips such as Guangzhou to Hainan Island or pleasure boat journeys along the Yangtze River, for example, the experience can be quite memorable and nice. Boats are clean, offer plenty of sight-seeing opportunities, and usually have an on-board restaurant. As with other modes of transport during the holiday season in China, ferries are usually overbooked and crowded.

Metro and Trains

Unlike the older, nosier, dirtier, and often non-air-conditioned metro system in most developed countries (London Underground and the New York subway are prime examples), China's metro system (called Subway in Beijing) in comparison seems much more advanced in terms of technology, very safe, much cleaner (graffiti-free and free of bad odors), and very comfortable. The metro does have slight drawbacks; with China being the world's most populous country, it is no surprise that trains are likely to be extremely crowded in rush hours. Be on guard against thieves, both on the train and on the platform, especially when it is particularly crowded. Thankfully all metro trains in China are air conditioned—which is a relief, especially in the summer. On-board announcements in both trains and metros are made in Chinese and English.

There are stations where several metro lines meet. Be careful not to confuse the words **interchange** and **transfer**. An interchange station is a station where you can change for other lines without having to go through a ticket barrier, and a transfer station is one where you have to leave the first line through a ticket barrier and then be charged for another line.

Trains in China are still the preferred mode of travel over long distance for the vast majority of the population, and more so during the national holidays when seats need to be booked well in advance. Bear in mind that trains can

Guangzhou Metro

be subject to delays and/or cancellations due to severe winter weather, as was the case during the 2008 Chinese New Year season when thousands of people were left stranded at train stations across the country. Most trains in China have glass windows, are air conditioned, and have an on-board restaurant or trolley service for snacks and refreshments. As opposed to air travel, trains in China are exceedingly efficient in getting off the station platform on time. Trains for long-distance journeys are not overcrowded as they used to be (exceptions can still be made for the hard seat compartments!), as only passengers with seat bookings are accommodated on board. There are four types of ticket available for all long-distance journeys in China:

1. Hard Seat

This is the cheapest ticket on offer; however the seat is not comfortable because it's similar to a hard wooden bench with no cushion or headrest, except maybe the window seal. Bear in mind that for many people this is more than enough as people look for the cheaper option and seats are booked well in advance during the holiday season or at weekends. There is also no privacy and compared with western standards it is dirty and smelly.

2. Hard Bed

This is similar to a hard bench seat except you have room to stretch your legs. There is no bedding provided; although on some routes you can rent bed sheets and pillows for a small charge. There is no privacy as the berths are arranged in a bunk bed configuration with no separate cabins. For long journeys it can cause a headache for those of us who are not used to the Chinese way of living. It can also be very noisy as people start playing cards, conversing loudly, and perhaps even enjoying a drink or two; mix all of that with babies crying, the stench of body odor or people smoking like chimneys and I'll leave the rest to your imagination.

3. Soft Seat

Depending on the train used and the length of the journey, seats may be leather padded or just soft cushions; nevertheless it is considerably much more comfortable than the hard seats, and less noisy.

4. Soft Bed

The soft beds are very comfortable and in quiet cabins, with each cabin having its own separate lockable door and four berths arranged in a bunk bed configuration. Each berth has its own reading light, a comfortable and clean pillow, bed sheet and quilt provided, along with a coat hanger. On some routes a toothbrush, disposable pair of slippers and washing-up soap are also provided. If you have time on your side, then for an overnight trip this may seem a comfortable alternative to air travel. As opposed to air travel there is no need to check in for domestic train journeys, end to end journey time is reduced because the train stations are in the heart of the city, unlike airports, which are located in the suburbs. There is more room to sleep or stretch your legs, it's roughly the same price as a flight on that route, and a nice hot complimentary dinner is provided, which actually tastes better than airline meals!

For business travel it may not be convenient to take a day journey from Guangzhou to Shanghai, for example; however, some people do take sleeper trains for journeys involving less than twelve hours of travel, so they can reach their office in the morning the following day. I once met a German businessman on a sleeper train from Beijing to Shanghai. He told me he found it much more comfortable and convenient to take the sleeper train than to take a two-hour flight between the two cities. His reasons for choosing the sleeper train were understandable too: From Beijing the train leaves at seven in the evening and arrives twelve hours later straight in the heart of Shanghai, with enough time at the destination to get him refreshed before going to his office.

Passengers on long-distance journeys can purchase a western breakfast or a Chinese one. From experience, I would recommend eating your breakfast once you arrive at your destination or try the Chinese option, unless your train journey takes you past breakfast time. The western breakfast is expensive and would most likely contain just two pieces of white bread with a spoonful of fruit jam placed in the middle or a fried egg liberally soaked in cooking oil — not appetizing at all.

With the opening of the 714-mile Qinghai to Lhasa (Tibet) rail link, train travel has become among the most modern in the world and includes some unique features that have been introduced for the first time in China.

These include having cabins that are fitted with oxygen masks (because of the high altitude that the railway line goes through), temperature control to keep the temperature warm in sub-zero freezing conditions (outside temperature can go as low as minus thirty-five degrees Celsius with crosswinds of over 50 mph), signs and announcements in three languages (English, Mandarin, and Tibetan), the train's crew include both Tibetan and Chinese nationals, for the on-board meals there is a choice of western, Chinese, and selected Tibetan dishes on offer, and the stunning views of the Tibetan plateau provide the

Beijing to Shanghai Train, restaurant inside

perfect icing on the cake for the passengers. The plateau covers approximately 2.3 million square kilometers and is situated on average four thousand meters above sea level.

Private Jets – The Future of Flying in China?

With an increase in the number of China's super-rich businessmen who earn serious amounts of money, affluent Chinese travelers are becoming more choosy because as their numbers continue to increase, and their average age becomes younger, they want their own private jets to be able to save them the hassle of waiting at airport queues. Of course the beauty of private jet travel is that travelers can go anywhere, any time of the day, and without the hassle of aircraft delays.

Many aviation analysts believe that China is set to become a booming market for private jets in the coming years, as important events beyond the Beijing Olympics will contribute to China's rising economy. China's private jet industry is destined to offer a more efficient, affordable means of traveling in a world that is becoming ever more congested.

The line between business and luxury travel is not clear because workaholic Chinese travelers, who have grown accustomed to being constantly in contact wherever they are, continue to conduct business even while they are on vacation. I remember one of my former Chinese directors had his phone on "standby mode" twenty-four hours a day so that colleagues in China can contact him anytime for work-related issues, even when he was on holiday with his family in Europe. Put this into perspective—with the fact that by around 2020, it has been predicted that China will have a staggering five million "super millionaires" with assets of more than $2 million. Given that the private jet business is booming in Europe and the USA, it will undoubtedly boom further in China.

Taxies in China

Taxies are metered and available 24/7 throughout the country. There is no need to book in advance or go to a designated taxi stand as all can be hailed on the street. Available taxies have a bright red light displayed on their front panel behind the windscreen.

Most taxi drivers cannot speak English, so it is best to get a friend to write down your destination in Chinese so you can show it to the taxi driver. Most hotel staff would be pleased to assist you on this matter and you can always show the business card of the hotel or your destination address.

Travelers should have small bills (RMB 10, 20 and 50 notes) for travel by taxi. Reports of taxi drivers using counterfeit RMB 50 and RMB 100 notes to make change for large bills are increasingly common. Be sure to get a receipt from the taxi driver. Taxi drivers can refuse to take you if you are drunk and behave disorderly. Generally speaking taxi drivers will not cheat you deliberately. Unlike in some western countries where you can pay your taxi fare using a credit card, in China you can only pay using cash.

Taking a taxi in China is, on the whole, safer than in most parts of Europe and the USA. Nevertheless there have been some reports of illegal taxi drivers who either spray passengers with a gas or turn on the air conditioning system that contains a gas to make the passengers fall asleep. This is in order to take the passengers to secluded locations where their partners in crime are waiting for the purpose of mugging. If possible inform your friends or hotel staff about where you are going. In any case it is wise to use only licensed taxies, avoid carrying large amounts of cash or walking alone, and exercise due caution in public areas.

CHAPTER 5:
EMPLOYMENT AND BUSINESS

Job Hunting

If you are sent to China as an expatriate on a contract through your employer in your own country, then you don't need to worry about the material in this chapter as it won't apply to you.

On the other hand if you have just arrived in China and are looking for work then there are a few options you can consider. If you are not looking for a job as a language teacher, then as a foreigner you will find it somewhat difficult to look for corporate employment, but it's not impossible. You have to keep trying hard to find the job or career you are looking for. The following information offers a few helpful tips that may assist you in your job hunting:

1. LOOKING FOR A JOB AS A TEACHER

There is a great demand for teachers who can provide tuition in English, Russian, Italian, Spanish, Japanese, Portuguese, French, or German. Most educational establishments would be willing to reward you handsomely if you can also teach a scientific or humanities subject in these languages. Teachers are respected in China and there is even a Teachers Day when students present gifts to their teachers and sing songs or read poems. Please note that this chapter does not apply to those who will be teaching in International schools because International schools have different standards that are compatible with "International educational law." This section is only for those foreigners who are thinking of teaching in a Chinese school.

English, being the international language, is in more demand than the other languages mentioned above. There are number of channels you can use to find the job that you want. You can apply directly to local schools, either by paying an ad-hoc visit to meet members of the staff, or by telephoning the school beforehand and asking them for vacancies. Don't be afraid of gate crashing into a school and asking the staff politely if they have any vacancies. Staff members at Chinese schools are generally more than happy to see a foreigner enter their school offering to teach a language. It would of course benefit you to wear a suit or look smart and take any proof of your credentials (certificates and similar documents) with you.

There are various websites on which you can register your resume, and some of these websites (listed below) provide direct links to the colleges and universities in most cities in China. You can also try applying to the list of schools and colleges that are provided in this book. Due to the increasing number of language teachers applying for openings, the minimum requirements to be a qualified language teacher in any school/college or organization include having a TEFL certificate and at least a Bachelor's degree, and being a native speaker of the language. The reason why organizations have become strict about requirements is that in recent years there have been quite a number of individuals, native speakers or not, who don't hold the relevant qualifications to teach language. This has been a nuisance for schools/universities especially when the language involved is English. Because most foreigners can speak English, Chinese schools used to be fooled into thinking that any foreigner who can speak English would be a good teacher. In actual fact this is not true at all and, thankfully, organizations that need teachers are realizing this.

Salaries can range anywhere from 3000 RMB per month up to approx. 10,000 RMB a month for those with extensive experience. There may be better offers than these; it just depends on the organization. An Australian expat teacher whom I met in Beijing said that he was offered an all expenses and accommodation paid English teaching job for 9000 RMB a month. Then there was an American teacher who was offered a similar all expenses paid job, but for only 3000 RMB per month.

When you are offered a job as a language teacher here are few things you should be on the look-out for:

- Read your contract carefully before accepting the offer and don't sign anything until you are fully satisfied with the package. Except for the basic salary, the benefits vary for different schools, with some offering any or all of the following:
  - Furnished accommodation with paid bills
  - Paid telephone for local calls
  - Free Internet
  - Drinking water supplied weekly or monthly
  - Three free meals a day provided
  - Five-day or six-day working week
  - One return flight back home (normally this is given after you have completed your contract)

- Be sure to know how many hours of teaching you would be required to do per week. There have been cases in China where the numbers of teaching hours are changed without notice after the contract is signed. This has resulted in teachers being asked to do overtime without being paid.

- There was one case where a foreign teacher gave his one-month notice to his employers; however, the university did not pay for his flight (as stipulated in the contract) and did not pay his one-month salary.

- If you are going to be working outside the major cities, be well prepared for additional culture shocks such as possible power cuts, foreign food, dusty air, blocked sewage system, the weather, and of course language problems.

- If you are going to provide private tuition then be sure you confirm the hourly rate for tuition with the establishment or your student before you start teaching. As a rough guide, hourly tuition rates range from 120 RMB to 250 RMB in the mainland (this depends on the teacher's qualification as well as to whom you are providing tuition—whether it's on an individual basis or to corporations). This may change according to the individual agreement between schools or students and their teachers.

- Foreigners teaching in China, particularly at newly established private secondary schools and private English training centers, have often found their employers unable or unwilling to honor contract terms or to assist in obtaining Chinese employment-based visas and other permits required for foreigners to teach lawfully in China.

- Potential teachers should always ask for references from other foreign teachers who have completed a contract teaching term and have returned to their home country.

- Potential teachers should certainly not arrive in China without receipt of the proper "Z" or work visa from the Chinese Embassy in their country. In some cases, it may be that you will arrive in China with a one-month tourist visa and then your school will provide a "Z-Type" work visa for you.

- Potential teachers must not accept any pledge by a school or institute to acquire the proper visa after their arrival. Health insurance that is provided by Chinese employers ought to be supplemented as described in Chapter 8.

- Prospective teachers should always insist that they be given a contract from their employer rather than from an agent or any third party member. These agents or middle men often get a large part of the monthly pay promised to the teacher. This leaves the teachers without significant financial income. These "fees" are at times not disclosed until after the prospective teacher arrives in China. To date, courts and police in many authorities have declined to interfere in these cases on behalf of foreign teachers.

The most popular English Tuition organization is English First. They have a myriad of opportunities around many cities in greater China and they are very professional in their approach to sign on English teachers. Here are a few websites where you may be able to find a job as an English teacher in China.

www.cbw.com/teaching China Business World
www.chinaeducationexchange.com
www.chinaprogram.com
www.china-tesol.com
www.daveseslcafé.com
www.englishfirst.com English First is the world's largest professional organization for learning English.
www.englishforums.com
www.englishteaching.com
www.eslmonkeys.com
www.teachingabroad.com
www.teachingjobchina.com
www.teachingmania.com

English Corners

When employed as an English teacher you will most probably be asked to attend an English corner. Basically it's an informal open session outside of teaching hours where Chinese students can discuss and ask you, as their English teacher, anything and about any subject. This is designed to improve the students' practical spoken English because they have no other chance to do so. It does test the teacher's patience and professionalism, especially when different sets of students will ask the same questions over and over again. And not surprisingly, most of the time, you are the one who is doing the talking because you have to explain lots of meanings, whereas it should be the other way around.

2. LOOKING FOR A CORPORATE JOB

The saying goes that if you have a degree, can use the computer, and can speak English, then you can get a job anywhere in the world. In China that is also possible, however it can be a little bit tricky because the corporate language is Mandarin. Even in multinationals the staff members discuss all problems in Mandarin. Most of the documents are also in Chinese and meetings are conducted in Chinese. The PowerPoint slides might be in English but the discussion is in Chinese. So therefore it can be a bit of a lonely feeling if you are asked to attend the weekly meeting and you are ignored. It can also cause a few problems if you are an engineer and need to look at technical documents for reference.

While the average salary in China is still around 1800 RMB per month, the corporate sector has started to see an increase in salaries during the past few years, especially in the major cities.

Depending on experience and qualifications, foreigners in general can demand more than the natives. Taxable income from corporate employment includes salaries, wages, and bonuses. A universal stipend of 900 RMB per month is deductible by the Chinese employers from taxable employment salaries.

Foreign nationals are entitled to an additional allowance of approximately 3000 RMB per month, which would bring their total allowable deduction per month to 3900RMB. Here are a couple of salary examples I know from personal experience, but salary is a negotiable matter between the recruiter and the employee.

Case 1: A foreigner with five years of experience and a master's degree was employed by a foreign investment bank in Guangzhou for approx 20,000 RMB per month before tax.

Case 2: A foreign graduate engineer with a bachelor's degree was employed by a multinational in Beijing for approx 6,000 RMB per month before tax.

Apart from the national holidays, especially the Chinese New Year (February), May Day (May 1) and the Mid-Autumn Festival (October 1), employees of foreign multinationals can enjoy anything up to twelve paid holidays a year, while those working for Chinese companies may get a few days less. In the old days of Chairman Mao, people seldom used to take holiday, hence most senior executives have an ethos based on working hard and saving lots of money.

A few companies, such as Philips and Siemens for example, encourage their staff to discuss problems in English and organize team exercises in English. However, language is not the only problem reported by most of the foreign staff members with whom I have worked. Some of the challenges and problems experienced by foreign employees working in China:

Corporate buildings in Shanghai

- Normally in China you cannot just go and see your manager or senior member of staff, and most certainly you cannot argue over any point with your seniors—irrespective of how professional you are in your approach. The corporate environment is built around a hierarchical structure where seniority comes first. That employees have to do what they are told, without their bosses giving them a chance to ask questions, is shocking for most foreigners. Even in corporate meetings, ideas may be shared amongst colleagues; however the final decision has to be made by the Manager or Director. It gives the image that the juniors treat their seniors like father/mother figures, and this is very much true because the Chinese are very status conscious in all business matters.

- If an employee wants to make a point to his or her manager, then the usual channel of communication is through email. It fits in better with the Chinese style of business negotiating and ethics because if their English is not good enough then it saves them from being embarrassed in front of clients for example, and it allows them to reflect more on their answer. If you are doing a good job, your managers will not mind you contacting them on their mobile phone, whereas on the other side of the coin, it would be better to go through the secretary or email. Also, Chinese managers usually don't reply to emails. This is again a sign of seniority and it may be the case that you first have to send an email and then follow up that email with verbal communication.

- In China the corporate culture is such that the Manager or Director does what he/she thinks is best for their employees. In some companies if the employees don't agree with their senior's advice then they risk being fired on the spot. This is common in Chinese companies, especially state-owned ones. This poses a challenge for foreign employees because if you are Manager, your employees will expect you to give them tasks to carry out and they won't use much initiative.

- On the other hand your manager will not expect you to ask him or her questions directly about your work; this can also pose problems because you are expected to know how to do your job or else your manager will probably think that you are not qualified enough for the job.

- There tends to be certain amount of jealousy amongst the Chinese staff members about a foreign staff member's salary. Staff members will openly say to you "I think you get a higher salary then me!", "What's your salary?"—don't be shocked to hear such questions as in China it is considered normal to build trust between your colleagues. The best way is to use diplomacy and try to change the subject.

- There is a certain lack of trust and underestimation of the ability of foreign employees to carry out their duties. Your duties may be changed because your manager may not know what task to give you. You must be aware of the constant reserve (or ridiculous laughter) Chinese display in front of foreigners due to bewilderment at what we might do next. This can be very upsetting, especially when you know what you are doing and how to do it and then someone tends to openly criticize your work to give the image that they are more intelligent than you. Despite any misunderstandings, it is best to present a positive, friendly, and professional image to your peers and your manager and most important not to openly criticize anything or anyone. It is better to keep your integrity and professionalism rather than to let the boat sink.

- If Chinese staff members do something wrong, they shouldn't be openly criticized for their mistakes because losing face for the Chinese is a very important thing. Criticizing them won't do any favors for your career. It is best to just go with the flow and focus on the task that is given to you.

- If you are working for a Chinese company then you may run the risk that on paper you are employed as a Engineer, for example, but in reality they may just use you as a English tutor to assist the department with its advertising or other English documents. This means that you won't be given much exposure or advancement contributing to your career. Definitely you will gain some excellent international experience by working in a Chinese company; however, don't expect to be promoted or given a salary increase every 6 months to a year, as you might in a multinational corporation.

- Flattery is common in all parts of corporate culture in China. Praising your peers in front of other colleagues is a way of keeping trust and negotiation going. It is also common to express reverence to the senior management in front of them.

- If you can communicate in Chinese then this is a huge advantage in your favor because then you will most likely be given real work and responsibilities, rather than just be a PR stunt for the company to show that they are international.

- In some corporations, especially state-owned traditional Chinese companies, the meetings will start off in a formal manner; however, take care not to be shocked to see people spitting or interrupting the speaker by talking loudly on their mobile phones. The worst I have observed is women cutting their fingernails in the middle of corporate meetings!

- Business hours are from 8 am till midday and from 2 pm until 6 pm. Some companies, including multinationals, operate a five-day work week; while most factories, Chinese corporations, and state-owned companies are open six days a week.

- When negotiating in a corporate meeting, a Chinese person may feel that he or she will risk embarrassing both parties by directly offering a negative response. Normally the response from the Chinese side is to remain silent or offer a vague smile.

- In the west, it is usual to ask questions of the speaker if someone is unclear about something. In China, however, audience members rarely ask questions of the speaker, even if they don't understand a point. This is because not being able to understand something is a possible loss of face. On the other hand, if the speaker is saying something wrong in his or her presentation, the audience will also remain silent and not criticize or correct in front of others to save the speaker from losing face. In one meeting when this happened (speaker making mistakes), the audience did not question or correct the speaker, but instead just started leaving the meeting.

- During meetings, the Chinese can be very argumentive and competitive in their approach to make a point. As a foreigner you may not notice this at once; however, if you are around in the company for a while then you will become familiar with this whenever you attend meetings.

- You may find that meetings or a simple talk with your colleague in China may seem to drag on for ages. People actually like this because since childhood, the Chinese are used to listening and observing the other party's views very carefully. Trying to rush the meeting would give the impression that you are not taking your job seriously and it will also seem rude if the speaker talks quickly. In the west people like to wrap things up quickly and not sound boring. For these reasons, in China meetings take some time.

Recruitment Agencies in China

ChinaHR (Monster.com of China)
4/F, CITIC Building 2
19 Jianguomenwai Dajie
Chaoyang District, Beijing, 100004
Service Hotline: 400 888 4567
Phone: +86 (0)108526 1188-1637
Fax: +86 (0) 10 8526 2139
Email: Service@corp.chinahr.com

Wang & Li Recruitment
Room 1801, Tower A, Jian Wai SOHO
39, East 3rd Ring Road, Chao Yang District
Beijing, P.R.CHINA 100022
Tel: +86 (0)10 5869 4671
Fax: +86 (0)10 5869 4672
Email: beijing@wang-li.com
Website: www.wang-li.com/

Zhaopin.com
Building A4, Huitong Office Park No.
71 Jianguo Road District
Beijing. PR China.
100025
Tel: +86 (0)10 5863 5888
Fax: +86 (0)10 5863 5864/65
E-mail: feedback@pub.zhaopin.com.cn
Website: english.zhaopin.com/

Recruitment Websites That Expats Can Use

www.jobchina.net
www.dragonsurf.com/careerwise/index.cfm
www.newchinacareer.com

Afternoon Siesta and Exercise

In most workplaces, including some multinationals, employees (including senior managers and directors) usually take a lunchtime siesta (Xiuxi) either on their chair or under their tables. In some of the traditional Chinese companies, employees are encouraged to buy a mobile mattress and pillow when they join the company. If you are working for a traditional Chinese company, you may even end up having to do group exercise in the morning or after sleeping in the afternoon. This is to boost staff health and morale. The secretary will put on the cassette player and with the vocals "Yi, Er, San, Si... etc. (One, Two, Three, and Four...etc.), the employees take part in an army style exercise!

Networking (Guangxi)

Although networking takes place all around the world, in Asia, especially in China, it has a special meaning to it altogether. Networking, or Guangxi, in China is used for everything from finding a job for your friends or relatives to acting as a matchmaker. If you are looking for a job then Guangxi can work greatly in your favor because it is very common for friends to consult each other if they have an open vacancy or if they know someone who is offering a job. It can be much better than sending your resume through a company corporate website where it may not even get more than just a quick glance by HR.

In China, when a foreigner meets another foreigner on the street, or on public transport, it's a great opportunity to network and you never know who you are going to bump into. You may end up meeting people who you would normally not come across in your home country because in your home country you are in a majority, whereas as an expat you are in a minority that have things in common. These people may be company directors, CEOs, or key HR decision makers within corporations. All of this, of course, provided you are a good networker and comfortable with meeting new people. But on the whole, in China, gaining the skill to "guangxi" with new people would come naturally even if you are not a good networker.

Business Formalities

The Chinese can be exceptionally formal when it comes to corporate events, especially if it involves the participation of foreign clients. Most professionals (including lawyers, corporate executives, investment bankers, and civil servants) wear formal dress to the office. In southern China, where it's hot (and other parts of China where it's hot in the summer), people generally dress down. In some companies, men usually roll up their shirt sleeves and trousers in the summer (especially engineers!).

Whenever two business persons meet for the first time, the formalities are instigated by first shaking hands and then exchanging business cards. Although shaking hands is common with everyone, irrespective of their age or gender, in business terms it is very important to bear in mind that when you are introduced to a colleague or client, you should stand up and shake hands. Even if you are familiar with your Chinese colleagues and even if it is common in your culture to do so, avoid kissing your Chinese colleagues (male or female) anytime during the beginning or conclusion of a meeting or dinner.

Friends or colleagues who know each other quite well will often shake hands firmly and for a little bit longer than in Europe or America. When you give someone your business card, it should be held at the top with two hands, and the person receiving the card also takes it with two hands. It is customary to read the card once someone gives it to you, and maybe even try to repeat their name in Chinese and their position. This will give them a feeling of importance in front of their colleagues and will show that you are giving them your absolute attention. If there are a group of people in the meeting then it is polite to go around the table and meet everyone one by one and not just a few people.

During the meeting people keep the business cards in front of them on the table to remind themselves of who's who, rather than store them away—which again can be seen as impolite. Almost all meetings are held in Chinese, even in multinationals. English may be spoken with foreign clients, although most companies have professional translators present, in case the client's first language is also not English. If you are giving a presentation in English, it would be polite for you to talk slowly, patiently, and clearly, so that those who understand English can follow what you are talking about. It would be an error to shout or talk loudly, and most certainly never show any signs of frustration when talking or explaining to your audience. Even a little sigh may seem rude and will make the Chinese feel embarrassed or uncomfortable.

Maintaining long eye contact with your counterparts is a good sign of business. Constantly looking away from the person you are talking to will give the impression that you are being rude, impolite, and not interested in the business meeting. It can also make your interlocutor lose trust with you. In the west it is different, where too much eye contact can be uncomfortable.

Business cards in China have a double side print, one side in English and the other printed in Chinese. In case your colleagues find it hard to pronounce your name, then you will most likely be given a Chinese name. Normally this is chosen by your colleagues and sometimes you are given a number of Chinese names to choose from, as was in my case. It's a good thing because if you are a sales guy constantly in contact with Chinese clients, then it saves them the hassle of pronouncing your English name! In return your friends and colleagues may ask you to give them a good English name (see the section on Chinese Names in Chapter 11).

Most professionals keep an album for their business cards, and in time you may end up with quite a number of albums, as I noticed from personal experience! Having a business card collection is very useful for the purposes of Guangxi; when you may want to look for a business opportunity or a new job, you can always flick through your album to find any useful contacts that may be of assistance to you.

Business Meals

A business lunch is normally taken within the time frame that is allocated by the company for a lunch break. Business dinners however, tend to take a much longer time because there is no need for anyone to go back to the office. Employees usually sit with their colleagues rather than according to which department they belong to. I do remember, however, a time when one of my colleagues kindly whispered to me that "the Engineers are not so sociable as the Sales & Marketing guys, so they tended to sit separately during formal dinners."

During formal dinners and events senior management start by giving a short speech and then go around carrying out the toasts with every employee. Normally non-managerial employees don't make a speech; however exceptions may be made to welcome new foreign employees to the company. So if you are asked to make a speech then it's best to make it short, offer gratitude to your senior managers, and make a few comments as to how you will contribute to the company's success.

In the west people normally only offer a loud "Cheers!" maybe once during a meal. In China, during a formal meal, the first "Cheers!" is offered by the senior management, and thereafter during the meal follow several toasts, usually starting by everyone banging the table with spoons or holding their glasses together high in the air over the table and loudly shouting "Gambei!" (the Chinese equivalent of saying "Cheers!").

Taxation of Personal Income in China

Economic reforms since 1979 have brought China step by step into line with other economies. In December 2001 China finally joined the WTO.

China imposes individual tax on the basis of a person's residence and domicile. In China a person is considered domiciled if they are resident in the country due to personal commitments such as family relationships or because they hold a registered householder with a personal residence record.

Any person who resides abroad for reasons such as education, employment, work assignment, visiting relatives, or touring, and who thereafter must return to China is regarded as being domiciled in China. Expats must be aware that western style (UK, USA, and European) pension schemes are not available to foreigners working in China.

The extent to which persons who are not domiciled in China are liable to income tax depends on their period of residence in China. After five consecutive years of residence in China, foreign individuals will be subject to individual income tax (IIT) on their global income (income paid from their native country), just as a Chinese domiciliary is liable. Subject to the approval of the tax authorities, however, foreign nationals who have been resident in the PRC for between one and five years are liable to be taxed on their Chinese sourced salary (paid in RMB) or if they choose the non-Chinese income paid by a PRC establishment. (This applies if you want your company to pay your salary in a foreign currency—usually this is in USD or Euros.)

Foreign nationals who have been resident in China for under a year are liable to pay the IIT on their Chinese-source income only. Foreign nationals who are employed in China for less than ninety days during a calendar year are exempt from the IIT if their income is paid by a foreign establishment and not paid by a Chinese company.

The following shows categories of income that are subject to the Chinese IIT, they include:

1. Wages and Salaries – 5% to 45%;
2. Income from personal services – 20% to 40%;
3. Business income from sole proprietorships, contracting and leasing – 5% to 35%;
4. Interest, dividends, royalties, and other income (including capital gains) – 20%.

Income is computed separately for each category of income and IIT is levied at the appropriate rate on taxable income of each category after deducting allowable expenses. The tax year is the calendar year, but tax returns must be filed and tax paid monthly.

In China, interest and dividends for investments are taxable with no allowable deductions. The tax rate is 20%. Income from investments in real estate property is taxable, and after deduction of a standard 20% of the gross income, in respect of expenses.

In terms of double tax treaties, China has over seventy solid treaties in force with other countries for the elimination of double taxation on the income, including treaties with the UK and the United States. In terms of keeping your money safe, Hong Kong would be the nearest best place for this. Most expats in China have a monthly stipend (more commonly known as a local allowance), paid for them to use on a daily basis while they are on the mainland (this "stipend allowance" is taxed according to Chinese laws as stated above) and a tax-free salary (paid in £UK, $US or Euros) in an off-shore bank account in Hong Kong or one of the offshore islands (such as Jersey, Isle of Man, Bermuda, Barbados, or the Cayman Islands).

Business Interests with China

With the economy booming, most western economic pundits believe there is no better time than now to either set up a business in China or directly do business with China while being based in their home country with the assistance of affiliates on location in cities like Shanghai and Beijing.

Setting up in China is by all means not as easy as setting up in Europe, India, or anywhere else where there is a sense of "internationality" in people's thinking and operability on business and cultural terms. Also setting up a new business in China requires a lot of homework and preparation. It's not a simple case of one or two trips and you are in; it has more to do with commitment by your company's senior management to have strategically set inroads into China where an expat or a number of expats from the European or American office need to relocate and live in China on a long-term basis and manage the resources on location rather than remotely from the HQ, which simply won't work. So companies must be able to work out whether they are actually up to this market place. Knowing your company's limitations, strengths, and weaknesses would be of great advantage.

Another good approach is to find local partners because it is inevitable that you will have to work with local partners when the business is up and running, and in China networking, as mentioned before, is, in most cases, more important than a brand image of the company. Chinese society is about building and sustaining trust between people. It is quite different from western history, which alternatively raises a caste division to control society or relies instantaneously on punishment to enforce conformity.

Global economists have come up with a general prediction that China's future is bound to accommodate an augmented shift of technology and proficiency, a larger inflow of foreign capital, and huge amounts of productivity, both in the manufacturing and financial business sectors. In a nutshell, to do business in China, one needs to have a plan of staying in the country for a long period. Building trust, relationships, and "Guangxi" with local partners are all equally important, as well as finding a location where you can have competition and repeat business (i.e., one of the major cities).

Here is just a guide to what you can expect to be the advantages or disadvantages. This list is by no means intended to make it look as if China is a very difficult place to do business for foreigners, because it's not. The advantages actually outweigh the disadvantages, and it's always the challenges that make the fruits of the labor taste sweet afterwards.

Advantages of Doing Business with China

- Reach – world's largest population (1.3 billion people) makes it one of the largest consumer markets in the world. Doing business in China can be quite lucrative.
- Exposure – The majority of Chinese people, especially the younger generation, like to try western consumer goods such as food, clothes, and so on.
- Opportunity for investment and sales at a large scale.
- New market – There is enormous opportunity for business growth for both Chinese and western companies.
- Cheap labor costs – at a fraction of what it costs to manufacture the products in the west (total cost of ownership is improved vastly).
- The sheer size of China and its capability to "compete right across the price chain" makes it a much more of a strategic threat than any other competitor in the world, past or present.
- China is no longer a massive cheap sweatshop; instead foreign companies are flocking to China and setting up manufacturing plants and research centers in major cities without the need of having large "sweatshops" – Chinese high tech is on its way.
- WTO membership allows China to stop the granting of zone and industrial based allowances to foreign business ventures. Foreign businesses can make their judgments around cost strategy (such as tax, labor, corporate and employee insurance).

- The Chinese pay close attention to detail, especially when dealing with foreign companies. Presentations and corporate meetings are well prepared in advance and are much better ordered than in the west.

Disadvantages of Doing Business with China

- Great time differences with Europe, North and South America, and Australasia.
- Language problems – A major obstacle for many western companies when they want to open an office in China. Even the newly styled "Chinglish" is difficult to for westerners to understand!
- Cultural differences – Losing face, giving an impression that everything is ok when it is not. This can lead to challenges such as lack of trust among Chinese colleagues and their counterparts in the business world.
- Laws regarding import/export of goods are strict, and the costs are one of the highest in the world.
- In case of any company legal issues, the legal process can take a long time; even for the smallest of cases it can take months, if not years.
- Western businesses remain worried about having their intellectual property (IP) stolen. The Chinese government is working hard at stamping down on Chinese companies/individuals who are involved in the abuse of IP; however there are always holes left unfound.
- If you are an exporter then you may find it difficult to find the right business partner.
- Many western economies are strong in professions such as financial services in consumer and investment banking, accountancy and engineering; currently very few if any of these markets are open in China. This provides a tough challenge for western companies.
- Strict guidelines in regards to advertising and marketing of foreign goods on the mainland. Because Chinese companies are not used to dealing with western markets and vice versa, there can be many misunderstandings in terms of what products are sold and how they are sold. For example one western company that specializes in offering travel incentives carried out a marketing campaign in China, with offerings such as "When customers purchase a one-year contract deal with a particular telecom company, they can take advantage of a "two return flights for the price of one with an airline company on any of their destinations." The Chinese telecom company management were very confused as to why the western company was offering a free flight to its customers because they had never heard of

such a thing before. What they did not realize is that the customers are not being offered anything free, but they have to actually buy.

- The increased competition within the mainland can lead to the shut-down or closure of smaller enterprises because they simply lose out in the market.

- Be careful when entering the China market because all the excitement of China being the "world's fastest growing economy" may lead one to think that one could get left behind; however, the truth may be far from that. There are a lot of hidden dangers such as the high cost of setting up the business, the high amount of import/export tax in China plus all the other problems that are highlighted in this chapter. It's a challenging market but it can be equally rewarding provided you hit the right notes and meet the right people at the right place.

- Contract terms may be changed by the Chinese side even after both parties have signed and agreed on the terms and conditions. It would be in the best interest of both parties to have documents in both Chinese and English.

- Christmas and Easter are treated as normal working days in China, whereas in the other countries (except in SE Asia), the long Chinese national holidays are not accounted for.

- There are no trade unions present in China, thus leading to moderately nonchalant rules and regulations regarding health and safety. Many companies do not have Health and Safety as part of their induction for new employees.

Business Consultancies in China

Foreign companies that are planning on entering the Chinese market would be strongly recommended to carry out their research thoroughly even before entering China, including getting plenty of advice from their respective Chambers of Commerce (list of Chambers of Commerce of most countries is provided in this book), from their embassy, from their country's trade and industry department, and from international management consultancies.

One of the most central concerns faced by western businesses making strategic decisions in China is of obtaining accurate market information. James A. C. Sinclair, Senior Consultant at Interchina Consulting in Shanghai, comments in his report "Market Information Paradox":

> *China is an enormous, complex and dynamic market. In the West, the market information structure is such that businesses have often been operating in their markets long enough to have developed a strong understanding of their markets. In contrast, the market information*

structure in China is relatively weak. Many western businesses are new to their markets in China, and for almost all the first impression is one of opaqueness rather than transparency. Western businesses can't just turn to their investment bank analysts, as the view from the ivory towers in Shanghai looks quite different from the reality on the ground in say, Sichuan for example.

Western governments are taking China very seriously (the other country being India of course), and so if you have a strong proposal to trade with or invest in China, you will need to know who does what and how to go by the more strategic routes. A deep support mechanism will be provided by your Chamber of Commerce as well as governments. There are various organizations that specialize in providing professional assistance to individuals or companies who want to move into the China market.

A list is included in this book of some consultancies that provide assistance to foreign businesses in China.

Quality of Goods

These days almost everything from designer clothes to the latest electronic gadgets that are sold in the USA and Europe is imported from China, and the labels proudly declare "Made in China." The standard of quality of those goods is equally high. However, ironically, goods of the same brand names that are sold domestically in China do not conform to the same international standards of quality as do the goods that are sold internationally. This is because manufacturers can get away selling bad quality products in the domestic market. Nevertheless with increasing competition from foreign companies that are choosing to manufacture goods on the mainland, as well as running a rat race with local "copy cats," Chinese manufacturers are taking steps to polish up the image of bad quality goods on the mainland.

Some Chinese companies are taking further steps to form international corporate partnerships with western companies in order to give the "good-looking" image to the consumer. Their efforts are duly paying off as this does bring the quality of goods in China up to scratch with global standards.

While you are on the mainland, if you are going to buy your children toys or electronic devices such as an MP4 player, it would be advisable to check if the products conform to ISO9001 quality standards and especially if they have full money back international guarantee, in case you want to return them. It's important to check this because if you buy most electronic goods on the mainland such as laptops or mobile phones, then they are only covered for guarantee in mainland China, not even Hong Kong or Macau. Some goods are covered under international guarantee; it's just a matter of finding the right shop that sells them. In Hong Kong, most electronic goods are cheaper than on the mainland and are covered under a world-wide guarantee.

Some fakes are so good that it is hard to detect if they are real or not. Even though the price of the goods may be reasonably low compared to your home country, there is a fine line between quality and pricing of the products. Poor quality can be a particularly important issue for items such as children's toys and shoes because toys can break easily and are harmful to young children if they swallow small parts or are exposed to lead paint, especially because infants and toddlers are apt to put anything into their mouths.

CHAPTER 6:
FINANCE—BANKS AND INSURANCE

The national currency is the Renminbi (People's Money; abbreviation is RMB) and is also known as the Yuan. It comes in denominations of 5-, 10-, 20-, 50-, and 100-Yuan notes, and there are coins in the denominations of 1 Yuan and 5 Jiao. The Renminbi is broken into 100 Fen and 10 Fen make up a Jiao or Mao. When buying goods you can refer to the money as "Kwai." So RMB 5 is referred to as "Wu Kwai" ("Wu" stands for five in Mandarin). A full translation of essential Chinese is given towards the end of this book.

In banks, foreigners are given respect and special attention by the staff. If, for example, there is a large queue in a bank, the chances are that a staff member will take you to the VIP counter and deal with your problem promptly. Service is generally fast and efficient. All banks in China have at least one security guard at the entrance and closed-circuit TV is in operation twenty-four hours a day. Even cash machines that have twenty-four hour access are manned by security personnel twenty-four hours a day. At the time of this writing, the maximum amount that can be withdrawn from cash machines is 20,000 RMB in one day. If in doubt, please check with your bank.

Banks in China

There are five main banks in China as follows:

Agricultural Bank of China (state owned)
Global HQ
Jia 23, Fuxing Road
Beijing, China, 100036
Tel: +86 (0)10 6821 6807/ 6842 4439
Fax: 86 (0)10 6829 7160/ 6842 4437
Website: www.abchina.com

Bank of China (the main state-owned bank)
Bank of China Global HQ
1 Fuxingmen Nei Dajie,
Beijing 100818, China
Swift: BKCH CN BJ

Tlx: +86 (0)10 22254
Tel: +86 (0)10 66596688
Fax: +86 (0)10 66593777
Website: www.bank-of-china.com

China Merchants Bank
Global HQ
News Palaza
2 Mid Shen Nan Road
Fu Tian District
Shenzhen, China
Website: http://english.cmbchina.com/

China Merchants Bank is a private bank and is widely considered a bank with a high level of professional service that conforms with international standards.

Construction Bank of China (state owned)
24-hour hotline: 95533
Website: www.ccb.cn

ICBC (State Owned)
Global HQ
55 FuXingMenNei Street
Xicheng District
Beijing, 100032, P.R.C
Nationwide 24-hour Service Hotline: 95588
E-mail: webmaster@icbc.com.cn
Website: www.icbc.com.cn

Then there are various other banks:

Bank of Beijing (Government)
Headquarters
17 Finance Street
West City District
Beijing, 100032, China
Website: www.bankofbeijing.com.cn

Bank of Communications (Government)
188 Yinchengzhong Road
Shanghai, 200120
Tel: +86 (0)21 95559

E-mail: 95559@bankcomm.com
Website: www.bankcomm.com

China Citic Industrial Bank

Block C, FuhuaMass
8 Chaoyangmen Bei Dajie
Dongcheng District
Beijing 100027
Tel: +86 (0)10 6554 2388
Website: www.ecitic.com

China Minsheng Bank

2 Fu Xin Men Nei Road
West City District
Beijing 100031
E-mail: service@cmbc.com.cn
Website: www.cmbc.com.cn

Shanghai Pudong Development Bank
Global HQ

12 Zhongshan Dong Yi Road
Shanghai
Tel: +86 (0)21 6329 6188
Fax: +86 (0)21 632 32036
Website: www.spdb.com.cn

Shenzhen Development Bank

5047 Shenzhen Development Bank Palaza
East Shen Nan Road
Shenzhen, Guangdong
China 518001
Email: netbank@sdb.com.cn
Website: www.sdb.com.cn
Fax: +86 (0)755 8208101

In smaller banks the service may not be as efficient and the number of offered services may be less than at one of the larger banks. Smaller banks may not be as well represented in the major cities. ICBC is the largest lender on the mainland and in early 2007 applied for banking licenses in the USA and Russia as part of its roadmap plan to expand into the foreign markets. While foreign banks have been making significant inroads into the booming Chinese economy in recent years and pushing hard for access, Chinese banks on the other hand are excluded from foreign markets. This is simply because of a history of poor risk management and corporate governance.

China's banks are cash-rich and ready to take on the world, just as the Japanese banks were doing half a generation ago. In actual fact the Bank of China is the only one of the nation's state-owned lenders that has any significant offshore presence—and the vast majority of the operations are in neighboring Hong Kong and Macau.

Peoples Bank of China
32 Chengfang Street
Xi Cheng district
Beijing
China 100800
Tel: +86 (0)10 6619 4114
E-mail: webbox@pbc.gov.cn
Website: www.pbc.gov.cn/english/

Foreigners Opening Bank Accounts in China–Requirements

If you are coming to China through your employer in your country, then your employer should be able to assist you in setting up a bank account for your salary and personal income.

If you want to open a normal savings account, then as a general requirement, all that is needed is your passport with a valid residence permit or work permit if you have one.

You can open a credit card account in China only if you are a Chinese and have property in China. Further details may be obtained from www.bankofchina.com

Most of the banks in China are open seven days a week and are busy with long queues. Sometimes the queues start to form outside the bank even before the bank has opened. Cash machines are available everywhere just like in the west.

With the rising Chinese economy, a large number of poor migrants are pouring into the major cities (especially Shenzhen) in search of fortune and fame.

If you are without money in China, the best option would be to get in touch with your consulate or embassy. They can advise you on how to transfer money from your country or elsewhere, and they maybe even able to contact friends and relatives if you wish.

International Banking

While Beijing has many branches of international banks, there has been an increase in the number of western banks in the other three major cities in China within the past few years. HSBC, Citibank, and Standard Chartered Bank have branches in all the major cities (Guangzhou, Shenzhen, Beijing, and Shanghai). There are plans to open branches of these banks in some other cities in the next few years as well as having some other western banks in the major cities.

All the above listed banks have cash machines in selected areas in all the major cities mentioned. These cash machines accept international bank cards and there is a charge for their service.

American Express has branches in Beijing, Guangzhou, and Shanghai.

Money Transfer

International money transfer is possible with Western Union. Most post offices have a Western Union counter inside their branches. The procedure is simple and does not take long: www.westernunion.com.

The Bank of China, ICBC, and China Merchants Bank also can transfer money internationally at a small charge. However it is best to use Western Union for money transfer because there may be delays in using the banks.

Currency Exchange

The Bank of China, ICBC, and the China Merchants Bank all have foreign exchange counters. You should not have any difficulty exchanging American Express travelers checks in the majority of the western banks or in your hotel.

It is best to keep the receipts with you of all your money-changing transactions to make sure you have no problems when you change the currency back to your own country's when you leave China. At the time of writing the maximum amount of hard currency you can take out of China is 20,000 RMB (equivalent to approx. $2500).

Foreigners are known to be rich so be careful not to be deceived by conmen approaching you with a laptop or the latest mobile phone in the shopping malls! Be careful of being handed counterfeit money (especially 100 RMB and 50 RMB notes), and there seem to be a lot of "on the street" money changers in the black market—this can get you in deep trouble with the Chinese police as it is illegal to exchange dollars for RMB except at banks, hotels, and official exchange offices.

Due to the large volume of counterfeit currency in China, unofficial exchanges usually result in travelers losing their money and possibly facing charges of breaking foreign exchange laws. If detained by police under suspicion of committing an economic crime involving currency, an individual may be delayed for weeks or months while police investigate the allegations.

Insurance in China

Many insurance companies in your own countries can provide short-term insurance if you are going for a month or so. However for longer periods as an expat, the following two Chinese companies provide insurance:

- Ping An Insurance Company (www.pa18.com) is the famous, largest, and most reliable insurance company in China. The staff at Ping An Insurance are very professional and there is always someone who can speak good English.
- China Life Insurance Company Ltd is China's second largest insurance company after Ping An.

You should have insurance provided by your employer automatically; however, if you need insurance for your personal belongings or life insurance for yourself then Ping An Insurance is the best option for you. In China it is no longer compulsory to buy insurance with your mortgage.

The AIA insurance company is internationally renowned and has branches in all of the main cities throughout China.

CHAPTER 7:

INTERNATIONAL EDUCATION—SCHOOLING FOR EXPAT CHILDREN IN CHINA

A child's education is of main concern to parents when they relocate to China. Unlike in most European countries where parents have a choice of state-run (free education) or private schools, in China you will have to pay for your child's education. With the growing number of expats flocking to China, there has also been an increase in the number of international schools. Some expats have children's education included in their job package, as this can be very expensive. Prices can range anywhere from approximately $10,000 per annum up to $25,000 per annum depending on the school and the age of your child. Scholarships and bursaries are available in some schools, and realistically these are not easy to secure as the competition for places can be demanding.

When choosing a school for your child's education, it is vitally important to be aware of the curriculum that is available in the various institutions. It may go against your child's interests and future career if, for example, they are introduced to a totally different curriculum from the one they have been used to studying back in their country. The majority of international schools teach the American or British curriculum and the age ranges are from Kindergarten up to International Baccalaureate (or A-Level if a British curriculum–based establishment). Some schools are specialized only for children of a certain nationality, such as French, German, Japanese, and Korean schools. The teaching and the curriculum in these schools is provided in their native language rather than English. The teachers in international schools are highly educated professionals, normally with extensive international teaching experience, and are usually hired from their native countries.

Presently government laws don't allow Chinese nationals to attend international schools in the mainland. The majority of the foreign schools are located in the major cities of Shanghai, Beijing, Guangzhou, and Shenzhen. A comprehensive list of international schools in the major cities is included under the listings in this book. It may be better to send expat children to an international school that really is international, rather than send them to schools that call themselves international but may have a higher proportion of students from one particular background.

Remember that children are just as vulnerable when joining a new environment as you would be when you join your new office environment in China. Children need to feel comfortable and happy in their new school, so that they can start making friends with other children who are in the same situation. Otherwise, if they feel lonely and "left out of the crowd," they may start feeling homesick, which can of course have a devastating effect on their education.

International schools should not be seen as just examination factories that intend to churn out the brightest of expat kids; rather, they are grooming grounds for providing expat children with the same education that they would get back home, which should better prepare them for entrance to British and American universities.

Dulwich College Management (DCM) is one of the leading organizations providing consultation on the establishment of international education in China. Based in Shanghai, DCM has in recent years assisted in the establishment of some of the most famous international schools in China, such as Dulwich College International (for which DCM is the franchise holder). DCM used

Dulwich College, Beijing

to be formally known as the GEICC. Richard Barnard, senior consultant at DCM in Shanghai, comments:

> *By Chinese law the schools can only enroll foreign national children, thus the strength of the schools' enrolment is a reflection of the high number of foreign families who settle in China for work. DCM is therefore in the process of developing education projects that will target Chinese nationals. These include United High Schools (joint ventures between Dulwich and local High Schools) enabling Chinese students to graduate with an internationally recognized high school diploma, and bilingual kindergartens.*

Dulwich College Management

601 Aviation Center
1600 Nanjing Xi Lu,
Jing'an District
Shanghai 200040 China
Tel: +86 (0)21 6248 7878
Fax: +86 (0)21 6248 6899
Website: www.dulwich-management.com
E-mail: info@dulwich-management.com

Effect on the Children

When moving to a new country, the environment can be stressful for you as the parents, and equally stressful for the children. Some children find it exciting to travel abroad and experience a new environment, and will look forward to making friends with other foreign children, while others can be trapped by homesickness and missing their life back in their country. Of course, if you are offered a job in China through your company, then before accepting the contract, it is best to talk it through with your family and research the many options of what may and may not be right.

For the children, it would be exciting for them to know that they will be flying halfway across the world to China and experiencing a new culture and a new environment. They will of course feel proud that they will be gaining a little bit extra advantage over their classmates by going overseas, and that not every child has the chance to study and live overseas. However, once they get to China, it may be the case that they either enjoy being there or they don't. This can depend on many factors such as whether they like the new environment (food and language can be the most important things for children when making these decisions), whether they are following up with their studies or are falling behind their peers from back home, whether they have made many friends in China—local or expatriate—and how long they can manage to live happily in China.

It is worth pointing out that children should be told that once they are in China, they will most probably remain in China for the majority of the year rather than coming back and forth frequently—unless the parents have a large wallet! It all depends on your personal budget or what expat package your company has provided you with. While most packages include just one or two return flights a year, some corporations can provide up to three or four return flights a year back to your country.

I knew one Canadian couple in Shenzhen who had left their jobs in Toronto, sold their house, and moved with their four children to China. For the parents it was a long break that they always had wanted to take from their careers and do something special, while for the children it was more homesickness than anything. I asked them how the children were coping and the father responded hazily:

> They [the children] don't seem to be enjoying it. They have not made many friends in the expat community and they find life here very boring because there is not much for them to socialise except the odd day away to a touristy place with the family. The kids didn't like the local food, the weather was too hot for them, and they found it difficult to make friends because of language and cultural problems, and majority of the time they just stayed at home playing computer games. We could not bear to see them suffer like this so we looked at all the various options again.

The children were signed up for daily remote "online" education tutorials from their school in Canada. This made sure that they didn't miss out on the curriculum and it's a much more economical solution than sending them to a local international school. However it proved challenging, and it was obvious that sadly the China trip did not work out for them as they had intended before they left Canada.

Libraries and Book Cities

There is no charge to become a member of a public library in China or to borrow books. The majority of the books are in Chinese. There are a handful of English books as well; however, most of these are for learning the language rather than being a novel or any other particular genre. Most libraries have a separate section for international books; however, these books may be considered boring or out of date. The majority of them are about scientific subjects such as Mathematics and Physics.

Most libraries also have an Internet room and the rates at the time of writing are ranging from approximately three to five Yuan per hour. The only problem may be that computers are installed with a Chinese Windows operating system.

China is heaven for budding bookworms as people will read just about anything and especially if it is concerned about foreign countries or written by western authors, all translated into Chinese of course. Another new phenomenon in China is the abundance of "book cities"—buildings which double as bookstores and libraries (as well as English learning centers). There is a "book city" in almost every major city. Most of these books are in Chinese except English tutorials and some movies. These "book cities" are busy, overcrowded, and noisy (not your ideal "quiet" place to read a book).

CHAPTER 8:
HEALTH CARE

Doctors and Hospitals

The old saying "Health is wealth" is very much true when it comes to looking after yourself in a difficult environment such as China. No matter how healthy you think you are, it would still be a good idea to go and see your doctor about two to three weeks before you arrive in China so that if there are any vaccinations or medication (such as for malaria, in case you are visiting the southern state of Hainan Island) that you need to start taking in advance, you can have enough advance notice.

As an expat you should have the contact details of your doctor given to you by your employer. If you happen to fall ill in a hotel, then consult the hotel staff, who would be happy to arrange a doctor to visit you. In China normally patients have to go to the hospital's Accident & Emergency unit. There is normally a small charge for registration upon your arrival at the hospital and depending on the illness; you may have to pay for the medicine too. Above all else, it is best to make sure that you are covered by adequate medical insurance either before you enter China or get medical insurance as soon as you arrive. Most expats are covered by medical insurance automatically as part of their employment contract before they arrive in China (such as the BUPA Gold scheme). If not then it's best to ask your employer for advice on this. It's important to have insurance because medical care is not free in China as I realized on one occasion:

In the first few months of my stay in China, I sprained my ankle by falling down a set of stairs on an overhead walkway bridge in Shenzhen. In deep pain and panic, I had no choice but to go to the nearest clinic (it was a small hospital doubling as a doctor's surgery in the Liantang area of Shenzhen). It wasn't clean and not too crowded either. I got to see the doctor, who was able to speak a limited amount of English. I immediately phoned one of my English-speaking Chinese friends, who was very helpful in exchanging translations between the doctor and me. To my amazement, after looking at the injury, the doctor just told me that I'd need an x-ray and left it at that. Then my friend on the phone advised me that the doctor will only carry on further if I paid first. I was lucky to have company medical insurance to claim back the expenses, even though they weren't that much. But this example goes to show the bureaucracy that patients have to deal with in order to get what they require.

Friends and/or neighbors would be more than happy to assist in any way possible in case you fall ill in your home, and it may also be helpful to have a friend who is a doctor. The Chinese doctors are very helpful and professional, and they treat foreigners with great respect. This is especially true if a foreigner falls ill in their country—they feel it's their duty as a host to look after you properly and they will do whatever is possible so that a full recovery is made quickly. Most doctors can speak "technical" conversational English.

If in the unlikely event that you are involved in an accident, get a taxi and inform friends. Ambulances are just used as a fast mode of transport from the scene of the accident to the hospital; they do not carry sophisticated medical equipment, and ambulance personnel generally have little or no medical training. Therefore, it is recommended that injured or seriously ill foreigners take taxies or other immediately available vehicles to the nearest major hospital rather than waiting for ambulances to arrive.

In rural areas, only rudimentary medical facilities are generally available. Medical personnel in rural areas are often poorly trained and have little medical equipment or availability of medications. Rural clinics are frequently reluctant to accept responsibility for treating foreigners, even in emergency situations.

If the injury or illness is serious try to get in touch with your consulate at the first instance so that they can get hold of your next of kin back home or friends in China. Your consulate or embassy should visit you in hospital, if friends and family are not available.

If you need to be medically repatriated, it can be very expensive, particularly if a medical escort or special equipment is required for the journey.

Hospitals in China are clean and spacious with separate wards for inpatients and outpatients. The queues are not as long as they used to be in the past. The one thing you may find a bit annoying is that there is a certain lack of privacy when you visit the doctor. While you are in a private consultation with a doctor, other patients will come into the room and openly listen to your conversation. This is something that you just have to get used to in China, especially if you are a foreigner—as people are always curious.

I went to a military hospital in Guangzhou once with a Chinese-speaking friend of mine. While the doctor was physically examining me and advising me what to do, there were three other patients who came into the room at the same time and while they were waiting for their turn to be seen, one of them started giving me advice too! This seemed a bit strange to me as there was no privacy and the doctor just told me to relax. It can be an unbelievable situation for first-time visitors.

If you are not accustomed to traditional Chinese medicine, you should be aware that Chinese doctors will tend to give you lots of tablets to take even for the most minor of ailments. For example, I had a slight fever in Guangzhou once, and the doctor prescribed me to take eight tablets a day for one week. Another one is where a friend of mine was prescribed to take six tablets a day for four days for a normal cold. In both cases, the medicine seemed to work, however in my case, I did find it hard to stay awake for almost a couple of days!

As a foreigner wishing to work in China you will be required to take a full body medical check-up before a visa is issued, including tests for HIV, Hepatitis B, and Syphilis, and ECG/Ultrasound. You will be issued with a Certificate of Health Examination in paper form and as a booklet. The paper certificate needs to be handed to the PSB when applying for the work permit, while the booklet form should be kept with your passport at all times in case of inspection.

China has one of the world's highest incidences of Hepatitis B and HIV, especially in migrant cities such as Shenzhen. Indeed, it was reported by the Shenzhen daily newspaper on World AIDS day in 2006 that there had been a 30% rise of HIV infections within one year. Recently there have been worries about bird flu and SARS.

If you are admitted into a hospital, you will be given a uniform to wear in the ward. Normally these clothes consist of white pyjamas with a blue or black stripes design. Pharmacies in China are different from those in Europe and the USA. They sell medicines only. Do not expect suntan lotion or deodorant or any toiletries from them. The largest difference may be that you can buy prescription drugs at any dosage on the street

Beijing United Family Hospital and Clinics ("BJU") is the first and remains the only foreign-invested full service international standard 50-bed hospital operating in Beijing, China. BJU was opened in 1997 by Chindex International, an American company, which in 2002 was awarded the US Secretary of State's Award for Corporate Excellence. BJU offers the full range of specialties including Family Practice, Internal Medicine, Surgery, Obstetrics/Gynecology, Pediatrics, Dentistry, Psychiatry, and Physiotherapy, in addition to a twenty-four hour Emergency Room staffed solely by expatriate staff specialists. These physicians are all board qualified (or equivalent) in their respective fields and include specialties such as Anesthesiology and Intensive Care Medicine. Additionally, staff are fluent not only in English but also in a wide range of languages including French, German, Japanese, Spanish, Swedish, and Finnish.

Beijing United Family Hospital (北 京 和 睦 家 医 院)
2 Jiang Tai Lu
Chao Yang District
Beijing 100016
Tel: +86 (0)10 64333960/1/2/4/5 (24-hour number)
Fax: +86 (0)10 64333963
Emergency Hotline: +86 (0)10-64332345
Website: www.beijingunited.com

Beijing United Family Clinic – Shunyi (北 京 和 睦 家 诊 所 – 顺 义)
Pinnacle Plaza, Unit 818
Tian Zhu Real Estate Development Zone,
Shunyi District
Beijing 101312
Tel: +86 (0) 10 80465432
Fax: +86 (0) 10 80464383
Website: www.bjunited.com.cn

Amenities include two operating theaters, international standard five-star LDRP birthing suites, neonatal ICU, a four-bed adult ICU, general inpatient facilities, and standard support services such as digital radiology, ambulance services, pharmacy, laboratory, and a 24-hour on-site blood bank with emergency blood prescreened to the International Blood Bank standard.

Global Doctor, Ltd. has opened clinics staffed by English-speaking doctors within the VIP wards of government-run hospitals in Chengdu, Nanjing, and Beijing. Global Doctor can be reached by telephone from China at +86 (0)10 8456-9191 or on the Internet at www.eglobaldoctor.com

Birth

Giving birth in China can be a trouble-free experience for the expat expectant mother, provided the quality of the medical care is excellent. It is absolutely essential that a good hospital is chosen, one where the doctors and midwives can communicate in English and where the quality of the doctors is also on a par with international medical standards. A list of hospitals that cater to foreigners is provided in this book. You can also find more information from your consulate or embassy.

It goes without saying that locally trained Chinese doctors can be as good as doctors in the west, and remember that giving birth in a country where doctors are used to delivering on average fifteen million babies every year should not pose too many problems! China boasts some top-quality hospitals with world-class facilities catering to the middle class, and they charge good money too.

The first few weeks after the birth of a baby can be quite stressful and without a doubt can keep the new parents busy. In China, English-speaking midwives and nannies are available in the big cities; however there are costs associated with this assistance. It may also be quite useful for the new mother to have friends around to assist with minor but important chores such as cooking or cleaning the home. If you are living close to other expats or Chinese who can speak English, then this should be no problem at all as people are nice here and would take the first opportunity to help. Having close relatives, such as the newborn's grandparents, for example, fly over to China may be another option, however bear in mind that costs will be high especially if they are flying from Europe or the USA.

In China, childbirth can be a surprisingly expensive experience for foreigners, as all medical facilities and post birth care charge fees. Birth registration for foreigners is not compulsory in China. The baby may be eligible for a Chinese nationality if one of the parents is a Chinese passport holder. Otherwise the baby will have the same passport as that nationality to which the parents belong. That said, it purely depends on the rules and regulations of different countries because for some countries, the baby is disqualified from acquiring the same passport as their parents (such as the UK, where a child born outside the UK to holders of a UK passport, who were also born outside the UK, might not be eligible for a UK passport, unless one of the parents was born in the UK). Sounds complicated and for further information, the best source is your consulate or embassy.

Your consular birth registration may be able to provide your newborn child with a birth certificate in the same style that is given in your country. Essentially this means that your child can obtain any future duplicate copies of the birth certificate from the General Registrar's office in your country. Again it is best you speak to your consulate or embassy regarding this.

If your wife is Chinese, then both before and after birth, she may prefer to spend time with her parents in her hometown or village, unless of course, the grandparents are already in the same place as the newborn. This will provide a sense of care and comfort for the new mother and baby while the baby's father may be busy with all the other important household chores that are associated with childbirth. In Chinese culture, a child is considered to already be one year old at the time of birth as age is supposed to be judged from the moment of conception.

Death

In the unfortunate event of a foreigner's death in China, the hospital or the police must contact the appropriate consulate or embassy at the first instance, so that friends and family are informed. The death of a relative or friend is very distressing, particularly if it happens abroad.

Below are local procedures involved:

Death in a Hospital

1. A death certificate should be issued by the hospital stating the cause of death.
2. The Public Registry Office would then need to notarize the death certificate. There would be a charge for this service.

Death Elsewhere

1. The Public Security Bureau (PSB) needs to be informed of the death and details.
2. Once the PSB staff members have seen the deceased, a death certificate is issued.
3. The Public Registry Office needs to then notarize the death certificate. There would be a charge for this service.

Your embassy or consulate can provide you with a variety of services such as advising on burial costs, local cremation, and transport of the remains and personal property back to your country. A comprehensive list of some major companies that specialize in international relocation is provided in this book (please see Listings).

Should you have to attend a Chinese funeral, white is the color to be worn. Chinese people believe that the body should depart into the next life intact; therefore cremation is not a popular choice—although in recent years with the lack of space in major cities, people are starting to opt for cremation. People also believe that the older the person is at the time of death, especially if they are over the age of seventy, then they are considered to have lived a good life, and so not many people would grieve seriously.

Traditional Chinese Medicine

One Chinese friend courteously advised me that "Chinese medicine works slower and only on a temporary basis as compared to western medicine, but it still works!" Traditional Chinese medicine is widely accepted in western countries as well as in every province within China and is recognized by the World Health Organisation (WHO). It is based around the concept that in a healthy individual the significant "internal energies" that flow along the body (known as Qi) try to maintain a balance between the hot and the cold.

Normally the Chinese doctor will first look at your tongue and your pulse rate and then determine whether your body belongs to the "hot" or "cold" set of energies according to the color of your tongue and the speed of your pulse rate. This is similar to the ancient Chinese philosophy of "Yin" (Passive energy) and "Yang" (Active energy), where Yin applies to such things as cold and female and Yang applies to hot and male.

Whereas in the west you would normally take one or two tablets at one time, for the same medical condition, in China you would most likely end up taking maybe five or six tablets perhaps three times a day. Therefore don't be put off by Chinese doctors giving you lots of small packets of herbal medicine to mix with warm water and drink with your meals or to mix with your hot meal. Herbal medicine contains lots of vital ingredients, some of which may be derived from exotic plants, organs of animals or standard household ingredients found in western countries such as nutmeg, black salt, black pepper, and other spices. The filling of a traditional Chinese prescription ordered by a Chinese doctor is a fascinating process to observe. The pharmacist selects a few particular ingredients from the hundreds on his shelf. It may sound like a tedious task having to prepare the medicine every time you take it, but it can have a good effect. Most taste like bitter tea.

Be sure to ask the doctor if the herbal medicine has any side effects as Chinese bodies handle herbal medicine differently than western bodies. Normally Chinese doctors will shrug off any problems and give it you anyway. For example I once tried using herbal medicine as an alternative to paracetamol (acetaminophen) for a headache I had. It took the headache away within a few hours; however I also had to get by with a lot of unwanted deep sleep for a couple of days!

A traditional Chinese pharmacy has a unique smell made up of thousands of scents emanating from jars and cabinets stocked full of dried plants, seeds, animal parts, and minerals. Among them are the well-known ginseng roots, dried or immersed in alcohol and often looking like a human figure.

Tongrentang Pharmacy (同仁堂), in an old part of Beijing south of Tiananmen Square, has been in business for over 300 years. Founded in 1669, this pharmacy was once a royal dispensary during the Qing Dynasty and still produces all the capsules and secret mixtures once used by royalty. The enormous size of this pharmacy is overwhelming, as is the selection of remedies that contain among others: small and large eggs, snakes coiled in spirals, dried monkeys, toads, tortoises, centipedes, grasshoppers, small fish, stag antlers, rhinoceros horns, and testicles of various animals. And then there are the thousand kinds of dried and preserved herbs, blossoms, roots, berries, and fruits.

While in China, although you may be cautious about using Chinese medicine, it does boil down to personal choice. You can have peace of mind that there is no harm in trying it as Chinese medicine will not make your illness worse; however, it is highly likely that either it will take longer to have any significant effect or it will make no change to your current situation.

In drug stores and pharmacies you can purchase a range of traditional Chinese medicines that are readily prepared for various needs, such as if you have a muscular pain then "hot patches" are available. These "hot patches" are made up of a sticky plaster smeared with traditional Chinese medicine that you can apply to the affected area.

Acupuncture

Having needles stuck into your body may not be your cup of tea; however, it does work effectively for some conditions such as back or muscular pain. Using the principles of Qi along with the body's energy channels of Yin and Yang, needles are inserted into the body's acupuncture points that lie on these energy channels. It is a proven method of treatment and has been for the past 2500 years in China. The risks of getting any disease such as HIV are negligible as the majority of medical centers use disposable and sterile needles. Costs vary depending on the clinic you go to.

Some Chinese people prefer to be treated using the traditional method of **Moxibustion** for treating minor aliments such as a fever or back pain. Normally this procedure requires the dropping of burning Moxa (made from wormwood) onto the required points of the body.

There are various other methods including using **Suction Cups.** These are glass cups that are heated using a burning piece of alcohol-soaked cotton and then placed over the required point on the body. As unpleasant as it may seem to the observer, these suction cups cause the skin to be "sucked out" and leave a temporary mark on the body. Usually if you happen to see someone with circular marks the size of a small glass cup on their forehead, then most likely they have had the treatment for a fever or headache.

"Miracle Cures" for Illnesses

Some foreigners come to China to get affordable surgical treatment or even a "cure" for illnesses that would otherwise be untreatable, let alone curable, in the west. Some hospitals and private practitioners in China advertise internationally to promote experimental medical procedures to treat diseases such as Alzheimer's, epilepsy, Down syndrome, AIDS, and others. Other practitioners advertise that "new procedures" are available to extend life expectancy or to make people taller using traditional Chinese medicine, and to provide other cosmetic procedures.

These advertisements state that these procedures are safe, cheap, and effective. Formal complaints have been reported to the British and American embassies from foreigners with regard to many of these experimental practices. The embassies and consulates are aware of fatalities and permanent disfigurements that have sadly followed some of these treatments. Foreigners are advised not to enter China for treatment of advanced diseases without first consulting their physician in their own country. Others are prepared to take the chance, because to them, this could be the only hope that their illness may be treated if not curable.

"Mobile Doctors" and Pharmacies

In both rural and urban areas, doctors sometimes set up mobile surgeries to carry out diagnostic procedures—all free of charge. Diagnostics may include blood tests, eye tests, investigation of hair loss problems, and other minor, treatable problems that can be detected without the need for the patient to go to a major hospital. These mobile Doctors (or "street doctors" as they are commonly known) are highly unlikely to be real doctors but could be medical students or nurses who are taking an opportunity to practice their trade. If you have a minor ailment such as a cold or fever then it's no harm to go to your nearest pharmacy and get the required treatment but if it's something more serious, your best bet is to pop into the nearest hospital.

There is an ongoing problem with fake medicines and out-of-date medicines being sold in some pharmacies, something that the government is trying to clamp down on, but without much luck. You will also find in China that just about any medicine is available over the counter without prescription from the doctor (except some rare traditional Chinese medicines).

Personal Stores

It's only been in the recent years that personal stores have started to become popular in China. "Watson's" is available in every city and small town throughout the country.

Problems faced by westerners in China (especially men) include a lack of shaving tools and antiperspirants. Because Chinese people naturally don't sweat as much as non-Chinese people and most Chinese men are not as hairy as non-Chinese, you won't find much antiperspirant or shaving equipment around. With the increasing number of foreigners in cities such as Shanghai and Beijing, stores are taking note of this problem and imported goods are being gradually introduced.

The Chinese as a culture don't prefer strong smells, hence there are not many aftershaves or perfumes. However, things are changing slowly, and in the major cities most Watson's stores are stocked with Nivea Roll-on Sticks (antiperspirants) and Gillette shaving creams and blades (although the prices are international). Just recently I saw the introduction of Brut antiperspirants in a Beijing Watson's store; however it was double the price of what you would pay for the same product back in the UK!

Opticians

Prescription glasses are available widely in major opticians. On-the-spot free eye tests can be performed by the optician; normally it's best to take a Chinese-speaking friend with you as only a limited number of opticians can speak English. Again it may be a case of trial and error to see which ones are the best. Providing a list of opticians would prove difficult as there are too many around, although you should be careful which opticians you choose. Usually the ones where the staff members are wearing uniforms are recommended by the locals because they are more professional and have better qualified staff available to help you.

If you are a contact lens wearer then you need not worry about poor quality materials. Contact lenses manufactured by both Bausch & Lomb and Johnson & Johnson are widely available throughout the big cities. Nevertheless you should be cautious, as with everything else in China, about fakes in the smaller stores on the high street.

Beauty Salons

With rising salaries and a much more stressful work life, there has been a huge demand for beauty salons that cater to young professional Chinese women. Chinese women go to beauty salons to relieve the stress of the day or just to relax and chat with their friends and colleagues while being pampered. Normally staffed by young women dressed in 1930's style pink nurses' uniforms, offering facial beauty treatment as well as body, feet, and head massage for women only, these salons are becoming ever more popular with the middle-aged Chinese women too. Some salons offer a hair wash, perm, cut, and style as well.

As a foreign woman, you would be most welcome to try out the beauty treatments on offer—just take a Chinese lady friend with you as the staff is unlikely to speak English. The costs are much cheaper than in Europe and the States, and the hospitality is excellent.

Genetically the vast majority of Chinese men are not known for going bald; nevertheless due to work-related stress or other causes, there has been a huge demand in the mainland for hair salons. These salons (known as ZhangGuang 101 Hair Salon, www.101.com) specialize in herbal treatment of hair loss for both men and women and offer a variety of treatments to suit your health needs. Again if you want to try, it's best to take a Chinese-speaking friend with you. There is a 101 Hair Salon in almost every major city in China.

Companies that specialize in beauty and healthcare products, such as Amway and Pharmanex, have started business in China with promising results that have attracted the country's middle class, who appreciate these luxuries.

Smoking and Drinking

The Chinese are one of the world's largest consumers of alcohol and tobacco. There are more than 350 million smokers in China (according to Reuters), and cigarette smoking is widespread among men, much more uncommon among women. In restaurants and at formal meals, it is common for people to be offered a cigarette along with traditional Chinese tea—and smoking is considered a kind of status symbol amongst the wealthiest in China. When I took a domestic flight from Beijing to Guangzhou, I was surprised to see that both of the pilots started smoking in the cockpit when the plane landed at Guangzhou (with the window open)!

If you happen to be in a smoke-filled restaurant, then you cannot do much except perhaps change your seat as far away as you can or change your restaurant as it is very hard to escape from other people's cigarettes in public places.

The majority of Chinese people don't seem to be worried about the health risks associated with smoking. Nearly one million Chinese die every year from smoking-related illnesses and approx. 100,000 from passive smoking according to a recent survey from the Ministry of Health in China.

Alcohol is an important part of formal meals and wine is always offered to guests. In larger restaurants, normally there will be two or three glasses on the table, one for the beer (Tsingtao Beer, named after a town in northern China, is the most common brand in China), one for wine (Great Wall wine is one of the most popular red wines available, but be careful as some Chinese wines are strong, especially the one that looks like water but is almost 70% proof!), and another glass for a toasting liqueur such as Maotai, again this is approx. 70% proof. Maotai is normally provided in a small glass.

According to Euromonitordata, China has become the world's largest beer market by volume, overtaking the USA in 2002. With a desire for western style beers, Chinese consumers are gradually shifting from drinking spirits to beer. Carlsberg, Heineken, and Guinness "Stout" beer cans are widely available at local prices in convenience stores and supermarkets around the country. Plus there is increased domestic competition from Chinese brewers such as Tsingtao, Kingway beer of Shenzhen and Snow beer of Beijing.

CHAPTER 9:
FOOD

While shopping with an expat friend in Guangzhou one day, he told me, "There is more variety in China and the food is fresh, rather than being frozen as is in Europe or the States." Judging from what is available in supermarkets, his statement is correct. It is only in recent years that some ready-made meals have become available in the supermarkets (such as ready-to-steam dumplings) because, as a culture, the Chinese like to have their food freshly cooked rather than frozen. Although in most Asian countries the perception is that westerners prefer to have their food frozen rather than freshly cooked, it shouldn't really be seen as a preference, as it may well just be that the British/Americans are more accustomed to "convenience" food. With the ever increasing number of western supermarkets such as Wal-Mart (American), Park n Shop (Hong Kong/USA), Carrefour (French), and Jusco (Japanese) as well as the numerous western food restaurants, there is certainly much more choice available for the expat than in the past. The British supermarket Tesco opened its first outlet on the mainland in 2007.

Don't be surprised to see live chickens, game, fish, crabs, and tortoise in supermarkets or in your local outdoor market, as they are killed only a short time before being cooked. In the supermarkets you will find a wide variety of meat available such as pig's feet, ears, face and hands; chicken feet; duck's head and eggs. The Chinese love pork and chicken eggs, and it's no surprise to find one of these two products in most dishes. Outside the major cities, the menus in most restaurants are printed in Chinese only, so if you are trekking on an adventure and become hungry, it would be advisable to keep a small dictionary with you at all times.

Red bean (Hong Du) and green bean (Lu Dou) are widely used in desserts such as ice creams and fruit drinks because they are healthy. Fresh mixed fruit juice is also widely available, either sold by roadside hawkers or in shopping malls. Rice is the staple food, usually plain boiled.

If you are not too adventurous with your meats, then the best way to stay healthy is to stick to eating plenty of fresh fruit, vegetables, and fish. In China, freshly cooked and uncooked seafood is available in abundance and there are restaurants that are dedicated to just serving seafood.

A typical Chinese food restaurant in Beijing

There are numerous amounts of dried fruits and pickles, usually packed in tight plastic bags. Unfortunately there are also a lot of fake-branded goods available openly in supermarkets and convenience stores; these include everything from copied "Red Bull" energy drinks to copied "Great Wall" Wine—these goods are copied so well that it is very easy to confuse them with the genuine products as everything abut the products, including the packaging and the taste, is the exact copy of the genuine article.

In 2006, there were a number of reported cases on state TV of shoddy and unsafe goods such as toothpaste mixed with industrial chemicals and eggs tainted with dangerous dyes. There was one case where a man in Guangzhou was "manufacturing" eggs in his home that looked and tasted like real chicken eggs.

The government is taking stiff measures to improve nutritional safety and China's dismal food safety record. The Health ministry openly reported in 2005 that there were more than 34,000 food-related illnesses and in 2006 a state-owned journal reported that a survey by the quality inspection administration found almost one-third of China's 450,000 food production companies had no licenses.

Breakfast—Chinese and Western

A bowl of warm congee (Zhou) is a favorite among the masses. It's great because you can mix it with anything. Some people like to mix congee with instant noodles and pickles, while some like to mix it with powdered milk and cereal packets to make it into a sweet porridge. Soy milk with simple bread or a steamed bun is another favorite. Then there are other treats such as a steamed bun with a sweetened egg yolk inside (Lai Huang Bao) or fried bread sticks (You Tiao).

If you are feeling homesick there are a variety of cakes (Dan Gao), bread (Mian Bao), and preserved milk available in supermarkets and convenience stores. The most popular brands of milk are "MengNiu" and "Yi-Li Niu Nai," both of which can be purchased in 250ml cartons. Nestle 250ml carton milk and powdered milk (550ml packets) are also widely available.

Green tea comes in all different tastes and brands. Outside the major cities, black tea and coffee are still quite a rare luxury. Lipton "yellow label" black tea is available, both ready made with milk and sugar (just add hot water) or in tea bags. Recently, imported cereal packets, oats, Earl Grey tea, and McVities Digestives, HobNobs and Rich Tea have started to become available in western supermarkets such as Carrefour, Wal-Mart and Ole.

Dim sum (Dian Xin in Mandarin) is eaten all over China; however, it is still the favorite in Guangdong (Cantonese) province, where Chinese tea is served with hot and steamed dumplings (Jiao Zi) filled with either vegetables or pork meat.

Chinese Cuisines

Westerns will be shocked to find that the Chinese food in China tastes nothing like what is available in Europe or the States, and that's because the Chinese food outside China is catered for the tastes of the western mouth. Obviously, chicken chow mein and prawn crackers are not staples in China! If you have not already got used to it, then the art of eating with your chopsticks will be a new experience for you—don't be embarrassed to make a fool of yourself in a restaurant. Even for Chinese people it is tricky enough when they start using the chopsticks for the first time in their childhood. When I used chopsticks for the first time, I had a competition with my friend to see who could eat the greatest number of peanuts quickly—it was a good way to practice and master the skills!

An essential part of any Chinese diet is ginger and garlic because they are cheap, available in abundance, and act as a natural cure for minor ailments such as headaches. Some Chinese believe that if you are experiencing nausea, the best treatment is to mix Coca Cola with a little bit of ginger or salt.

Unlike in the west, the experience of going to a restaurant in China can be a bit of a noisy affair and very busy indeed — with waitresses dressed in brightly red colored Qi Piao's standing at the entrance to greet guests. Foreigners will notice that despite most of Chinese food being healthy, some regional dishes can also be very salty, oily, or sugary (sugar-coated tomatoes are a prime example). So considering this statement, amazingly, the vast majority of Chinese people are slim and appear healthy compared to westerners. One of the many reasons for this may be that Chinese people naturally have a better metabolism than non-Chinese (although there is no scientific proof of this and don't take my word for it!), and the other reason may be that the people tend to eat small amounts of everything that's on the table, rather than eating large bowls of one dish.

Cantonese Food

Considering the content available on most of the menus in restaurants in Guangdong province, Cantonese food may be classed as the most varied in the whole of China. There is a saying that the Cantonese "will eat anything with wings, except a plane, and anything with four legs, except a table." If you venture around restaurants in the major cities such as Guangzhou, Shenzhen, Zhuhai, or Zhongshan, you will observe that this statement is very much true. In outdoor markets, buying fresh meat is defined in an entirely different way, as you will find all kinds of game, snakes, rats, snails, insects, and seafood; all waiting to be sold while still alive. In one market in Guangzhou, I was shocked to observe a woman sitting on the pavement on a busy crowded street, killing and then scooping the insides of frogs right in front of impatient customers.

In a restaurant, the most shocking sight I have come across is people eating a very expensive dish called "Buffalo's Penis" accompanied by drinking snake wine, which is served in some of the high-class restaurants. The chef brings in a glass of wine (usually Great Wall wine) in one hand and a live snake in the other hand. Then within seconds the chef severs the snake's head to pour the blood from the body into the wine glass. Utterly distressing for the faint-hearted observer and not recommended if you want to sleep peacefully without having nightmares.

Some other famous Cantonese dishes include cactus cat meat, chilled monkey brain, casserole mountain turtle, and hot pot dog. Unlike in Europe and the USA, where hot dog refers to pork meat, in China, a hot dog is actual cooked dog meat and is usually served in the winter months, as dog meat is known to provide a warm feeling. Then there is also pig's blood, which looks like thick brown jelly and is eaten as a delicacy in Guangdong province. Many foods are believed to have medicinal properties, such as black chicken soup with coconut being good for heartburn.

Sichuan Food

Sichuan province is famous for a number of things, including the giant panda and some of the most beautiful scenery throughout China. But all of them are incomparable to the exquisite cuisine of this province because Sichuan is known throughout China for producing spicy food. Sichuan cooking relies on the heavy usage of chilies and spices in dishes, so those of you who are not used to hot food should take precautions.

There are also other regional cuisines such as Shangdong food (a high concentration of seafood), Shanghai cuisine (sweet and sour), and flavors from northern China, including Inner Mongolia.

Muslim Food

Throughout the country you will find Muslim restaurants that are owned and operated by the Chinese Muslims, namely the Hui and Uighur people, from the Xinjiang province. They are famous for making delicious halal food such as lamb koftas, lamb and vegetable kebabs, thick noodles (known as "La Mian"—that means pulled noodles), Peshwari naan breads and Ma-Dang, which is a very sweet sticky toffee-like dessert that is sold by peddlers. It contains a mixture of exotic fruits and nuts. Naturally, you won't find any pork dishes in a Muslim restaurant.

Vegetarian Food

Vegetables are available in abundance everywhere and have been popular for over 2500 years in Chinese cuisine; however, because China is a nation that loves eating meat products, if you are strict vegetarian, you will find it a bit of a challenge as most dishes contain meat, usually pork, in some form or other (except of course if you go to a Muslim restaurant).

Normally during formal meals, it is considered a status symbol to offer the guest meat dishes rather than "simple and cheaper" vegetable ones. Vegans would be disappointed to know that even McDonald's in China does not offer a veggie burger. Nevertheless there are many other options available such as "Subway sandwiches." "Mian Dian Wang" is another Chinese fast food outlet that offers vegetarian options including various noodles and dumplings.

You can politely mention "Wo bu yao rou" or "Wo bu che rou" (both mean "I don't eat meat") to the waitress in the restaurant, and she would be more than glad to show you the myriad vegetable options including lotus root, boiled cabbage leaves, and shredded carrots ("Bai/Hong lobo" — white/ red carrot). Bean curd (Tofu) is made from soy beans and is widely served in restaurants. It's delicious eaten either with rice and pickles, or just plain with any other dish.

International Cuisine

In the major cities, there is plenty of choice for international cuisine that includes Japanese, Korean, Indian, Italian, French, Mexican, and Midde Eastern food. There are a few American steak houses in the cities of Beijing, Shanghai, and Guangzhou. Most of these restaurants are managed by natives from those respective countries with well-trained Chinese cooks. Don't expect to see an expat bar in every city and it may be that you will have to stick to Chinese beers such as Tsingtao or Kings Beer, which are comparable to most foreign beers. Foreign beers are available (such as Carlsberg, Heineken and Guinness made under license) but not in every city.

Fast Food Outlets and Coffee Houses

Western fast food outlets first started operating in China during the late 1980s as an experiment in a market that had no previous experience of this kind of food. It was either make or break for companies like McDonald's, KFC (KFC celebrated twenty years of operation in China during 2007 with a nationwide marketing campaign), and Pizza Hut. These days you will have little problem finding your nearest KFC, McDonald's, or Pizza Hut in any major city and this trend is on the increase. In 2005 McDonald's opened its first ever "drive thru" in Dongguan city (halfway between Guangzhou and Shenzhen), and since 2006 pizza express home delivery has become available in some of the larger cities. With the increasing number of fast food chains and sugary brands such as Coca-Cola, Nestle (chocolates and ice creams), there is also the rising risk of young Chinese children becoming obese. Evidence of this is clear in the larger cities, where young overweight kids take their parents and grandparents into the local KFC/McDonald's.

Subway Sandwiches and Croissant de France can be found in the major cities as well. You may prefer to try Chinese fast food, from outlets such as "Real Kungfu" — whose corporate logo consists of Bruce Lee doing a karate kick. Chinese fast food consists of healthy steamed vegetables and meats cooked without the usage of oil.

Shanghai fast food shops

Coffee is still a relative luxury in China for many people as green tea is the preferred option. Starbucks has managed to break this culture barrier by opening quite a number of outlets in the major cities, much more rare in the rural areas, for now. There are a number of other coffee houses such as "Mingtian Coffee," "Kosmo," and "SPR Coffee" among other local outlets.

Drinking Tea and Water

Chinese people drink large quantities of water (usually boiled) as it is believed that water helps to wash away the pollutants in the body as well as keeping the digestive system flowing. When you enter as a guest in anyone's home or an office, usually the first thing that is offered is hot water in a plastic or paper cup from the water tank. Every household and office in urban China has a mobile water tank. The water tank can be ordered from the supplier once the container is finished. If your company has provided an accommodation for you then most likely your apartment will contain a free supply of drinking water. Bottled water is also available ubiquitously throughout the country; the most popular brands are Cestbon, Watson Water, Nanfeng Spring Water and Ginten Water. Western brands such as Evian or Vittel mineral water are available, but, as expected, cost more.

It goes without saying that the Chinese drink large quantities of "green tea," without adding sugar or milk. Tea shops are widely located everywhere and sell beautifully decorated boxes and hand-painted tins full of various types of traditional Chinese tea. The Chinese drink tea frequently in offices, homes, restaurants, and formal gatherings. Tea bags are a relatively new thing and only available in the major cities. Small amounts of fresh tea leaves are mixed with boiled water and require about five minutes to infuse before you start drinking. Trying to drink Chinese tea without swallowing the tea leaves is a skill in itself, and for this reason Chinese tea should be drunk in a mug with a lid in the shape of a Chinese pagoda roof. Every time a tea leaf gets to the top of the mug, you should push it away with the lid before you end up swallowing it.

Tea houses (Cha-dian) are places where Chinese people can go, usually in groups with friends or colleagues, and relax after a long day in the office. Tea houses are located in quiet and beautiful surroundings, usually with the presence of traditional Chinese music being played with a Zheng instrument in the background, either a recording or live. Chengdu, the capital of Sichuan province, is famous for teahouses and they can be found in most parks, theaters, and narrow lanes in cities. The most popular tea house in Beijing is the "Xi Bei Cha" located in the northwestern area of Shangdi—which is also known as the Silicon Valley area of Beijing. The unique aspect of this tea house is that you can get your feet massaged while you are sipping your tea and chatting with your friends.

CHAPTER 10:
RELATIONSHIPS

Personal Relationships—Boyfriend and Girlfriend

Unlike in the past, when it used to be rare for couples to be together before marriage, times have changed and China has become a bit more liberal and open minded with regard to relationships. While holding hands is common, kissing in public is still very rare. This has nothing to do with being a taboo; it's just not in the culture. Asians generally (including Indians, Thais, etc.) are shy when it comes to romance in public because you would get "onlookers," and it may seem offensive to the elders and traditional people. That said, modern China is presenting a few surprises, as a recent trend has been for couples to head for parks or get romantically attached in quiet neighborhoods.

Nevertheless, living together before marriage is rare and arranged marriages are still widely practiced in China. However with the emergence of the internet and modernization, couples in urban areas are more and more often choosing their own partners.

Foreigners ought to be aware that if they are in a relationship with a Chinese national, normally this may be assumed to be a strong indication for marriage, both by their Chinese partner and their respective parents. For example, if a couple are seen romantically tied together in a neighborhood, people start gossiping and asking the parents whether they will be getting married, and so for parents to marry off their children is a matter of respect and honor. So what may seem to be a "casual friendship" to a westerner may be considered something a bit more serious by his or her Chinese partner.

Marriage in China

Weddings in China are normally held in a local registry office followed by a lavish reception for friends and family at a restaurant or hotel.

Most marriages in China are still arranged by the parents, relatives, or friends of the family who may act as matchmakers; this is very much the case in the rural areas. In some remote villages often the bride and groom only meet each other on the day of their marriage, although this practice is slowly fading away as increasingly couples have the freedom to choose their own partners, and usually start dating before marriage.

Unlike in the west, engagement ceremonies before marriage are not practiced on the mainland. Even though things are getting a bit more liberal, nevertheless both the bride and bridegroom have to get consent for the marriage from their respective parents. In some parts, especially the rural areas, the bride and bridegroom wear traditional costumes according to the part of China where they are from, such as Mongolia or Shannxi for example.

In the major cities the bride and bridegroom usually wear western style wedding clothes, with the bride wearing a beautiful white dress and the bridegroom wearing a tuxedo. Irrespective of the weather conditions, newlywed couples flock to parks and lakes to take photos, posing in front of beautiful flowers and sculptures. All in all, getting married in China can be a rewardingly romantic experience.

One thing that you may find confusing is that Chinese women don't change their surname when they get married, and the children adopt the father's surname. A Chinese woman married to a foreigner may or may not change her surname depending on the couple's personal decision.

Marrying a Chinese National

An increasing number of Chinese nationals, more women than men, are marrying foreigners. Indeed some expats whom I have met have come to China for no purpose other than marrying a Chinese girl, and then they don't leave China. Either they have met their Chinese partner in their home country and followed them to China or they just come to China, usually leaving their life behind in their own country, in search of true love; of course that's not to say that they could not find true love in their own country. I have managed to gather information on what steps are required in order to get married in China, either to another foreigner or to a Chinese national.

Basic Information About Getting Married in China

Foreign nationals planning on getting married in China, either to a Chinese national or to another foreigner, should review the following general information provided by the Chinese Government for the proper procedures. All marriages, by foreigners and natives, in China are registered according to the laws of China, regardless of the nationality of those being married. Contrary to popular belief, the diplomatic and consular officers from your embassy or consulate do not have the authority to perform marriages and are not required to witness the marriages of foreign nationals.

The current Marriage Law of the People's Republic of China was approved in September 1980 and came into practice in January 1981. Under this law, marriage registration procedures are administered by the local civil affairs office (minzhengju), in each authority. Individuals planning to marry ought to visit one of these offices for explicit information. There will be a charge for this visit. If one of the spouses is a Chinese national, the appropriate civil affairs office will be the one in the authority in which the Chinese national is registered (the location of the *hukou*).

The marriage registration process may take anywhere from several days to several months to complete, depending upon how quickly the required documents are obtained. For example, some Chinese citizens have difficulty getting a "release" from their danwei to obtain the "certificate of birth" or the "certificate of marriageability."

The **danwei (work unit)** is the basic-level organization through which party and government officials control the social, political, and economic activities of inhabitants. The danwei typically controls the share of accommodation, grain, edible oil, and cotton rations; the issuance of permits to travel, to marry, and to bear or adopt children; and permission to enter the army, Communist party, and university as well as if an individual wants to change his or her job.

It is recommended that the couple dress up (coat and tie for the male). From past experience, it appears that whenever a couple appeared in jeans and trainers the registration process took over a month whereas couples who dressed formally and displayed a "correct attitude" were usually registered within a few days.

If both are foreigners, it will be the civil affairs office in the city in which they live. In general, at least one of the partners must reside in China. Two foreigners visiting China temporarily on tourist visas are unlikely to be able to register a marriage.

Certain categories of Chinese nationals, such as diplomats, security officials, and others whose work is considered to be crucial to the state, are not legally free to marry foreigners. Chinese students generally are permitted to marry if all the requirements are met, but they can expect to be expelled from school as soon as they do. Foreign nationals wishing to marry Chinese students should bear this in mind. It also should be noted that the school may require Chinese students to reimburse the school for hitherto uncharged tuition and other expenses upon withdrawal from school to marry foreigners. The school will not release documents the student needs to register the marriage until the fees are paid. Some work units may also demand compensation for "lost services."

Upon the receipt of an application to register a marriage, the civil affairs office will ascertain that both parties are of minimum marriageability age (generally this is twenty-two for men and twenty for women, although a higher minimum may be established by the local civil affairs office) and that both parties are single and free to marry. Previously married persons will be asked to submit original or certified copies of final divorce or of death certificates if widowed.

Foreign nationals who want to marry in China will generally be asked to submit the following:

- A current passport
- A Chinese residence permit
- A health certificate from the local hospital designated by the civil affairs office
- A "certification of marriageability," which can be prepared at your consulate on the basis of an affidavit in which the foreign national swears or affirms before a consul that he or she is currently legally eligible to marry.

Individuals who have previously been married need to show a certified divorce decree, annulment decree, or death certificate both to their consulate when preparing this certificate and to the local authorities. Since proof of termination of all previous marriages will again be required when you file an immigrant visa petition on your spouse's behalf, it is highly recommend that you do not surrender the certified copies of death certificates or divorce or annulment decrees to the civil affairs office. You should take a good photocopy with you when you go to register the marriage. Generally, if you present the certified copy with the copy for their review, the Chinese authorities will accept the copy. This is also true for your spouse if he or she has previously been married.

- Three photos of the marrying couple, taken together
- A registration fee

The Chinese partner to the marriage will be asked to submit the following:

- A certificate of marriageability (obtainable from the office that has physical control of his or her file)
- A certificate of birth
- Household registration book
- Health certificate (obtainable from a regional level local hospital)

- A letter from the parents of the local partner giving permission for their child to marry a foreigner (this letter should include the index fingerprint of both parents below their signature and date).

All English-language documents must be translated into Chinese. Translation of documents usually takes about a month, but can be completed within 10 days at double the original cost. Translations should be obtained from and certified by a Public Notary office or a lawyer (list provided in this book) in your city.

It takes the marriage registration office about an hour or so to review the submitted documents and approve the application. Once the marriage registration office approves of the application and registers the marriage, it will issue a marriage certificate to be picked up by the couple.

For some nationalities, the rules to get married to a Chinese national vary slightly. For example British citizens have a requirement to obtain a Certificate of No Impediment in order to get married in China. It's a British legal requirement to confirm that a British national has been resident in China for twenty-one consecutive days before swearing an Affidavit and completing a Notice of Intent to Marry. The notice of intent to marry will be displayed at the British consulate for a period of twenty-one days, after which a Certificate of No Impediment will be issued in both English and Chinese languages. This certificate is valid for three months from the date of issue.

Divorce in China

Divorce is still quite rare and seen rather as a taboo, although in the big cities, just as Chinese couples have the freedom to choose their partners, they also have the freedom to leave them—so much so that in the big cities divorce is providing quite good business for lawyers.

Adopting Children in China

Whenever I used to go to the Shamian Island of Guangzhou, I used to come across quite a number of expat families with Chinese children I used to think to myself that those children looked nothing like either of the parents. Then someone told me that it is common to adopt Chinese children in this part of Guangzhou.

Interested foreigners should be aware that the process of adopting a child in China and bringing the child to their country may be expensive, time-consuming and difficult. The number of Chinese children adopted by foreigners has steadily gone up since 1988 when only eight adoptions were on record; in 2006 when almost 5,000 children were adopted in China. Most of the information listed in this chapter is obtained with kind permission from the American and British Embassies in Beijing. All the information is correct at the time of writing this book and neither the author nor the Embassy authorities are responsible for any misapprehensions that may arise after consulting with or relating to any adoption organizations.

Chinese Organizations/Agencies Involved in the Adoption Process

There are many child adoption centers in western countries. Anyone wishing to adopt children in China should first start doing research by consulting their local adoption center in their country. Responsibility for the various procedures necessary to adopt a child in China in accordance with Chinese law is divided among the following Chinese government authorities:

The China Center for Adoption Affairs (CCAA)

The China Center for Adoption Affairs, a branch of the Ministry of Civil Affairs, is the central authority for adoptions in China. Since its establishment in 1996, the CCAA has taken measures to regulate adoption procedures and make them clearer.

CCAA
103 Beiheyan Street
Dongcheng District
Beijing 100006
Tel: +86 (0)10 6522 3102 or 6513 0607
Fax: +86 (0)10 6522 3102.

Department of Civil Affairs

China's provincial and county Civil Affairs Bureaus are officially in charge for orphaned and abandoned children. The Ministry of Civil Affairs administers the Civil Affairs Bureaus.

Department of Civil Affairs
147 Beijeyan Street
Beijing 100032

Children's Welfare Institute (Shehui Feli Jigou)

The Ministry of Civil Affairs, through provincial Civil Affairs Bureaus, administers the Children's Welfare Institutes. These are government-operated homes for orphaned and abandoned children. Children can only be placed in welfare institutes if their parents have died or abandoned them. For abandoned children, the authorities do make efforts to trace the parents before allowing adoption from the institutes.

Notaries Offices

The provincial Notaries Offices, which are managed by the Ministry of Justice in Beijing, issue the concluding adoption certificate. That process terminates the parental rights of the birth parent(s). Each adoption certificate comes with a notary's birth certificate for the child and either a statement explaining the reasons for desertion or notary's death certificates for the orphaned child's parents.

Public Security Bureau (PSB)

The local police station in China or Public Security Bureau (PSB), as known in China, in the locality where the adoption takes place, is responsible for issuing Chinese passports and exit permits to children adopted by foreigners.

Hospitals

Chinese law states that it is not permitted for a hospital to release a child directly to prospective parent(s) for adoption. Prospective adoptive parents have to go through the correct channels for adoption.

Children Eligible for Adoption

Only children processed by the CCAA are available for international adoption. The CCAA matches individual children with prospective adoptive parent(s) whose completed applications have been submitted to the CCAA by a licensed adoption agency in your country. Only applications submitted by agencies whose credentials are on file at the CCAA will be considered. A list of these adoption agencies is available from any one of the websites listed at the end of this chapter. An important issue that is made is that prospective parents *may not* choose the child they wish to adopt because the CCAA does not consider requests to adopt specific children.

Adoption Categories

The Adoption Law of the People's Republic of China, adopted by the twenty-third meeting of the seventh National People's Congress Standing Committee in December 1991, presented that, with a few exceptions, children under the age of fourteen in the following categories may be adopted by foreigners:

- Orphans—Any child whose parents are deceased or who have been declared deceased by a Chinese court.
- Abandoned children—These are children who have been abandoned by their parents or guardians.
- Hardship cases—These are children whose birth parents are incapable of looking after them because of unusual hardship such as financial or other valid reason(s).

Definition of a Special Needs Child

As the time of writing this document, no legal definition of a special needs child (or "disability") was developed by the CCAA. In the absence of a specific definition of special needs for the purposes of foreign adoptions, the CCAA relies on the criteria for disabled people approved by the State Council in October 1983. There are five kinds of handicaps as defined here:

(a) defects in vision
(b) defects in hearing and language
(c) mental deficiency (such as low I.Q. and development)
(d) handicap/impairment of arms and legs
(e) mental illness

The determination is made on the basis of "obscurity or loss of social function." Financial hardship is not classed as a disability.

Some illnesses that may be considered to cause an individual to become disabled in western countries may not necessarily be considered to be so in China. Potential adoptive parents should be very clear in their applications as to whether they are interested in adopting a disabled child. The medical report provided by the CCAA gives specific details about any disability or medical abnormality which does not comprise a disability under Chinese law. If and when in doubt about any specificity of information received, prospective adoptive parent(s) should feel free to request clarification from Chinese authorities directly or through the adoption agency in their country. If, prior to signing the final contract, adopting parent(s) believe that a disability or medical condition that has not been considered a disability under Chinese law may be more serious than otherwise presented, an independent medical examination may be considered and can be requested.

Foreigners traveling to China to complete adoptions will ultimately have to stay a period of time in China during the immigrant visa process. Foreign citizens interested in adoption in China have often inquired about inexpensive housing in the city where the child is located in China. Your adoption agency or travel agent may be in the best position to assist you in this regard.

Outline of Requirements for Adoptive Parents (table provided courtesy of the American Embassy in Beijing)

Section of China Law	Adoptive Parent(s) requirements	Adoptable Children's requirements
Article six	a) Age thirty-five or over b) Childless c) May adopt only one child	a) Abandoned child (Parents cannot be found or have relinquished parental rights to control)
Article eight, Paragraph two	a) Age thirty-five or older b) Not childless c) May adopt more than one child	a) Orphaned child (Requires proof that both parents are deceased) b) Handicapped child
Article seven	a) Age thirty-four or under b) Not childless c) May adopt more than one child	a) Orphaned child (Requires proof that both parents are deceased) b) Handicapped child
Article ten	Unmarried	All above age restrictions, limitations *re* number of children and category of children apply (implied)
Article nine	Unmarried Male	If adopting a female child, the adoptive parent must be at least forty years older than the adoptee

Chinese Documentary Requirements and Authentication Procedures

As stated in article twenty of the PRC adoption law, a foreigner interested in adopting a Chinese child must present proof of age, marital status, occupation, financial status, health condition, and police check record. It is advisable to bring several copies of the authenticated documentation with you to China in addition to the package of documents forwarded by your adoption agency to the CCAA for approval. Authentication means that the documents must bear the seal of the Embassy or Consulate of China in your country in order to be acceptable in China.

Required Documents for Adoption

1. **Birth Certificate(s)**: Certified and authenticated copies of the adoptive parent(s)' birth certificate(s). The birth certificates should include the applicant's name, sex, date of birth, place of birth, and parents' names. Please note that only original certificates would be accepted.

2. **Marital Status Certificate**: A certified and authenticated copy of the adoptive parent(s)' marriage certificate (if applicable) and/or proof of termination of any previous marriage (certified copy of spouse's death certificate or divorce decree). Single adopters must submit a document attesting to single status—this is obtainable from a public notary in your country.

3. **Health Examination Certificate(s)**: A medical certificate(s) for adoptive parent(s) executed by physician before a notary public and authenticated. Each applicant should submit a completed "General Physical Examination for Adoption Applicant" form. This form may be available from any adoption agency in your country. Please note that medical reports will only be considered valid if sent to the CCAA within six months of the date of issuance.

4. **Statement of Childlessness**: A notarized and authenticated statement is needed that clearly states that adoptive parent(s) is/are childless and has/have not adopted other children.

5. **Certificate of Infertility**: If this condition is present, a medical certificate (executed by a physician before a notary public and authenticated) is required. Note that infertility is <u>not</u> a requirement for adoption in China any longer.

6. **Certificate of Criminal or No-Criminal Record**: A certificate of good conduct for the adoptive parent(s) from a local police department in the country of the adoptive parent(s), notarized or bearing the police department seal and authenticated, is required. For example an FBI report (USA) or a Criminal Check Bureau (UK) is acceptable in lieu of a local police record; however, this is separate from the criminal records checks that are conducted by INS as part of the petition process.

   If the adoption claimant has lived overseas, away from his or her country of regular residence for one year or more during the last five years, the claimant must put forward a corresponding certificate to indicate whether the applicant has any criminal record in the overseas locality.

   It must be noted that certificates of criminal or no-criminal record will be considered valid only if sent to the CCAA within six months of the date of issuance. A criminal record does not automatically mean a rejection from the adoption process for the adoptive parent(s) as it depends on the seriousness of the crime committed. Needless to say, any individual who has been convicted of sexual offenses, irrespective of whether the case involved children or not, would be automatically rejected from consideration for adoption. For more details you can consult your embassy or consulate in confidence about this issue.

7. **Certificates of Profession, Income and Property**: Every applicant must submit a certificate of profession issued by his or her employer. This would include the applicant's position, the length of employment, and annual salary denominated in local currency. If the applicant is self-employed, the certificate must be submitted by a certified public accountant; if the applicant is an accountant, another certified accountant must submit the certificate.

8. **Letters of Reference**: Two letters of reference, notarized and authenticated, are required.

9. **Certificate(s) of Property**: If applicable, copies of any property trust deeds are required.

10. **Home Study Report**: A home study prepared by an authorized and licensed social agency must in all cases be submitted. The report must describe in detail:

   • the applicant's motivations and reasons for adopting; whether the applicant has children, including any from previous marriages or any other adopted children; any conditions the applicant places on the adoption, including whether special needs children are acceptable (and indicating what kind of special needs); and whether older children are acceptable.

   • the applicant's family background, including education, experience, and relationships with parents and siblings.

   • Whether the applicant has a history of alcoholism, substance abuse, pilferage, domestic violence, child abuse or other harmful behavior, or whether the applicant has a criminal record or any penalty meted out against him or her.

   • The health status of the applicant, including whether the applicant suffers from any mental or psychological illness or any unfavorable elements that would affect the bringing up of the child. Licensed physicians in connection with the conditions mentioned above should supply the health certificate.

- The marital status of the applicant should include a description of the relationship between husband and wife, any previous marriages, the number of divorces and their causes.
- Who shall act as guardian for the child in the event of an accident or health problem, or premature death of the applicant(s)? What will be the commitment on the part of the guardian?
- The reason for any cohabitation between family members or others living with single applicants, in order to ensure that the single adopter is not a homosexual. Homosexuals are prohibited from adopting children in China.
- The community environment in which the applicant lives, and in particular the attitude toward accepting children from other cultures and ethnic groups.

The Home Study should be investigated and completed by a certified, licensed social worker. The social worker should provide an assessment as to whether the applicant is qualified to adopt, as well as suggestions for the adoption.

11. **Bank Statements**: This is to prove that the applicant has enough funds to take financial responsibility for the adopted child.
12. **Power of Attorney**: This is required if only one spouse will travel to China. In the case of married couples, if only one adopting parent comes to China, the spouse traveling to China must bring a power of attorney from his or her spouse, notarized and properly authenticated by the Chinese Embassy or one of the Chinese Consulate Generals in your country.
13. **Letter of Intent to Adopt**: describing the child the adoptive parent(s) is/are willing to adopt, notarized and authenticated. Please be mindful of Chinese law regarding those children that are eligible for adoption by given applicants.
14. **Certificate of China Adoption Approval**: All applicants must submit a Certificate of China Adoption Approval, or its equivalent, by the competent department of the applicant's country of constant residence. The applicant must also submit a certificate of effective approval of travel to China for adoption.

What to Bring for Your New Baby

It is difficult to predict how long it may be obligatory for you to remain in China with your adopted child. Many stores, including foreign supermarkets such as Wal-Mart and Carrefour, sell products for babies. Most hospitals and western style hotels have personal stores and shops that sell some products for babies. It may also be useful for you to bring your own things from your own country in advance. This would save you time and the effort of looking for the right products that may be difficult to buy.

These items may include:

- Plastic or cloth baby carrier
- Bottle nipples
- Disposable paper diapers
- Baby wipes
- Baby blankets
- Infant wear
- Thermos bottle—for hot water to prepare dry formula
- Milk bottles (plastic, glass, and disposable)
- Disposable plastic bags for milk bottles

Resources

The following websites may be of assistance to those wishing to find out more about adoption:

http://www.china-babies-dev.com/
http://www.childrenshopeint.org/china.htm
http://www.chinaadoptionresources.com/link.htm

CHAPTER 11:
WOMEN IN SOCIETY AND IDENTITY

Attitudes Towards Women

Women in twenty-first century China, irrespective of whether they are white collar professionals or not, are treated the same as males. In the major cities, there has been a significant increase in the number of women opting to focus on their career rather than marrying in their early twenties and starting a family, as was the case in the past and still is in the rural areas. Even though China does not have official laws in place that define equal opportunities, as they do in the west, the people still have the common ethos built into them, through years of communism, that everyone should be treated with unity and equality irrespective if they are rich, poor, male, or female.

Women participate in all kinds of professions, such as police officers, judges, lawyers, doctors, engineers, senior corporate executives and even politicians. Nevertheless, some male-dominated professions still exist, such as firefighters, construction workers, or taxi drivers, where the absence of women is due to personal choice or other reasons rather than on discriminatory grounds—which is not the case.

As a foreign woman in China, you will be treated with respect and no different from how a male foreigner would be treated. Sexual harassment towards foreign women (even locals) is rare, and you don't need to feel unsafe walking on your own, for example, late at night. When it comes to interacting with foreign women, the majority of Chinese men are shy, although they would be most willing to jump at the first opportunity to become friendly. In saying this, caution should always be practiced, as you would anywhere else in the world.

Wearing a bikini on the beach should not pose problems, although it would be common sense to avoid wearing revealing clothes (i.e., short skirt for example) in busy shopping malls or late at night as you will be likely to attract unwanted attention. The worst you may encounter is giggling men saying such things like "Hello, English/American women!" from a distance (with a hint of shyness).

Chinese Names

Around the world we have perceptions of various surnames such as that most Muslims and Arabs are known as Mohammed or Ali, Smith is a popular western name, and most Indians can be distinguished by the surname Singh, Patel or Shah. However, no country can quite match up to China's record for the contest of most used surnames in the world. If you happen to be in a bank or a hospital or anywhere where there is a genuine need for customers to book business appointments, then it's not surprising to hear the names of two people with the exact surname and forename being called up.

With 1.3 billion people sharing about 430 surnames, it can get pretty confusing. In contrast to the growing economy, China is also going through a name crisis, which means there are too few names for too many people. The number of Chinese people named Wang is 94 million, a number that exceeds the population of most European countries including France, Germany, or the UK. There are a staggering 88 million people surnamed Zhang. The most popular Chinese names are Li, Wu, Xiao, Zhang, Wang, Hu, Jiang, Zhou, and Guang.

In my Shenzhen office, there were twelve colleagues named Wu and 3 of them had the same exact full name only to be set apart by having them called Wu junior (Xiao Wu, where Xiao means Small or Junior), Wu senior (Lao Wu where Lao means Old or Senior) and Wu number two (Er Wu)! The idea of addressing your seniors by putting "Lao" in front of their surname and your juniors by putting "Xiao" in front of their surname, is a more respectful but informal way of greeting people. It's best to only start using this once you know someone well enough. Sometimes the Chinese find it easier to solve the "too many people with the same name" problem by putting their job titles before their names, so for example Professor Jiangzhi, Captain Xiaopang (for Pilots etc.), Dr. Deng. or Nurse Yixia.

The government has started making efforts to propose a few changes to the law in order to allow parents to create double-barreled surnames for their children. The Chinese put their surname first followed by the forename. So for example the name "Deng Xiao Ping" would be known as Mr. Deng and not Mr. Xiao Ping, and "Mao Zedong" where Mao is the surname and Zedong is the first name would be called Mr. Mao and not Mr. Zedong.

Most Chinese students, people who work in multinationals or those who live in the major cities, tend to have an English nickname that replaces their Chinese first name. When using an English nickname, a Chinese name can be written in a western style, for example if someone is called James Wu then they would be, of course, known as Mr. Wu.

A Chinese may not be offended if you pronounce their name wrongly; however they will appreciate your effort to try to say it correctly. The most frequent mistakes that westerners make is reading "Ang" as "Aen" as in Bang, instead of "Ah-n."

In the corporate office, unless you know your colleagues quite well, it is best to be formal when addressing someone (as in Mr./Ms./Mrs.) regardless of whether they are senior or junior to you. It all depends on how you are introduced to your colleagues when you first join.

When I joined my first corporate position in Shenzhen, all the colleagues (including the senior management) were known by their first name. Even I was given a Chinese name (Lei-Xinge) and some colleagues asked me to christen them with an English name. Chinese people can be quite adventurous when choosing English nicknames—I have met people who have decided to call themselves "Top Gun," "Milky," "Magic," "Stone," "Spark," and "Punjab" just to name a few.

Mistaken Identity?

Even though there are officially fifty-six ethnic minority groups in China, the country is not considered a multicultural society as such because those minorities are still Chinese by blood rather than being from other parts of the world, as is the case in Western Europe, Australia, and North America.

Foreigners are known as a "Wai Guo Ren" (外国人) and anyone who looks mature or is generally over the age of thirty is known as a "Lao Wai," meaning old foreigner. In Hong Kong and Guangdong province, a rather blatant curse word, "Gweilo," is used, literally meaning "white ghost." Africans or people with a dark complexion are known as "Hei Ren" (黑人, black person) and white people as "Bai Gwe" (white person). Irrespective of your race, you will be attracting friendly attention just by being a foreigner in China, with your differences in facial features, body shape, and hairiness.

If you are a non–white skinned foreigner or even a "foreign born Chinese" in China, then this is something which you may end up explaining to people if they ask. Because of many years of poverty and low incomes, the vast majority of the people have not been abroad (although this is changing nowadays); therefore it is most likely that people will judge your origin from what you look like rather than your nationality.

Foreign born Chinese, more commonly known as "Overseas Chinese" or "Non-Resident Chinese" (NRCs), are treated with great respect when they return to China, just as any other foreigner is.

However if NRCs have relatives who live in China, usually they are expected to bring back gifts or money when they return to their motherland. It is usually the case of emigrant Chinese going to the USA, Australia, or European countries and working hard to save as much as they could, so that when they returned back to China, they could build a new home or set up a business in China. Although this is the same with most emigrants including Indians and Pakistanis in Europe and the USA, the NRCs actually contribute to the growing success of their country and work hard.

Therefore it is best to politely mention your nationality as well as your ethnic origin, whether you are a British Indian, British-Chinese, and so on, otherwise people get confused. Don't take it personally if someone consistently refers to you as an Indian or a Chinese, even if you are a British-born Chinese or an American-born Indian for example. Most Chinese people still have an image in their minds that London is foggy and industrialized, that British people are gentlemen wearing a bowler hat and carrying an umbrella, and that the ladies are elegant and wear posh hats and dresses.

Personal Story

In my experience I have noticed on many occasions that Chinese people got very confused about my ethnic identity when I met them for the first time. During my time in China, people have mistaken me to be an Arab, Latin American, Pakistani, Mexican, Malaysian, and even an African. It's only when I opened my mouth that people started thinking of countries like America or Britain! Even then I have to explain clearly that I am a British Indian and not entirely British. To my amusement, I have had people come up to me and curiously put forward questions that may seem to be completely unreasonable in the west, such as "Are you a White man or a Yellow man?" or "Why don't you talk like Tony Blair?"

To some extent it can be an enormous advantage to look Indian (and be Indian by blood!), speak Chinese, and have a British education and upbringing. It can be the perfect intelligence tool for any foreign corporation!

I remember thinking about going swimming for the first time in a public pool in Guangzhou, where my Chinese girlfriend teasingly asked me to shave my legs and thighs because most Chinese people see an unusual amount of body hair as an abnormality.

CHAPTER 12:
CHINESE LAW

The Chinese police force (known as Jing Cha) is one of the largest and the best in the world. The police in China have more power than the courts and lawyers. There are numerous plain-clothed C.I.D. (Criminal Investigation Department) officers patrolling the streets, shopping malls, and even state-owned companies/offices. China has one of the toughest criminal laws in the world. The death penalty by lethal injection or the firing squad is used for serious crimes such as murder, rape, engaging in sexual activities with a minor, bribe of a large amount, fraud of a large amount, and drug-related cases. For other crimes, the penalty can range anything from a simple warning to imprisonment.

Policeman in sunglasses in Shenzhen

145

Entry and Exit

It is highly prohibited to carry out any of the following while passing though any ports of entry/exit within the People's Republic of China:

1. To forge, alter, misuse, lend, buy, or sell visas.
2. To be in possession of illegal, pirated disks (CD/VCD/DVD/Cassette/ Computer hard disk/video tape, etc), or pornographic disks.
3. To smuggle out of the country protected cultural relics, gold, silver, diamond, ivory and other previous metals; rare animals and rare plants and their derivatives; contraband goods.
4. To be in possession of or consume illicit drugs—this is a very serious crime and punishable by death.

While in China

All of these are highly prohibited within the country:

1. To assault someone or to instigate a quarrel; to infringe on someone's rights and freedom.
2. To steal, rob, gain by deceit, vandalize public or private property, or purchase stolen goods (be very careful what you buy because in China the buyer also gets punished if the goods don't belong to the real owner).
3. Prostitution and having a massage by women are illegal activities in the PRC. Sexual harassment and rape are also very serious crimes, as is having sexual intercourse with a minor. If you are found guilty, these crimes can all lead to serious trouble.
4. To log onto pornographic websites, or to distribute or trade in pornographic or obscene materials, is strictly illegal.
5. Don't disturb the peace and order in public places, especially train stations, airports, shops, cinemas, or market places. Please take note that being intoxicated doesn't constitute a proper defense and doesn't reduce responsibility and liability.

Note: The above examples are only a partial list of prohibited activities in China. You need to pay attention to all the laws, although, like anywhere else, just be careful and sensible in life. Your behavior in China should be no different from how you behave back home. A good rule of thumb from an old Chinese idiom is: "Ruxiang Suisu"—When in Rome, do as the Romans do.

CHAPTER 13:
FESTIVALS AND RELIGION

Chinese festivals are split according to either the solar calendar or the lunar calendar. There are nine holidays according to the former while there are five official holidays according to the lunar calendar.

Christmas day in China is no different from any other day as it is not officially celebrated here. Foreign hotels and multinational corporations have a Christmas tree in the foyer along with a Santa Claus. Christmas celebrations are not quite like what they are in the west as in one particular example I saw in Shenzhen: The foyer of the Hilton Hotel was decorated in silver and blue instead of the usual red and green that is associated with Christmas in the west, plus the dragon was used instead of the reindeer and the legendary Chinese monkey king replaced Santa Claus.

During the official Chinese holidays, streets are decorated with the national flags, and special entertainment shows are provided in cities, where famous singers and actors mingle with the crowds and promote a sense of nationalism. Crowds are encouraged to participate in the singing of patriotic songs, as well as traditional songs that tell stories about village life and the struggles during the Cultural Revolution.

Chinese New Year (Chun Jie)

Chinese New Year (known as the Spring Festival) usually falls towards the beginning of February and is the highlight of the year for everyone. During the official three-day holiday, China is effectively closed for business in banks, law courts, and other government offices. Companies normally offer seven days, so employees have to compensate by working the following weekend.

Many people take extended leave from the office for about three weeks. It's the time of the year when people get the chance to return to their villages and hometowns and have large family reunions. People clean their home the day before the start of the New Year and this may include relocating the furniture in the home to give the home a new look for the New Year. Old clothes and furniture may be thrown away and replaced with new ones. If you are planning on traveling within the country, it would be a good idea to book your holiday in advance as it is very difficult to get a seat on any form of transport at the last minute.

Weeks before the start of the Chinese New Year, streets, shops, homes, and offices are decorated with red lights in the shape of Chinese lanterns, the legendary monkey king, or other things associated with Chinese culture. People put up red and yellow colored decorations on their front doors and inside the house to bring good luck for the coming year. Loud firecrackers are set off, in a belief that they will scare away evil spirits and bad luck.

In the major cities, especially Shanghai and Shenzhen where there are a considerably high number of migrants, be wary of thieves and gang robbers who try to look for anything expensive like laptops and mobile phones so that they can take them back to their villages or hometowns and give them as gifts to their families.

Qing Ming

This is in the third month of the Chinese calendar. It's a day when people visit the cemeteries and burial sites to pay respects to their ancestors.

October Mid Autumn Festival (Zhong Qiu Jie)

Also known as the golden week holiday or the moon festival, the mid autumn festival is a time when people eat lots of delicious moon cakes. These are round cakes made with the standard ingredients of wheat, sugar, and one or two dried egg yolks. Other moon cakes come with a variety of stuffings, according to the area of China in which they are sold, including dried fruit, nuts, and meat (usually ham, duck, or chicken). The legend goes that you should climb your nearest hill or mountain late in the evening to admire the full moon and eat moon cakes with friends, family, or your loved one.

Rather expensive in some places, these cakes can be an ideal gift for anyone. Foreigners often find them very heavy and they are considered quite fattening.

The story behind this holiday reverts to a legend called Hou Yih, who was an officer in the Imperial Guards in the year 2000 B.C. It goes that one day there appeared a sighting of ten suns in the sky. The Emperor, greatly concerned and afraid that this sighting foreshadowed some great evil to his people from the almighty, ordered Hou Yih, who was an expert archer, to shoot nine of the suns. Hou Yih did not let the emperor or the Goddess of the western heaven down, for he did exactly as requested and accomplished the feat with impressive results.

Knowing that Hou Yih was also a renowned architect, the Goddess asked him to build her a remarkable palace made of multicolored jade, as jade is a very important stone in the Chinese culture. He did not fail and with that the Goddess rewarded him with a capsule that would give him a chance of having everlasting life. The legend states that he was not to take this pill until he had undergone a year of prayer and fasting.

Hou's wife was not aware of the capsule that Hou had hidden away safely. Or so he thought, because his wife, a very beautiful and charming young lady named Chang Oh, found it and swallowed it. By the time Hou found out, it was too late. His wife was already airborne and was sent to the moon. Ever since, the legend has it that Chang Oh's face gleams in the moon on the 15th day of the 8th month of the Chinese lunar year—hence the moon festival!

May Day Holiday

The May Day naturally falls on the 1st of May. It's not much of a celebration of any sort; however the relief for many people to get a three-day official break from the office is welcome.

Dragon Boat Festival

Apart from Chinese New Year, the dragon boat festival, known as the "Duan Wu Jie," is perhaps the best known symbol of a traditional Chinese festival. It falls on the fifth day of the fifth lunar month. The highlight of the festival is contestant teams racing on their local river in slim wooden boats in the shape of a dragon (usually with the front part representing the dragon's face and the back part in the shape of a tail). Each team may have up to eight contestants, all dressed in colorful traditional costumes and chanting patriotic songs to the beat of drums in the background.

On the ground, shops sell boiled rice (known as "Zhongzhi") mixed with vegetables or meat and wrapped in a banana leaf, made to the shape of a pyramid (known as "Ketupat" in some parts of SE Asia such as Malaysia and Brunei).

The festival is said to commemorate the death of a minister and great poet of the State of Chu (Qu Yuan) during the Warring States (475–221 B.C.), who according to legend, drowned himself in protest in the river after learning that his king did not accept his advice. To avoid sea life consuming his body, the people of Chu launched their boats and threw rice dumplings wrapped in bamboo leaves into the river where he drowned to feed the fish.

It's a very colorful event in cities such as Shanghai, Guangzhou, and Hong Kong, where people line up on the banks of the rivers and cheer on the contestants. At the end of the race, in a gesture of good humor, the captain of the winning team is jubilantly thrown into the river by his teammates before collecting the trophy from the mayor of the city.

Religion

In China, people are allowed to practice their religious beliefs in places of worship; however, it would go against the government's wishes if those beliefs were spread around or if others were encouraged. Several cases were reported of foreigners that have been detained and deported from China for passing out nonauthorized religious literature. Sentences for distributing this material may range from three to five years' imprisonment, if convicted.

For these reasons, many Chinese keep their religious beliefs a private matter. There are of course many beautiful Buddhist temples around, as well as Christian churches and Muslim mosques. The main religions are Buddhism, Taoism, and Confucianism. While the majority of Chinese people don't believe in God or any particular religion, China is home to approximately 102 million Buddhists, approximately 9 million Muslims and around 14 million Christians.

Shop selling religious items

CHAPTER 14:
HOBBIES/INTERESTS

There are plenty of open air and indoor swimming pools. Most real estate developments have their own in-house gym and swimming facilities that can be used by the residents for a minute cost compared with public facilities.

Every major city and town in China has numerous beautiful parks and lakes. These parks are kept clean and have a small entrance fee. The country has approximately 2,800 natural lakes with a total area of more than 80,000 square kilometers. Some of the more popular parks and lakes have traditional Chinese instrumental music being played, normally with the recorded sound of a "Zheng," an 8- or 25-stringed plucked instrument. The speakers are camouflaged in shrubs and flowers, creating a romantic atmosphere. Public parks are extremely congested during the holiday season with families, tour groups, and couples.

Chinese people have in the past been known to save money for future investments and not spend on holidays or unnecessary purchases because it was thought of as a waste of money. Nevertheless, with increasing salaries and more free time on their hands, Chinese families are starting to enjoy all the kinds of entertainment and lifestyle choices that would normally be seen in other more advanced developing nations in Asia. Everything from artificial skiing slopes to traveling abroad is on the activities list for the modern Chinese person.

Irrespective of the city you are living in, there are things to see and do everywhere in a country that is host to at least 33 official UN World heritage sites, including the Beijing Great Wall, the Giant Panda reserve in Sichuan, and the Xian Terracotta warriors.

During the winter months, hot springs, some natural and some man-made, are popular tourist attractions for families and couples alike. Hot springs are normally located in beautiful rural surroundings next to mountains, parks, or lakes. Most hot springs offer special packages that provide hotel accommodation, breakfast, and unlimited access to the pools. As with other parks, tea houses, and lakes in China, hot springs also have beautiful Chinese instrumental music being played in the background, usually the stringed "Zheng." An ideal way to take away your stress in the winter.

Excursions can be easily booked through travel agents, some of whom can speak very good English. There is the risk that some expats can make themselves fall into the trap of just staying around their expat neighborhood because they are afraid to wander around the country due to lack of language or cultural knowledge.

Cats and Dogs

Chinese people, especially women, love to keep small dogs as pets. Chihuahuas seem to be a favorite choice and in many neighborhoods people normally go for an evening stroll with their dogs. For unexplained reasons, Chinese girls get very excited when they see dogs, not so much with cats. Even if a girl is walking hand in hand with her boyfriend, and if she sees a cute dog, she will almost forget her boyfriend and focus on the dog! On the other hand if you are a young single man walking with a cute dog, then girls will take note of you too, not just the dog!

Mah-Jong

There is a general belief among the Chinese elders that by playing Mah-Jong, they can help eliminate any irregularities that are usually associated with the brain's functionality as a person gets older (such as Alzheimer's or Parkinson's disease for example). So because of this physiological effect, blended with the fact that the elders have nothing else to do all day, they often play Mah-Jong all day. The phrase "all day" implies exactly that— most people start playing the game early in the morning and carry on until sunset with the occasional break for essentials or to have a quick snack at lunch time. These pensioners play for fun of course.

The Chinese as a culture like to gamble and some serious players like to indulge in this rather addictive game for financial purposes. There is plenty of this going on in the Las Vegas of Asia, Macau.

Little Emperors/Empresses!

China's one child policy may seem to be working well in the government's roadmap to having a smaller population; however it has also tended to create a large population of spoilt and discourteous kids. This is much more apparent within China's middle class where each young kid has the close attention of their parents, both sets of grandparents and all other relatives who are willing to buy anything for their loved ones. Hence these middle-class Chinese kids have been given the nickname "little Emperors" or "Empresses." On the whole children are treasured in China. The subject of children is probably the best starting point of your talk with your host. Therefore when you do ask about children, always start with your own kids, or your friends' kids. It a nice way to get into the inner circle with your host and mix in well with your Chinese friends.

CHAPTER 15:
ENTERTAINMENT

Chinese Opera

Chinese opera comes in various styles, such as Beijing Opera (more formally known as Peking Opera and "Jiangxi" in Mandarin), Cantonese Opera, from Guangzhou, and Sichuan Opera. Of all the Chinese operas, the most famous is Beijing opera, which is thought to have been established around 1790.

Chinese opera requires the actors to go through hours of preparation in skilled face painting, which itself is like a work of art. Chinese opera is performed by actors who express their singing and moods with prolonged high-pitched notes lending a very strong emotional connection to the story they are performing. Even some Chinese people cannot understand what the actors are saying when performing the opera. If you come to China and you don't get a chance to watch a genuine opera show, then it may be said that you have not experienced the real China.

Tickets can be expensive during the holiday season. In touristy places such as Beijing, almost all shows are fully booked. If you love watching Chinese opera then you can either head off to your nearest theatre or find out more or watch it on Channel CCTV 11, which is dedicated to nothing else but Chinese opera.

KTV Bars

The Chinese usually like to relax in the evening either at home with their families, or go out with their colleagues and friends to a KTV (Karaoke Bar). KTV venues have rooms to hire of all different sizes depending on how many people want to rent the room for singing. The prices for hiring a room per hour depend on the type of service you want, such as food and the number of songs. Each room consists of a couple of televisions with microphones to sing with and a PC from which you can choose the songs that you want to sing. Convenience food, such as snacks, fruit, and drinks, can be ordered. For those who cannot understand Chinese, or who are not budding singers, then KTV may prove to be a boring affair. Some KTV machines do have a limited selection of English songs.

Unlike in Japan and Korea, where KTV bars also double as "hostess bars" for exhausted businessmen in search of some of the unmentionable pleasures of life, in China the KTV culture has not reached such adventurous altitudes. Nevertheless in some big and modern cities such as Shanghai, Shenzhen, or Harbin, such KTV bars do exist in minute numbers with the majority of "hostesses" being migrant girls from the villages, attracted to the neon lights.

In the northern cities they are usually young women from Russia or Mongolia. Normally the trend is for businessmen to go to a KTV bar after work and perhaps act as host to their counterparts from the overseas offices, staying there until the wee hours of the following day, not doing much except singing songs, drinking, and watching TV. Quite monotonous actually but it's effective if you just want to while away the time after a stressful day.

Theatre & Cinema

There are a number of good cinemas in the major towns and cities. In smaller towns and villages sometimes there is a common television set up in the middle of the street where everyone can come to watch the latest movie. Hollywood movies are normally shown a bit later than in the rest of the world because of license reasons. While Chinese cinema has not quite hit global popularity as Hollywood and Bollywood (Indian cinema) have, there is a general interest in Chinese movies throughout Southeast Asia. With the rise of modern Chinese stars making their mark in Hollywood movies; such as Jackie Chan, Jet Li, Gong Li, Zhang Ziyi, and Chun Fat Yuan, Chinese movies are no longer stereotyped for being full of just simple kung fu action. Increasingly foreign filmmakers are looking towards China to choose their locations because of its beautiful and magical landscapes.

Most of the theatres and cinemas are large, clean, modern, and have a roof, although some have open sides, which makes it difficult in the winter because there is no heating system—this more applies to southern China because of the hot weather for most of the year. The other thing that you may find annoying when in a theatre or a cinema is that people will talk with each other and on their mobile phones right through the entire show only to stop if there is an important scene or something special happens in the show. All of this seems discourteous to the foreigner. But be assured that the Chinese see it as simply a way to enjoy a good day out with the family.

CHAPTER 16:
COMMUNICATION

Email and Internet Access

China has plenty of Internet Service Providers (ISPs) who will be happy to help connect you.

There are a surplus of private and joint-venture ISPs, many of which have their own World Wide Web sites, some of them bilingual, others Chinese only. The total number of Chinese surfers reached almost 120 million in 2006, according to a report from US-based research and consulting firm eTForecasts. Data published by eTForecasts suggested that the American share of the world's online population declined from around 20% in 2004 to about 18% in 2006, while China's share increased steadily from about 10% to just over 11%.

Broadband is widely available through China Mobile or China Unicom, the two main state-owned service providers on the mainland. It's best to take a Chinese-speaking friend with you to a local China Mobile store. For a relatively small price, between approx. 100 RMB and 200 RMB a month at the time of writing, you can have unlimited internet connected through broadband access plus your China Mobile landline. They even install the equipment for no extra charge. In a nutshell, internet access in 21st-century China is much faster and cheaper than in the west. Another success story is that China is now Skype's biggest market. In September 2005, Skype had just over 13 million registered Skype users in China, approximately 13% of the total, and more than in any other country.

When you apply for your Internet access account, it's best to take your passport and a copy of your passport with you. Although you're technically required to register with the Public Security Bureau (PSB) before you can open an account, many ISPs will do this for you.

Internet Cafés (Wangba)

Internet cafés are located in all the main cities. Some of them are in coffee houses such as Starbucks or Illy but the vast majority are in dark and smelly rooms accompanied by a cloud of cigarette smoke—unhygienic and to be avoided if possible. It gives a whole new meaning to surfing on line, as in any internet café, you can find an army of at least fifty people, usually teenagers, all playing Counter-Strike with each other! Be careful as some of these internet cafés are operated without a proper license and are prone to random checks by plain-clothed police. Costs at the time of writing are about four Yuan per hour. As there aren't many smoke-free cafés in China, a nice and clean internet café can cost between seven and ten Yuan per hour.

International Calls

You can request access to making international calls from your home phone when you set up with China Mobile. Calling internationally from China is not cheap, because there is only one provider, so therefore no competition for prices. International Calling cards provided by either China Satcom (known as 17970 or "Yao-Qi-Jiu-Qi-Ling") or by China Unicom (known as 17910 or "Yao-qi-jiu-yao-ling") are available at street kiosks in values of 50 RMB or 100 RMB. Most people at the kiosks don't understand English, so you can ask them in Chinese as follows:

English: I would like to buy the "17910 International Calling card" for 50 RMB/100 RMB please, thank you.
Mandarin Pinyin: "Wǒ yào yì zhâng yâo-qî-j ǐu-yâo-líng guó jì diàn huà kǎ- Wǔ Shí Kuài dç/Yî Bǎi Kuài de, xiè xiè"
Mandarin: 请我要一个17910购机点卡 50快的/100块的

English: I would like the "17970 International Calling card" for 50 RMB/100 RMB please, thank you.
Mandarin Pinyin: "Wǒ yào yì zhâng yâo-qî-j ǐu- qî-líng guó jì diàn huà kǎ- Wǔ Shí Kuài dç/Yî Bǎi Kuài de, xiè xiè"
Mandarin: 请我要一个17970购机点卡 50快的/100块的

Phone Lines/Modems

As is the case in other developing countries, phone lines in China can be awkward, so your ability to dial in to a server may depend on how your office (or hotel, home, university, or work unit) is connected. If you're in a western-style business office, you should be able to dial in easily. If you're at a university or some other state-run organization where the telecom equipment is old, you may have problems since phone lines are frequently overloaded. Keep trying, however, and you can usually connect.

On the whole, China has a very high bandwidth compared to most European and Asian countries. Internet connection is fast, reliable, and much more efficient.

Chinese phone kiosk

Photo Processing Shops

Getting your photos processed should not be a problem, as there are photo processing studios everywhere in most towns and cities. These photo processing studios also double as "luxury photo" studios, where you can go and have your photos taken in various poses, with super Kodak type quality and much cheaper than what you would pay for the same quality in the west. It's also a kind of fashion among the unmarried couples or Chinese girls to have their photos taken complete with a wedding dress or a tuxedo—just so they can see what they will look like when they get married!

Newly wedded couples as well as toddlers can often be found in parks and lake areas during the weekend having their photos taken, rain or shine.

Newspapers and Media

Chinese media, including the internet, is censored by the central government. The news pages of the BBC, CNN, and some other selected news websites are blocked.

The state owned CCTV (China Central Television Channel) has twelve official channels, with CCTV 9 (www.cctv-9.com) being the only English-speaking channel in the whole of China. CCTV1 and CCTV5 are the main flagship channels, and both show major sporting events live such as the World Cup and the Olympics. There are two other English-speaking channels that are available on cable TV, TVB Pearl broadcast from Shanghai and ATV broadcast from Hong Kong. BBC and CNN are available on cable TV or in four-star and five-star hotels. If you don't have STB (Cable TV), then the other 70 state-owned channels are all in Chinese. Apart from CCTV, every province, or cities in provinces, has its own state-owned television channels with local news and shows. Occasionally western movies are shown with subtitles.

China Daily is the major English-speaking newspaper and is available in hotels and reception halls of multinationals, but it's difficult to find it in a street stall. Then there are various state-owned newspapers that are available only in those particular cities or provinces, like for example the *Shenzhen Economic Zone* daily is only available in Shenzhen, and the *Guangzhou Nanfeng Daily* is only available in Guangzhou, and so on. All these newspapers are of course printed in Mandarin.

South China Morning Post (www.scmp.com) is a Hong Kong–based English daily that is only available in all major hotels and multinational offices on the mainland.

Glossy fashion magazines from the west have only started being sold in recent years, and not many are available on the market. *GQ, Marie Claire*, and *Good Housekeeping* are just a few that are available on street stalls, and are printed in Chinese. If you are coming to China with foreign magazines or newspapers, they may be confiscated at the entry/exit port if the customs staff members feel that the material is not appropriate to bring into China, which includes publications that contain pornography, are political in nature, or are intended for religious proselytism.

Foreigners seeking to enter the mainland with religious materials in a quantity larger than that required for personal use may be detained and fined. Chinese customs authorities may confiscate books, films, records, tapes, and compact disks to check whether they infringe Chinese prohibitions.

CHAPTER 17:
LEARNING CHINESE

The official Chinese language, known as Mandarin or Putonghua (common language), is one of the world's most complex languages. Unlike the ease with which foreigners can pick up languages such as French and Spanish with considerable fluency, this is not always the case with Chinese because no matter how expert you are at mastering this marvelous language, you will never be as good as a native Chinese, as one of my friends quite rightly pointed out:

No matter how fluent foreigners are at speaking Mandarin, they always sound funny to us because to us it looks strange that a foreigner is talking in Mandarin, but we are most willing to assist of course. It's all part of the fun of learning any new language.

Mandarin is spoken by approximately 95% of the population of mainland China and Taiwan. It is also known as *Hanyu* (the language of the Han people) and *Zhongwen* (language of the middle kingdom). The majority of the population keeps Mandarin as their first or second language along with their local dialect.

There are more than 150,000 foreign students in China, with the vast majority learning Mandarin. China's only English-speaking television channel, CCTV 9, quoted that in 2006 there were more foreign students in China than the number of mainland Chinese students (125,000) studying overseas.

Considering that one in five people in the world is from China, along with the fact that Chinese is one of the most difficult languages to learn, it would be a good idea to learn to speak some useful phrases before coming to the country. By learning Chinese you can begin to understand the cultural differences, and often it will help explain to you why those differences make you particularly uncomfortable.

Some schools in European countries, such as the UK and France, have already taken notice of the need to introduce Mandarin as an optional subject into their school curriculum. Clearly, European governments are realizing that they need to help equip the youth of today to handle the future challenges of working alongside their counterparts from emerging economies such as China.

Because of China's large geographical presence, many dialects are spoken in the different provinces. Apart from Mandarin, which is based on a northern dialect, with a few exceptions, with Beijing pronunciations as the standard, there are seven other dialects spoken widely throughout China, including Shanghainese, Hakka, Guangdonghua (Cantonese is spoken in Hong Kong, Macau, and Guangdong Province), Amoy, Fuzhou, and Wenzhou. In some of the villages and remote areas there are many minor local dialects spoken only within the tribes.

The Chinese phonetic alphabet is called the Pinyin and uses letters from the pronunciations of the Chinese characters. As the characters themselves don't correspond to the sounds, the phonetic alphabet is a well-established tool that helps overcome any problems in reading, writing, and remembering the characters.

Many of the letters have the same sound values as in English, however a few are different. Other Asian languages such as Vietnamese, Burmese, and Thai, for example, work in a similar way to Mandarin because they belong to the Sino-Tibetan family of languages as opposed to the Indo-Aryan family, to which English, Arabic, and Hindi, for example, belong.

The tone of the Chinese word is just as significant as its pronunciation. This feature of verbal communication of Chinese is the challenging part for foreigners to learn. In English, the tone of a word varies with the mood of the sentence; in Chinese, the tone stays the same whether the sentence is a question, exclamation, or a simple statement. The mood is signified by stress on some words. To use a wrong tone in a Chinese word would transform its meaning entirely.

There are four tones in Putonghua, expressed as 1st, 2nd, 3rd and 4th. The first tone is a relatively high level pitch (-); the second tone is a rising pitch (/); the third tone is a fall-rise pitch (V) and the 4th tone is a falling pitch (\). Now considering Mandarin has four tones, other dialects may have more, such as Shanghainese has eight in some words and Cantonese has up to nine. Therefore Mandarin may seem quite straightforward in that respect.

Many Chinese words are made up of one or two syllables, and each syllable is represented by one character. Even if two syllables have the same initial and final letters, the tone may give them totally different meanings. For example: Yī said in the first tone means the "number one" and Yǐ said in the third tone means a chair.

Besides the four basic tones, there is one special tone known as the neutral tone. The neutral tone is not a syllable that stands by itself; it occurs only in relation to the tone that precedes it. There is no tone mark written above syllables of the neutral tone. The neutral tone is considered short and weak, but don't think that neutral is far less important than the four main tones, since not many English speakers can master the language accurately and with a natural flow if unaware of how and where to use a neutral tone in communication.

Normally the tone mark is written on top of the vowel. In the case that there are several vowels in a word, then the tone mark is written on top of the major vowel that is pronounced clearly and the loudest (or the vowel that is visibly the most important). The structure of a Chinese sentence is relatively simple to understand and can be put as: Subject, Verb, and Object.

In some circumstances there are bound to be changes in the tones. Quite a number of words, such as Wǒ (Me, 我) are not necessarily at all times marked with a similar tone when they emerge in various phrases. The simple explanation behind this is that the tone of some words depends entirely on the tone of the word that follows it. So for example Wō ought to be only spoken in the first tone when it's used by itself; if the next word consists of either a 1st, 2nd or 3rd tonal word, then Wō can be spoken in the fourth tone, Wò; if then the fourth tone is present in the next word, Wō should be read in the second tone Wó.

Effectively, if the 1st tone is followed by a neutral tone, then it may be possible to stress the 1st tone, if however, there are two similar tones, then the tone on the first syllable should be short and then the tone on the second syllable can in actual fact be stressed.

Let's say if a syllable of a second tone is followed by a syllable of the 3rd, 4th, 1st or the neutral tone, then the second tone is pronounced with only the falling part of the tone without its final rise. However, in case the second tone is followed by another second tone, then the first second tone is read as a first tone. Sounds confusing—and it is for anyone who is alien to the language. Also note that all questions are normally followed with a "Ma" at the end.

Chinese Characters and Written Chinese

As pointed out earlier, the Chinese language is one of the oldest and most complex of languages to learn. Every Chinese character depicts a picture and it is upon this principle that the written form is based. Chinese characters are believed to have been created more than 3800 years ago out of simple pictures of things they represented. For example a person (Rén) looks like a little human with two legs as if he is running (人), and mouth (Kǒu) looks like a square (口). The written form is the same throughout most of the southeast Asian region where the majority of Chinese people reside. The complexity comes in the spoken form, where there are a myriad of regional dialects and forms of the Chinese language. Cantonese for example is only spoken in Guangdong Province and Hong Kong, while Hokkien is spoken in some parts of Singapore, Malaysia, and some parts of Fujian and Anhui provinces. The vast majority of the words are compounds that are created by joining two or more characters together. For example, the characters for the "sun" and "moon" put together make the word "bright," while the words "electric" (Dian, 电) and "shadow" (Yǐng, 影) make the word "cinema" (Dian Yǐng, 电影). Modern Chinese characters consist of two parts: the radical and the phonetic. The radical shows the class to which a word belongs, while the phonetic illustrates how a word is pronounced. Most of the characters without a phonetic component are believed to have been developed from simple pictures.

For example, the radical word "mouth" (Kǒu, 口) may be found in a whole host of words such as "to eat" (Chī, 吃) and "drink" (hē, 喝). There are approximately 250 radicals; some of them are common while others are rarely required for everyday usage. It's a very useful skill to be able to learn and practice using the radicals with phonetics.

The phonetic part of a character is often itself a character. Mastering the pronunciation of the core character from which some words are derived can often assist in the pronunciation of most of those words. Westerners frequently find it very difficult to distinguish between the various sounds of words when they are pronounced in Pinyin, even though they may look different when written. Just practice having a go and you'll be able to impress the locals sooner than you think!

For westerners, learning all these concepts can take a long time; indeed the spoken version of standard Mandarin is easier to pick up then the written version, where the latter may take years and even then it is difficult to master some words. Various sources indicate that there are around 60,000 characters, bearing in mind that for everyday use (perhaps to read a magazine, newspaper, or road signs) you will only require on average between 5000 and 7000 characters. Even this is a lot to swallow considering that in the English alphabet there are only twenty-six!

My personal Chinese class tutor in Guangzhou advised me that for any beginner to the Chinese language, the best way to study is to learn to write and pronounce one or two characters a day and keep on memorizing those characters on a regular basis, so by the end of a year you will have mastered at least 365 characters!

A Few Useful Phrases

Me
Wǒ
我

You (Singular)
Nǐ
你

You (Plural)
Nǐmen
你们

We
Wǒmen
我们

Hello
NǐHǎo
你好

How are you?
Nǐ Hǎo Ma?
你好吗？

I have a question
Wǒ yǒu yí gè wèn tí
我好一个问题

What is your name?
Nǐ Jiào Shén me míng zì?
你叫什么名字？

Can you help me please?
Nǐ néng bù néng bāng máng?
你能不能帮忙？

I don't understand
Wǒ bú míng bai
我不明白

I don't know
Wǒ bú zhī dao
我不知道

Excuse me
Láo Jià
劳驾

Yes
Shì, Duì
是，对

No
Bú Shì
不是

Sorry
Duì Bú Qǐ
对不起

Pardon Me
Qǐng yuán liàng
请愿 凉

Thank You
Xìe Xìe Nǐ
谢谢你

CHAPTER 18:
BEIJING OLYMPIC GAMES 2008

Towards the conclusion of the first decade of the twenty-first century, China will be attracting global attention at a huge scale. Shanghai is hosting the 2010 World Expo and at around the same time other Chinese cities are hosting various global sporting events; Guangzhou is hosting the 2010 Asian Games, while Shenzhen is hosting the 2011 Universiade. However, when the greatest sporting event on earth comes to Beijing in 2008, all of these events will surely be just icing on the cake for China's future economic prospects.

The Chinese put forward an ambitious bid to host the Olympics on the eighth day of the eighth month of the year 2008, because in China the number eight is considered to bring good luck and fortune. And luck was indeed on the side of the Chinese, when in 1991, the IOC formally awarded the 2008 Olympics to the city of Beijing.

The Olympic slogan making its presence felt
at the Badaling Great Wall, Beijing.

The coming of the 2008 Olympics in Beijing created tremendous economic and social opportunities for Chinese citizens as well as foreigners. To China, the Olympics mean more than just a showcase for the largest sporting event in the world. The Olympics open corridors for massive economic trade at the highest level between China and the rest of the world, opportunities that are expected to continue well after the games have concluded.

In their spare time, many expats have contributed to the Beijing Olympics national campaign as volunteers try to assist in the set-up of the games as much as possible. Some have been involved in promoting the capital city as a branding image for the various multinationals who will be acting as sponsors to the global event; a few expats have been giving some of their time to go around Beijing and report to the Beijing 2008 organizing committee any misspellings in public places such as on road signs or restaurants.

This is of course a very important issue because in order for Beijing to be a successful Olympic city, it must have correct English signs that are understandable by everyone.

In the run-up to the Olympics, the number of shops selling the official merchandise for the Olympics has increased.

Nobody should be blamed for the lack of correct English in the city; it's a natural occurrence because the Chinese language and the English language are totally different. It must be borne in mind that China has not been exposed to the international arena for a long time, and so English is still very much a new language. It's difficult for the Chinese people to learn English, just as it is for foreigners to learn Chinese. In general Beijingers are working hard at learning English and the government has made many efforts to assist its people in achieving this goal.

One of the recent trends to have hit the capital is taxi drivers practicing their English while driving around foreign passengers. Simple sentences such as "Where would you like to go?" or "It will cost you X amount of RMB" are played on the car cassette player and occasionally the taxi driver might like to practice talking with you too. It's all good fun and a great way for the drivers to enjoy their work because it's something new and exciting for them.

Beijing has been cleaned up and its citizens have been encouraged not to spit and shout. Some schools have started teaching children the basics of manners such as not to push in queues for buses and in shops.

The other major problem that the government is making hard efforts to tackle is the considerably high amount of pollution in Beijing. Smog and industrial pollution from factories have paved the way for Beijing to have an atmosphere similar to Dickensian London. Beijing's air quality was ranked 28th out of 113 cities worldwide in a report created in 2004 by Qin Jize from the *China Daily* newspaper. With the government's encouragement, the meteorological office has been monitoring the number of days a year that Beijing has a clear blue sky and early indications are that in recent years that number has been rising at a stable rate. To assist in reducing the pollution, some factories have been relocated to other industrial cities such as Tianjin and Shijiazhuang.

China has promised perfect weather to the Olympics organizers, planning to fire rockets into the sky to scatter any rain clouds. Beijing, which is chronically short of water, is well practiced at firing chemical infused rockets into clouds to prompt much-needed downpours, but recognizes that rain prevention systems remain a much tougher project. I was with another British expat in Beijing one summer day and surprisingly (quite rare!) the sky had no clouds, was blue, and featured beautiful sunshine.

Useful Links

http://en.beijing2008.cn/ Official website for the Beijing Olympics 2008

CHAPTER 19:
MOVING TO CHINA—DECIDING WHAT TO PACK

Once you know for sure that you are off to China, you need to decide what to pack up depending on the following factors:

- What time of the year you are going and which part of China you are going to—this is very important because if you are going to south China during the winter then you don't need to pack too many warm clothes. Winter in southern China lasts no more than two months at the worst and the majority of the year is warm and humid. On the other hand, winter time can present some exceedingly freezing conditions in the northern cities such as Beijing, Shanghai, and Xian for example.

- How long are you going to China for? Obviously if you are going for a contract that is lasting for at least a year then it would be wise to take quite a considerable amount of clothing with you.

- Take sensible amounts of clothes with you, maybe seven sets of clothes, one for each day of the week, with an extra set for other occasions. Don't fall into the trap that buying clothes on the mainland is necessarily cheaper than in the west because it's not surprising to see western-labeled designer clothes or other high-quality material available at more or less a similar price as you would pay back in the west. Of course on the other side of the coin, there are various outlets that offer high-quality "fake" designer labels at a fraction of the cost you would get in the west. Remember that you will have to bring the whole lot back again, so avoid over-packing at all costs!

- Some corporations offer a "relocation allowance" for those who are going to be moving abroad for a long period (anything from six months and beyond is considered as "long period"), while others might cover the cost of extra luggage on top of the basic amount that airlines offer (typically this extra luggage can be anything from 80 kg up to 180 kg, depending on your company's policy). It would be advisable to move as many personal belongings as you like and make the most of the allowance that is given to you.

- Even if you do qualify for a "relocation allowance," do bear in mind the small size of Chinese homes. Unless you are lucky enough to be put in a luxurious and spacious expat villa in Shanghai or Shekou, do try to keep your luggage on a small scale because storing it would be a problem. Most Chinese homes don't have the storage space that western homes do, and especially if you are moving from Canada or the USA, where many homes have a basement level that can store extra luggage, you will be in for a shock as there is no such thing in a Chinese home (even in the expat areas). You may need to pay extra to a relocation company to have your extra luggage stored in their warehouse. The costs associated with this are available from your China relocation company, and a list of these is provided in this book.

- There is no need to bring your furniture to China, unless you want to of course. There is IKEA and B&Q in some cities in China.
- Be careful of bringing electrical items into China. Although in Hong Kong and Macau you should have no problem with using western style three-pin plugs, in China the plugs are configured with either two pins, or narrow-type three-pin plugs. If you have to take an electric shaver, a portable games console, mobile phone/laptop charger, and so on, then it is advisable to buy an international plug adaptor. Electrical adaptors compatible with international standards are widely available in China. It would be advisable to purchase one from your home country or at an international airport.
- Bear in mind that import/export laws in China restrict certain items from being brought into the country, such as some publications. For example, a British friend of mine who relocated to China had copies of the *Sun* newspaper and men's magazine *Nuts* confiscated by customs officials upon arrival at Shanghai Pudong Airport—much to his embarrassment in front of on-looking locals, who, of course, had never seen such publications in their life.
- You might want to bring your favorite snack foods to China, such as Walkers crisps or chocolate—these are not widely available. Although they may not last long once you are there! "Dove Chocolate" (Mars group), "Snickers," "Cadbury," and "M&M's" are available on the mainland.
- For children, think about items such as toys, computer game consoles, books, and anything else they cannot live without. Involving children will help reassure them that they will find it comfortable living in China just as they did back in their home country. Important things such as favorite hobbies (stamp collecting materials, skateboarding shoes, favorite books, music, and DVDs) should also need to be taken into account.

- There is no need for you to bring your bicycle to China. After all, China used to be known as a "bicycle country"! You can purchase good quality cycles in many stores in every city at a reasonable price.
- You might want to bring your own cutlery and utensils to China because western-style kitchenware is not easy to find (except in Wal-Mart, Jusco, Carrefour, and Tesco supermarkets). Chinese-style spoons are not the same as western-style spoons, and even if you are in a western-style restaurant (except in five-star hotels and foreign-owned restaurants), then eight times out of ten you will probably get a fork and a sharp kitchen knife instead of a dinner knife matched to the fork! It's just like in the west, where supermarkets don't stock as many chopsticks as western cutlery, so the same in Chinese supermarkets, where they don't stock as much good quality western-style cutlery as they do Chinese ones.
- Don't worry about taking the bedding, because there are plenty of good quality pillows, quilts, and bed sheets available in China, and there is more variety too. You can easily purchase genuine silk bedding for a fraction of the cost you would pay in the west, plus it's a rare luxury to have silk material bedding in the west.
- In terms of your dress code, pretty much anything goes in China and you can dress however you feel comfortable. Because of history, there is no particular fashion style in China and it's especially the women who tend to wear an odd and interesting mix of clothes that might make you wonder for example, why someone in the office wants to dress in tight leather pants as if they were going to ride a motorbike! Of course as a woman, if you go out in a tiny top and shorts, don't complain if you get stared at more than you normally would as a foreigner, especially from construction workers who have not seen their wives/girlfriends for years!
- If you are on medication, it is advisable to take it with you, especially if you know that it may be difficult to purchase in China. Some medication (for epilepsy and diabetes for example) may not be available in China so talk this over with your doctor at home before bringing a reasonable quantity to China. If the medicine is prescribed in limited quantities, you may need to arrange the delivery of further prescriptions.
- Antiperspirants and shaving cream are available in stores such as Watson's, but rare, so it would be wise to take a sensible amount of stock with you. (These products are not available in abundance and are expensive because they are imported.)
- Pets can be brought into China as long as they are not endangered or protected wild animals. You should check with the Chinese Embassy in

your country and you should also check with the local Agricultural and Fisheries department in your country. Furthermore the Chinese Embassy in your country may be able to provide detailed information on any customs laws requiring the importing of pets into China.

- You may want to take along your favorite music tracks (either as a MP3/4 or CD format and your favorite DVDs as foreign music and films are still not widely available in China. Be aware of the customs restrictions on what to bring and how much.
- Minor but important things that you must take care of and need to take with you are listed here:

1. Mandarin phrase book and English-Chinese dictionary
2. Passport
3. Work Visa & Resident Permit
4. Your contract in English and Chinese (if you have one)
5. Birth Certificate, Marriage Certificate, etc. (although you can get copies in case you lose these)
6. Local Driver's License and International Driver's License
7. It would be useful to have contact addresses and phone numbers of people you know in China (friends, colleagues and so on)
8. Medicine and any medical certificates
9. Copies of credit card numbers, mobile phone Sim cards and local currency need to kept safe with at all times (never leave valuable belongings open in your home in China—thieves know where foreigners live and can target them in any case)
10. Take care of your mobile phone, laptop, and all other valuable belongings
11. Important numbers of the local police station and emergency numbers of your local consulate and embassy in China
12. International calling cards

CHAPTER 20:
CULTURE SHOCK IN CHINA

No matter how well you prepare yourself mentally, you will nevertheless experience culture shock. It's something that will stick with you irrespective of how long or how many times you travel between China and other countries because for you China will never be the same as your native country. In some way or another it will, without a doubt, affect you emotionally and perhaps even physically. The good thing is that the longer you stay in China, the more you get used to the surroundings and then you start treating it as your second home. This is when at least some of the emotional signs of the initial culture shock start to dissipate. Getting to identify what is acceptable and what isn't can at times prove to be tricky.

Settling in any foreign country for the first time can be challenging yet exciting. It's fair to say that for the first few months you are no more than an excited tourist taking photos everywhere, digesting the sights, smells, and sounds of China.

Before you go you need to think carefully about questions such as "How long do you really want to stay in China" and "For what reasons will you stay in China?" or "Is it beneficial for your future life or career?" You may be in a situation where you are going to China for the first time to experience what it's like before you embark on a longer stay there afterwards. The answers to all of these questions are vitally important because those answers will inevitably determine how you feel and react after returning from China. If you can, try to take a short break to go and experience what's its like in the country that you may be living in for a long time. It will be better than going there with no preparation and then not liking the place—you will just end up wasting your money and time. The other side of the argument may be that you don't have the time and/or money to go to China for a holiday.

There are a number of ways to overcome the initial homesickness. One way is to treat it like a lucky break or a working holiday because everyday you know that you are experiencing something new and different, something that your friends and relatives back in your native country never got the chance to do. Treat it as no different from migrating to a different city, that you had never been to, in your native country. The main difference is that when you are abroad you experience a different "culture" in terms of language and not just the environment.

The symptoms of culture shock occur naturally and start even before the journey begins in your home country, as you prepare to leave the comforts of your accustomed surroundings. It sounds like a sad love story but that's exactly how it may be viewed, because you are leaving something that you love and going to a destination that you are not familiar with, and in the process you will most likely end up making new friends and starting a new life. It's as much a physical experience as an emotional one, and it is something that any individual will experience every time he or she moves to an unfamiliar location anywhere in the world.

Try to look at it the other way around. Take a moment and just imagine how Chinese people feel when they come to your native country to work, for holiday, or to study. Of course it is not easy for Chinese people to settle into a foreign environment, especially a western culture such as Europe or the USA. Everything for the Chinese seems a challenge, from holding a fork and knife in a restaurant to not being able to mix in with the locals for entertainment. Thinking about this may put your mind at ease because you as a non-Chinese suffer the same culture shock when you are in China.

I remember when I was at university, I used to see lots of Chinese students going to the local supermarket and buying nothing but eggs, rice, and ready-made noodles. It seemed funny at the time but when I was in Shenzhen, I realized that I was in their shoes and the locals must have been wondering why this weird foreigner was buying lots of hamburgers and cereal bars!

Suffering from culture shock may include confusion, loneliness, disorientation, homesickness, anxiety, disliking the local food, missing loved ones or friends back home, and stress. This all takes its toll with the time difference (+8 hours GMT and +12 hours from New York) and the cost of international calls. For example, making that extra effort to telephone home can be a headache especially if you have had a long day and you need to call back to your parents or loved ones. For long-distance relationships, couples can find it stressful to say the least.

Quite amazingly you will be surprised that in China, you will end up making more friends than you ever did back in your home country. These friends may consist of fellow expats and locals alike. There are two reasons for this. The first reason is that you will be surrounded by a group of people from different countries and cultures but who have something in common; you are all expats in a foreign land. So there will be plenty of friends to make, to share stories about each other's experiences.

The other reason is that you will find it much easier to make friends with the locals because to them you are different, and being different has its advantages. Both you and your host friends can share stories about each other's culture and countries. Chinese people will often consider it a privilege to invite a foreigner into their home for a meal. Even on the street or in the office, it is very easy to make friends with the locals because you are different.

This "over-friendliness" by the Chinese and the VIP treatment given to foreigners can actually make foreigners become too spoiled in a way. For example, I realized that I got used to being treated like a VIP for everything and it got to the point where sometimes I expected it all the time, whereas this was not always the case. For example if I went to a bank and there was a large queue, then the bank staff would give me the privilege of jumping the queue simply because I was a foreigner; or if I went to a restaurant and there were no tables available, then on a few occasions I saw that the waitress took the trouble to ask some Chinese people to either move to another table or hurry up so that a foreigner could take a seat.

One side of me was always thinking that this is a good thing, while on the other hand I was always feeling a bit guilty of taking "liberties" to some extent in China. One day on a crowded train from Guangzhou to Shenzhen, a Chinese man offered me his seat; I politely kept on refusing but finally I sat down after he declined my refusals. At the moment that I sat down, another young Chinese man came up to me and spoke in an American accent: "I have lived in New York for over twenty years and no one has done this for me in America, why should we give up our seat to foreigners in China? Why? Can you tell me?" Meanwhile a lady, presumably his other half, calmed him down. I thought to myself that he did make a point and he was brave enough to say it. So I politely told him to take it easy, in Chinese, and then got up and changed carriages. He seemed surprised and I assume he wasn't expecting me to answer back in Chinese.

But my point is that the American-Chinese man made me think that most foreigners (including me) get sucked into the habit of being treated like a VIP everywhere we go in China (this is while under the influence of suffering from culture shock), but we don't realize that when foreigners come to our country we ignore the culture shock that they are going through. It's an interesting concept, one which I am sure many foreigners would wonder over!

Repatriation—The Effects of Reverse Culture Shock

Even though this book is aimed at expats who have not yet set foot in China, the issues involved when you do return from China to your home country need to be addressed. It's best to know what you may expect beforehand rather than later.

After spending a long time in China, coming back to your home country may seem strange, especially if it's in Europe or North America. For some people it may be a relief to come back while for others it can actually be more stressful to return than it was to move to China in the first place. No matter how long you have lived in China, you will without a doubt see things differently, think and behave differently, than you did before you left your home. Some people experience more of the reverse culture shock after returning from China to their homelands, while others experience more culture shock when they go to China. It purely depends on the individual.

A Dutch friend of mine who returned to Holland after spending nearly two years in Guangzhou told me that he didn't find much of a reverse culture shock when he returned to Holland, but he had suffered from culture shock when he first arrived in China because he wasn't prepared for the shock, mentally or physically—whereas he knew what it was like in Holland and nothing much had changed upon his arrival.

From my personal experience, every time I come back to the UK, it seems so boring and dull compared to the excitement and busy atmosphere of Hong Kong and China. Strange as it may seem but when you have been in a country like China for a long time, every time you come back to the UK it makes you think how life is more laid back and relaxed in the west. I suppose, apart from my parents, the second best thing I missed must be the food. It's always good to tuck into a bag of nice cod & chips or a cheese & onion pastie!

The beauty of it all is that most expats complain when they are in China, but when they are away they start missing their expat life so much that it hits them emotionally. This is because they don't get the same star "VIP" treatment in their home country that they became accustomed to as expats in China.

If you are living in the west (especially the UK, America, or some parts of Europe), you will definitely notice that it's much easier to make friends in China, simply because you are different. In the west people are more conservative and have an attitude of minding their own business, whereas in China or anywhere else in Asia, people may be nosy and curious, but out of that you will end up making more friends than enemies.

For example, in the UK, it is rare for someone to go up to a total stranger on a bus or train and start introducing themselves and becoming friendly; people will start having doubts about your character. But in China you will have to get used to Chinese people coming up to you and asking questions and trying to become friends with you. As an expat you may find out that it's easier to make friends with other foreigners in China, because as foreigners you are a minority in someone else's country; and through this networking opportunity you never know who you may bump into.

As an expatriate away from home for a long time, you will realize that you will have changed more than your family or friends who have stayed behind. Even though they have carried on with life without you, they generally would have maintained the same routine of life for the period that you have been away whereas you will have met many people from diverse cultures and backgrounds, experienced different environments, and faced different challenges and benefits of life, which actually can make someone more mature about life, especially if they are young.

Personal Story

I first went to China for a one-week holiday during the spring festival of 2004. I was lucky that I knew a very close friend there who welcomed me and showed me around because I knew nothing about China. I was not prepared for the culture shock. I could not speak the language, could not even hold chopsticks properly, and was just like a kid in a candy shop—very excited and running around Guangzhou with my camera taking photos of anything that seemed new and strange to me.

When I came back to the UK I felt like as if I had woken up from a dream because it was such a short trip and even though I had been away for only seven days, I was in actual fact experiencing the effects of "reverse culture shock." One of the many reasons for this could have been that I enjoyed my holiday so much and I did not want to come back to the UK.

I liked the place so much that I could not wait to go back. It was almost as if I had fallen in love with China and Hong Kong, because they are so far away from the UK and it's something exotic, something new and it's something special to have when you are moving around between Europe and Asia.

I kept my faith and I did manage to go back later in the same year after completing my degree, but this time it was for a longer period. This time around I did not know how long I was going to stay in China and where my future would take me with my job. Nevertheless after the first few months, when the "honeymoon period" was effectively over, the reality of living and working in China started to hit me.

The two major shocks that foreigners are likely to encounter in China are that of language problems and the lack of good-quality western cuisine. It's usually after the first couple of weeks that you start to realise that you have to live without eating cereal with milk in the morning or have a Sunday roast. The only places near the mainland where you are guaranteed to get some genuine western food are in Hong Kong or Macau. Thankfully living in Shenzhen meant that I could always nip across the border to Hong Kong for a day or two during the weekend and spoil myself with as much Marks & Spencer food as I liked!

Living so far away can, without a doubt, be exciting and life rewarding; however, there are other minor but important things that you have to worry about. For me the pressures of life such as worrying about my parents' health were always lurking at the back of my mind. It was the thought of "What if things went wrong." Of course I kept in touch through email, internet, and the phone.

Nevertheless, being so far away meant that naturally my parents would not disclose any bad news to me, such as if my mother was ill for example (which she was on one occasion and I only found out when I returned to the UK after a few months!). Of course I was livid with them for not telling me and they obviously didn't want to worry me so they kept saying everything was fine.

I was lucky to have a job that enabled me to effectively "commute" between China and the UK on a fairly regular basis and hence I got used to the thirteen-hour non-stop flights so much that after a few times it really felt no different than catching a long-distance coach with the exception that I had to deal with the effects of the time difference both mentally and physically!

I found out that having lived in China for a long time also made me effectively "become Chinese," and I only realized this when I came back to the UK. My parents and family were astonished that I could speak Mandarin, and it didn't end there. In the first week I came back, while assisting my parents with the weekly shopping in a local supermarket, after getting my change back from the cashier, without realizing it, I accidentally said thank you to her in Chinese, and she looked at me in surprise!

It is fair to say that I wasn't fully prepared for the shock that I got when I arrived in Guangzhou; however, I am glad that I wasn't because it has made me better prepared to tackle the culture shock no matter where I go in the future. I always maintain the principle that if you can survive in China then you can survive in any other country (except war zones, natural disasters, and so on of course!).

From my experience, I would certainly advise expats to go on a short crash course on Chinese culture before they come to China, if possible. It would certainly help to have friends or colleagues who are from the mainland and get to know as much as possible about the culture from them. Even speak with expats who have been resident in China for a long period of time and try to get useful advice from them. It will boost your confidence and morale tremendously.

CHAPTER 21:

HOW TO STOP CULTURE SHOCK FROM RUINING YOUR LIFE IN CHINA!

- Avoid rejecting the culture. You must remember that you are in someone else's country, so it's only fair to respect their way of living—no matter how strange you may find it. In England, there is a saying that an "Englishman's home is his Castle"; there goes a similar saying in China: "A Chinaman's home is his Imperial Palace." Trying to change local methods to make life easier for you will not work. Instead it will do you more harm than good and build up your stress and frustrations. The best way is to just go with the flow and accept the local practices and ways of living.

- Do as much background reading about China and in particular the part of China that you are going to. A good start would be to read the *The Rough Guide to China*, *The Lonely Planet* guides to China, and other useful travel guides. Go to Google or yahoo and just type in the name of the Chinese city you will be traveling to. Look at the photos, maps and so on to get a virtual feel of the place—to mentally prepare you. The physical preparation can come later when you are physically there and that should not be a problem as you will get used to it after a few days or couple of weeks at the most.

- Avoid whining and complaining about everything that makes you feel uncomfortable, such as people staring at you or asking you too many personal questions. The Chinese people are very nice and friendly towards foreigners and those that have seldom come across foreigners will want to be as hospitable towards you as possible. For these reasons people in the suburbs and rural areas (and even in some major cities where there's a large migrant community), will stare at you and will be curious to find out more about you. Most Chinese people are shy in front of foreigners—by all means you can meet the other end of the spectrum too. It will do you no good to take things personally, say for example if nobody sits next to you on a bus or train, despite that seat being the only empty one. Don't be upset by people staring at you or being nosy. Instead try to start a conversation if you can; in the process you may learn something new about their culture and life. If you smile, then 90% of the time you'll get a smile back.

- Most foreigners I have met in China are very careful about eating the meat, especially street meat. There is no harm in trying any new food for the first time, and then you don't have to eat it again if it doesn't tickle your taste buds. As long as you buy what the natives are eating or if there is a large queue of people including foreigners buying the food, then it should be no problem. As mentioned earlier, the Chinese are very careful of what they eat and where they eat—if a restaurant is empty then normally it means that the restaurant is under-rated by the natives.
- Learn the language—inability to speak Mandarin is a problem for most foreigners in China. To put your mind at ease, try to learn the essentials of the language before you go to China and then try to keep learning on a regular basis while you are there. Normally the best way is to learn one or two words a day and then memorize them after a few days. The Chinese language is very different from all the Indo-Aryan languages so therefore it is difficult to learn for westerners. Practice and repetition help.
- Even though China is changing and people are becoming a bit more liberal, nevertheless, do try to avoid kissing, hugging, or engaging in any other "touchy" behavior with your partner in public—as it will not go down well with the locals. For example, I once saw a foreign gentleman giving a piggyback ride to his girlfriend in Beijing's Tiananmen Square. This resulted in him being politely told by a guard to put her down as it caused offense to the locals.
- Try not to be put off by people spitting, clearing their throat with a loud noise, or sneezing loudly without a tissue in public places (including offices, public transport, etc.). This kind of behavior is normal among the deprived and those who have not been in contact with westerners. Unfortunately it is ubiquitous in China, caused either by excessive smoking, bad air pollution, or just an unpleasant habit. There is nothing you can do about this, because if you look at someone with disgust, they will get confused and think that something is wrong with you. Try to ignore the negatives and think of the positives and you will see the world in a different way.
- Just as in other countries in Asia where the midday sun is dangerously hot—especially from 12 pm to 3 pm (India, Malaysia, Vietnam, etc), Chinese women use an umbrella to protect their skin from the blazing hot sun. I have seldom seen men use an umbrella to protect against the sun because the Chinese believe that "the Man should be strong and face the sun!" If you are a foreign woman, it would be advisable that you use an umbrella to protect yourself. You will be the odd one out if you don't!

- If Chinese friends invite you to their home or to attend a dinner with them or their family, it's best to accept the offer if you have the time. The Chinese consider it an honor to invite a guest, especially a foreigner, to their home. Even if you politely refuse the offer, it may seem rude, so you should try to make an effort to attend because, as mentioned before, losing face in China is very important.

- Avoid getting upset and certainly don't verbally lash out at anyone if they push you and then they don't apologize for it. Since China is the world's most populous country, undoubtedly people are going to push and shove each other unintentionally in crowded places such as airports and train stations. People, especially those from the rural areas, are not used to saying sorry, as it is seen as similar to "losing face." In saying this, elderly people are given more respect than any other group of people.

- It is very easy for a foreigner to get upset in China, and for the smallest of things—all because of culture shock. What makes it worse is that the locals will usually start laughing and this would of course give you the impression that no one is taking you seriously. This is because in China facial expression goes a long way to show your emotions. When Chinese people are upset they normally open their eyes wide, their eyebrows are then pointing upwards and they stare with disgust. However when westerners get upset, they frown, have their eyebrows pointing inwards towards the eyes and start moving their arms and hands in all different directions to show anger and then the Chinese people start laughing because they think you seem confused and not upset.

- Avoid jokes or using sarcasm in the office, with friends, or at formal dinner gatherings/parties. Given that the vast majority of Chinese people have not been exposed to sarcasm, and mix that with language problems—you will not be doing anyone any favors—and if the joke is rude then you best be careful as people may take it seriously enough to feel insulted. In the process, you will end up feeling embarrassed and effectively "talking to yourself"—because not many people will understand what you are trying to imply. The sense of humor of westerners is just totally different from a Chinese sense of humor. In saying this, the best advice would be to "to keep your sense of humor," and in China it's a must to beat culture shock!

- The general sense of dressing is very informal throughout the country, partially because of the hot weather (in southern China) and partially because of cultural differences. People generally don't judge you on the way you are dressed although saying that, there is the chance that in their own circles and within their own class, people will tend to show off. Even in many multinationals, unless you are a senior Manager or Director, not many people wear a formal suit. Sales and Marketing professionals normally keep a suit in the office, in case a client visit is required at short notice. It does make you think how affluent people in Europe and the States are when it comes to dressing up. In the evening you may come across people going to the supermarket to do shopping wearing their night pyjamas and slippers and in hot weather the men usually roll their shirts up to their chest and rub their belly.

- Don't be shocked to see someone cleaning the road while wearing a blazer jacket, or someone dressed in tight leather pants in a corporate meeting in a multinational. It goes without saying that because of historical reasons, such as that people only started wearing western clothes around the early 1980s, many Chinese don't conform to Western concepts of how to dress up properly and for what occasion. This applies very much more for women than men and the proof is everywhere.

- As mentioned earlier, when conversing with your Chinese friends or colleagues, don't have any perceptions of rudeness or "no-manners," especially when words such as "Thank you," "Sorry," "Please," or "Excuse me" are not used as often in Chinese as in other languages.

- All over China, women outside hotels in tourist districts frequently use the prospect of companionship or sex to lure foreign men to isolated locations where their accomplices are waiting with the intention of robbing you. You should not allow yourself to be driven to bars or an individual's home unless you know the person who's making the offer.

- If you need a haircut, then be careful which hair salon you venture into. Don't be fooled by the numerous amount of so called "hair salons" that are actually illegal massage parlors or brothels, and the shocking thing is that they are everywhere in China. The government is taking great efforts to tackle this problem; however, like most things in China, it's easier said then done. It's sadly a vital ingredient for a waiting pandemic of diseases such as AIDS.

- You should take care and be wary of the fact that in the big cities, it is common for prostitutes to place nuisance calls to your hotel room number (somehow they know where foreigners stay!) in the middle of the night — the best defense is to disengage the phone from the socket. Some cases of theft of personal belongings have in the past been reported by foreigners, who have been either intoxicated or drugged in their hotel rooms. Hotel guests should refuse to open their room doors to anyone they do not know personally.

- On the whole learn as much as you can about China. Try to catch up on current affairs by watching the news, reading the internet and newspapers, and doing research on your embassy's website. Also try to read travel books to learn more. On the internet go to any search engine and type in keywords such as: "Expat + China" or "living in China" or anything about the particular city that you are going to travel to. This could range from any subject such as the availability of foreign foods to school options. Further website addresses are of course provided in this book for your reference.

- If you want, you might like to hire a professional relocation consultant who can advise you on any worries that you may have regarding settling in China. Your company may have resources and information for getting hold of a relocation consultant on your behalf, as the prices may be high if hired on an individual basis. If there are a group of expats in your company who have come to China for the first time, then perhaps a cost- and time-effective solution may be for your company to hire a relocation consultant for you. A good consultant will not only save your money and time but also provide encouragement to you to mentally take control of yourself and provide you vital information as to how you can achieve that in a way that's comfortable to you.

- Having a positive attitude can go a long way to diminishing the stress that is connected with culture shock. Having a good attitude toward most things can eliminate the bad and sad feelings that you may develop once you have settled into your Chinese environment.

- This one comes down to personal choice; however I would put myself in the situation of avoiding wearing too much perfume or aftershave. Chinese people are not used to wearing too much of these products. Although with the change of the times, the younger generation from China's middle class would jump at the first opportunity to try the latest CK1 or Christian Dior.

- As an expat in a foreign country you need to prepare yourself for challenges and benefits. However, no matter how bad you feel or how bad your experience has been, don't be taken too much by stories and experiences that other expats or repatriates (people who have returned back from China) tell you. They may not have been able to beat the culture shock in the same way that you may do or they may not be experienced travelers and so on. It's good to get different opinions and listen to other people's stories, and then you can judge for yourself of what the place looks like and feels like. Every country has good people and bad people and every country has good areas and bad areas.

- You will not be doing yourself many favors by just hanging around in expat bars and areas where the majority of foreigners (Laoweis) stay as this will not give you exposure to the real China. As a foreigner in China you have to go out and experience the country as the locals do—otherwise it's a waste of time and money. I remember venturing into a few expat bars in Shekou (Shenzhen) and Shanghai, where I happened to meet quite a number of foreign expats who proudly told me that they had been living in China for many years. I was, however, a bit shocked to find out that when I asked them if they could speak the language or know anything about general Chinese life, they shrugged their shoulders and said, "Nah, buddy, there is no real need, I have my free home, my expat bar, and my corporation looks after me well here; I don't need to speak Chinese or eat Chinese food!"
- Don't be put off by friends or family members who try to scare you with any ancient stereotypes that they may hold about China. On one of my trips back to the UK, I once met up with one of my university alumni friends, and they were stunned to hear that I was living in China for such a long time. They were telling me things like: "You'd better take care," "Do you know anyone there?" "Oh god, China? That's where they have public beheadings right?" It was the funniest thing I ever heard. I politely reassured the gentleman that he's probably thinking about Saudi Arabia and in my time in China I have never heard or seen such things. He was shocked to hear that I feel much safer walking on the streets of Guangzhou in the middle of the night than I do walking in broad daylight in some parts of London or New York.
- When putting down chopsticks on the table during dinners, avoid putting them facing downwards into a bowl of rice, as this indicates a symbol of death or bad luck. Normally a chopstick stand is provided for each person, where you can place the chopsticks on the side of your dishes.
- Avoid giving a clock to anyone as a gift, as this indicates death. I made this mistake when I gave a Millennium clock in 2000 to a Chinese friend of mine. Of course if a foreigner gives such gifts (unknowingly), then it can be taken with a laugh.
- There goes a saying that "Give a Chinese an Apple and he will in return offer you an Orange. If he does not have an Orange readily available, then

he will remember it and returning you the Apple will become one of his life's goals."

- The best way is to make as many Chinese friends as possible—which shouldn't be a problem because Chinese people will jump at the first opportunity to make friends with a foreigner. One American friend of mine put it into perspective:

I have been to so many places around China with my Chinese wife that I would not have been able to see had I been lurking around with other foreigners or by myself. Having a Chinese partner certainly helps in many ways such as language problems, food, companionship, a share of cultures and you get to experience China in a exciting way that can greatly eliminates any physiological effects that you get with the normal culture shock because you feel safe in the company of your Chinese partner.

CHAPTER 22:
LISTINGS FOR CHINA

Management Consultancies That Provide Advice to Foreign Companies in China

Accenture China (Beijing)
7/F., Capital Tower
6A, Jian Guo Men Wai Avenue
Chaoyang District
Beijing 100022
People's Republic of China
Tel: +86 (0)10 5870 5870
Fax: +86 (0)10 6561 2077
Website: www.accenture.com

APCO China
16th Floor, NCI Tower
12A Jianguomenwai Avenue
Chaoyang District
Beijing 100022
People's Republic of China
Phone: +86 (0)10 6505 5128
Fax: +86 (0)10 6505 5258
Website: beijing@apcoworldwide.com

A.T. Kearney (Shanghai) Management Consulting Co., Ltd.
HSBC Bldg., 42nd Floor
1000 Lujiazui Ring Road
Pudong New Area
Shanghai 200120
People's Republic of China
Tel: +86 (0)21 6841 2020
Website: www.atkearney.com

Bain & Company Consulting Group – China
Unit 2407-09, Office Tower 2
China Central Place
79 Jianguo Road
Chaoyang District
Beijing 100025

People's Republic of China
Tel: +86 (0)10 6533 1199
Fax: +86 (0)10 6598 9090
Website: www.bain.com

BearingPoint
Shanghai (China Headquarter)
31F CITIC Square
1168 West Nanjing Road
Shanghai 200041
People's Republic of China
Tel: +86 (0)21 5292 5392
Fax: +86 (0)21 5292 5391

Booz Allen Hamilton China
Suite 2511, One Corporate Ave
222 Hu Bin Road
Shanghai 200021
People's Republic of China
Tel: +86 (0)21 6340 6633
Fax: +86 (0)21 6340 6048
Website: www.boozallen.cn

Boston Consulting Group China
21/F, Central Plaza
227 Huangpi Bei Lu
Shanghai 200003
People's Republic of China
Phone: +86 (0)21 2306 4000
Fax: +86 (0)21 6375 8628
www.bcggreaterchina.com

CapGemini China
Unit 803-806
Capital Tower
5 Jia JianGuoMenwai Avenue
Chao Yang District, Beijing
People's Republic of China
Tel: +86 (0)10 6563 7388
Fax: +86 (0)10 6563 7399
Website: www.cn.capgemini.com

Deloitte China
Deloitte Touche Tohmatsu CPA Ltd.
8/F Office Tower W2
The Towers, Oriental Plaza
1 East Chang An Avenue
Beijing 100738

People's Republic of China
Tel: + 86 (0)10 8520 7788
Fax: + 86 (0)10 8518 1218
Website: www.deloitte.com

Droege Management Consultants China
Rm. 2001 Green Land Commercial Center
1258 Yu Yuan Road
Shanghai 200050
People's Republic of China
Tel.: +86 (0)21 6240 9090
Fax: +86 (0)21 6240 9881
Website: www.droege.de

EAC Management Consulting
Novel Plaza, Rm. 1403
128 Nanjing West Road
Shanghai 200003
People's Republic of China
Phone: +86-21-63508150
Fax: +86-21-63508151
E-mail: eac-sha@eac-consulting.de
Website: www.eac-consulting.de

Far Eastern Limited China
Rm315-319, 3 Floor,
HuaLian Development Mansion,
728, XinHua Rd.,
Shanghai 200052
People's Republic of China
Tel: +86 (0)21 6283 3322
Fax: +86 (0)21 6283 2277
E-Mail: Shanghai@far-eastern.cn
Website: www.far-eastern.de

Fiducia Management Consultants
Unit 0603, Landmark Tower 2
8 North Dongsanhuan Road,
Chaoyang District
Beijing 100004
People's Republic of China
Tel: +86 (0)10 6590 6108/6220
Fax: +86 (0)10 6590 6109
E-mail: info@fiducia-china.com
Website: www.fiducia-china.com

JLJ Management Consultants China
Unit 603-605
Shanghai Oriental Center
699 Nanjing West Road / 31 Wujiang
   Road

Shanghai 200041
People's Republic of China
Tel +86 (0)21 5211 0068
Fax +86 (0)21 5211 0069
Email: info@jljgroup.com
Website: www.jljgroup.com

LEK Management Consultants
Floor 34, CITIC Square
1168 Nanjing Road West
Shanghai 200041
People's Republic of China
Tel: +86 (0)21 6122 3900
Fax: +86 (0)21 6122 3988
E-mail: info@lek.com
Website: www.lek.com

McKinsey China
17/F Platinum Building
233 Tai Cang Road
Shanghai 200020
People's Republic of China
Tel: +86 (0)21 6385 8888
Fax: +86 (0)21 6386 2000
Website: www.mckinsey.com

Mercer Investment Consulting/HR Consulting China
Room 3601
HongKong New World Tower
300 Huaihai Zhong Road
Shanghai 200021
People's Republic of China
Tel: +86 (0)21 6335 3358
Fax: +86 (0)21 6361 6533
Website: www.merceric.com
Website: www.mercerhr.com

Monitor Consulting China
Unit 3905-3906, K. Wah Center
1010 Middle Huaihai Road
Xuhui District
Shanghai 200031
People's Republic of China
Tel +86 (0)21 6145 8900
Fax +86 (0)21 6145 8901
Website: www.monitorgroup.com.cn

PWC China
11/F PricewaterhouseCoopers Center
202 Hu Bin Road
Shanghai 200021

People's Republic of China
Tel: +86 (0)21 6123 8888
Fax: +86 (0)21 6123 8800
Website: www.pwc.com

**Roland Berger Strategy Consultants
(Shanghai) Ltd**
23rd Floor Shanghai Kerry Center
1515 Nanjing West Road
Shanghai 200040
People's Republic of China
Tel: +86 (0)21 5298 6677
Fax: +86 (0)21 5298 6660
E-mail: office_shanghai@rolandberger.
  com
Website: www.rolandberger.com.cn

Comprehensive List of Hospitals in China

Anhui Province

Anhui Provincial People's Hospital
1 Lu Jiang Road
He Fei City
Tel: +86 (0)551 2652 797

**Affiliated Hospital of Anhui Provincial
Medical Institute**
218 Ji Xi Rd, He Fei City
Tel: +86 (0)551 3633 411

Beijing

Alcoholics Anonymous can be reached
in Beijing at:
Tel: +86 (0)10 139 1138 9075
E-mail: beijingfellows@yahoo.com

Arrail Dental (瑞 尔 齿 科)
19 Jian Guo Men Wai Da Jie
Chao Yang District
Beijing 100004
北 京 建 国 门 外 大 街19 号
Tel: +86 (0)10 65006472/3, 85263235/6

Asia Emergency Assistance Ltd. (AEA)
14 Liangmahe South Road, 1/F
Beijing 100600
Tel: +86 (0)10 6462-9112, 6462 9100
Fax: +86 (0)10 6462-9111

Bayley & Jackson Medical Center
7 Ritan Dong Lu
Chaoyang District
Beijing 100020
北 京 朝 阳 区 日 坛 东 路7 号
Tel: +86 (0)10 8562 9998
Fax: +86 (0)10 8561 4866
Website: www.bjhealthcare.com

Beijing First Aid Center
103 Qian Men Xi Da Jie
Xuan Wu District
Beijing
北 京 前 门 西 大 街103 号
Tel: +86 (0)10 120 (24-hour), +86 (0)10
  65255678, 66014336

Beijing Red Cross Chaoyang Hospital Affiliated to Capital Medical University
首都医科大学附属北京
红十字朝阳医院
8 Bai Jia Zhuang Lu
Chao Yang District
Beijing 100020
北京朝阳区白家庄路8号
Tel: +86 (0)10 6500 7755 Ext. 2380, 6502 4704

Beijing United Family Hospital
2 Jiang Tai Lu
Chao Yang District
Beijing 100016
北京朝阳区蒋台路2号
Tel: +86 (0)10 64333960/1/2/4/5 (24-hour number)
Fax: +86 (0)10 64333963
Emergency Hotline: +86 (0)10-64332345
Website: www.beijingunited.com

Beijing United Family Clinic – Shunyi
Pinnacle Plaza, Unit 818
Tian Zhu Real Estate Development Zone
Shunyi District
Beijing 101312
北京顺义区天竺房地产开
发区日祥社区818号
Tel: +86 (0)10 80465432
Fax: +86 (0)10 80464383
Website: www.bjunited.com.cn

China Academy of Medical Science-Beijing Hospital (Peking Union Hospital) 协和医院
1 Shui Fu Yuan
Dong Cheng District
Beijing 100730
北京东城区帅府园1号
Tel: +86 (0)10 6529 5120; +86 (0)10 6529 5284
Fax: +86 (0)10 65124875

Friendship Hospital - GlobalDoctor Clinic
95 Yong An Lu
Xuan Wu District
Beijing 100050
北京宣武区永安路95号
Medivac Center in Bangkok: +66 2 236 8444

Tel: +86 (0)10 8456 9191 or +86 (0)10 83151915
E-mail: gdbjing@163bj.com

Hong Kong International Medical Clinic – Beijing
Swissotel 9 Fl., Beijing Hong Kong Macau Center
Dong Si Shi Tiao Li Jiao Qiao,
Beijing 100027
北京东四十条立交桥港
澳中心9层
Tel: +86 (0)10 65012288 Ext. 2346

Intech Eye Hospital (Dr. Hu) (英智眼科医院)
12 Pan Jia Yuan Nan Li
Chao Yang District
Beijing
北京朝阳区潘家园南里
12号
Tel: +86- (0) 10 6773 2909

International Medical Center (IMC) – Beijing
Lufthansa Center, Office Building
Suite 106
50 Liang Ma Qiao Rd
Chao Yang District
Beijing 100016
北京朝阳区亮马桥路50号
燕莎中心办公楼106室
Tel: +86 (0) 10 64651561/2/3 (24-hour number)
Fax: +86 (0) 10 64651984

International SOS Assistance (SOS)
Kunlun Hotel, Office Suite 433
2 Xin Yuan Nan Lu
Beijing
24-Hr. Number: +86 (0)10 6500 3419
Fax: +86 (0)10 6501 6048

MEDEX Assistance Corporation (Medical Evacuation Service)
871 Poly Plaza
14 South Dongzhimen
Beijing 100027
Tel: +86 (0)10 65958510
Fax: +86 (0)10 65958509
E-mail: medexasst@aol.com; medexws@sina.com

MEDEX Assistance Corporation
Regus Office 19
Beijing Lufthansa Center
50 Liangmaqiao Rd
Beijing 100016
Tel: +86 (10) 6465 1264
Fax: +86 (10) 6465 1267
Email: medexasst@aol.com

Ministry of Public Health-Beijing Hospital
1 Da Hua Lu, Dong Dan
Beijing 100730
北京东单大华路1号
Tel: +86 (0)10 65132266

No. 3 Hospital of Beijing Medical University
49 Hua Yuan Bei Lu
Hai Dian District
Beijing 100083
北京海淀区花园北路49号
Tel: +86 10 62016925, 62017691

Peking Union Medical Hospital
1 Shui Fu Yuan
Dong Cheng District
Beijing 100730
Tel: +86 (0)10 6529 6114 (registration)
Tel: +86 (0)10 6529 7292 (information)
Tel: +86 (0)10 6529 5284 (24 hours)
Modern Facilities with English speaking staff. Separate ward for foreign patients.

Sino-Japanese Friendship Hospital
Ying Hua Dong Lu
He Ping Li
Beijing 100029
北京和平里樱花东路
Tel: +86 (0) 10 6422/1122
Fax: +86 (0) 10 6421 7749

SOS International (Medical Emergency and Evacuation Service)
北京亚洲国际紧急救援
医疗服务中心
Building C, BITIC Leasing Center,
1 North Road
Xing Fu San Cun
Chao Yang District
Beijing 100027

北京朝阳区幸福三村北
接1号北信租赁中心C座
100027
Tel: +86 (0)10 64629100 (24-hour), +86
(0)10 64629112
Fax: +86 (0)10 6462-91111

Vista Clinic (维世达诊所)
Kerry Center Shopping Mall B29/B30
1 Guanghua Road
Chao Yang District
Beijing 100020
北京朝阳区光华路1号嘉
里购物中心 B29B/B30
Tel: +86 (0) 10 8529 6618
Fax: +86 (0) 10 8529 6615
Website http://www.vista-china.net

Dongbei Province (Including Liaoning Province)

Shenyang

Shenyang District includes China's three northeast provinces: Liaoning, Jilin and Heilongjiang. There are several hospitals which can provide services for foreigners in each province. Not all hospitals, however, have a designated English-speaking doctor for foreigners. This list is provided for reference only and does not constitute a recommendation.

American Medical Center – Global Doctor Medical Staff
54 Pangjiang Rd.
Dadong District
Shenyang
Tel: +86 (0)24 2433 0678; +86 (0)24 2432 6409
Fax: +86 (0)24 2433 1008
Emergency No: +86 (0)24 2432 6409

First Hospital of China Medical University
155 Nanjing North Street
Heping District
Shenyang 110001
Tel: +86 (0)24 2326 8760
Fax: +86 (0)24 2326 4417
Tel: +86 (0)24 2325 6666

He's Eye Hospital
128, Huanghe Bei St
Huanggu District
Tel: +86 (0)24 8653 1325(president's
office); +86 (0)24 8652 0800

The No. 2 Hospital of China Medical University
26 Wenhua Rd
Heping District,
Shenyang 110003
Tel: +86(0)24 2389 3501
Emergency: +86 (0)24 2389 2620
(day)/2389-2430 (night)

The People's Hospital of Liaoning Province
This hospital is designated for use by
foreigners
English-speaking doctors available.
33 Wenyi Rd
Shenhe Dist.
Shenyang, 110015
Tel: +86 (0)242414 7900 Director's Office:
+86 (0)24 2481 0438
Emergency: +86 (0)24 2481
0136/2414-7900

Dalian

Dalian Friendship Hospital
8 Sanba Square
Zhongshan District
Shenyang 116001
Tel: +86 (0) 411 271 8822
Admin office: +86 (0) 411 271 3281

Dalian Railway Hospital
6 Jiefang St.
Zhong Shan District
Tel: +86 (0)411 282 1120
Foreign Line Ward: +86 (0)411
2636293/2834447

The No. 1 Hospital of Dalian Medical University
222 Zhongshan Rd
116011
Tel: +86 (0)411 363 5963
Special Need Medical Department which
can meet medical needs of foreigners,

Ext.2126/2127/2128/2129 (night) or +86
(0)411 4394743.

Fujian Province

Fujian Provincial Hospital
134 Dongjie
Fuzhou
Fujian 350001
Tel: +86 (0)591 755 7768

Union Hospital Affiliated to Fujian University of Medical Science
11 Xin Quan Road
Fuzhou
Fujian 350001
Tel: +86 (0)591 335 7896 Ext. 8291, 8292
(Emergency)

Xiamen

Lifeline Medical System
123 Xidi Villa Hubin Bei Road
Xiamen City
Fujian 361012
Tel: +86 (0)592) 532 3168 (24 hours)
Fax: +86 (0)592) 532 6168
E-mail: lifelinexiamen@yahoo.com
Working Hours: Monday–Friday 8:00
am–8:00 pm,
Saturday 8:00 am–noon

Gansu Province

The People's Hospital of Gansu Province
160 Dong Gang Xi Lu
Cheng Guan District
Lan Zhou 730000
兰 州 市 城 关 区 东 岗 西 路
160 号
Tel: +86 (0)931-8416801 Ext. 203/302,
8822184

Guangdong Province

Guangzhou

Affiliated Hospital of Zhongshan University of Medical Science
58 Zhongshan 2nd Road
Guangzhou 510080

Tel: +86 (0)20 8775 5766 Ext. 8511; +86 (0)20 8733 0808 (Emergency)

Global Doctor Medical Center
Guangzhou City No. 1 People's Hospital Outpatient Department, 7-floor, 1 Panfu Lu
Guangzhou, Guangdong, 510180
Tel: +86 (0)20 8104 5173
Fax: +86 (0)20 8104 5170
E-mail: guangzhou@eglobaldoctor.com

Guangdong Concord Medical Center
9/F of the Guangdong Provincial Hospital
96 Dong Chuan Road
Guangzhou
This hospital is clean and modern and has a private inpatient floor. It has an in-patient and an outpatient unit located in a large government hospital. Outpatient visits are handled by staff physicians by appointment. Specialists are called in as needed or the patient is escorted to see the specialist. There is a membership fee. Be sure to make an appointment before going in for a check-up since this facility gives priority to its members and does not guarantee service to non-members.
Tel: +86 (0)20 8387 4283, +86 (0)20 8387 4293,
+86 (0)20 8387 4313
+86 (0)20 8387 4283 (Emergency)

Guangdong Hospital of Traditional Chinese Medicine (Ersha Island Hospital)
Da Tong Lu
Ersha Island
Guangzhou 510100
Tel: +86 (0)20 8190 4609; +86 (0)20 8188 9683

Guangdong Provincial People's Hospital
96 Dongchuan Road
Guangzhou 510080
Tel: +86 (0)20 8382 7812 Ext. 2603; +86 (0)20 8384 8627 (Emergency)
Tel: +86 (0)20 8188 5119; +86 (0)20 8387 4283

Guangzhou Can Am International Medical Center
5/F Garden Hotel
368 Huanshi Dong Lu
Guangzhou
The Guangzhou Can Am Medical Clinic offers a second choice for Guangzhou expatriates who wish to visit a Western standard health care setting. No membership is required, though those who are members ($120 fee) received a 20% discount on services. On-site laboratory, radiology, and pharmaceutical services are part of the operations. Four medical doctors, one dentist, and one professional counselor are on staff.
Visitors are welcome if you'd like to have a tour of their facilities. The clinic has also arranged direct billing with 10 insurance companies and is looking to increase this list.
Clinic hours: Monday through Friday 9:00 am to 12:30 pm and 2:00 pm to 6:00 pm. Saturday 9:00 am to 12:30 pm.
Tel: +86 (0)20 8386 6988 (24-Hour hotline)

Guangzhou Children's Hospital
318 Renmin Central Road
Guangzhou 510120
Tel: +86 (0)20 8188-6332 Ext. 5103 (Emergency)

Guangzhou Emergency Center
Tel: +86 (0)20 120
Anyone who needs emergency medical service can call the city Emergency Center (e.g. Guangzhou: 020-120), which will inform the hospital nearest the patient to arrange an ambulance and a medical team to the patient's location as soon as possible.

Guangzhou No. 1 People's Hospital
602 Renmin Road North
Guangzhou 510180
Tel: +86 (0)20 8108 2090; Tel: +86 (0)20 8108 0509

Guangzhou No. 2 People's Hospital
Tel: +86 (0)20 8181 4711

Guangzhou Red Cross Hospital
396 Tongfu Road Central
Guangzhou 510220
Tel: +86 (0)20 8441 2233x1108; +86 (0)20
8444 6411 (Emergency)

Guangzhou Overseas Chinese Hospital
Shipai, Guangzhou 510630
Tel: +86 (0)20 3868 8102 (Emergency)

Nanfang Hospital
Shahe, Guangzhou
Tel: +86 (0)20 8514 1888 Ext. 87287; +86
(0)20 8770 5656 (for foreigner service)
+86 (0)20 8770 6163 (Emergency)

No. 1 Affiliated Hospital of Guangzhou Medical College
1 Yanjiang Road
Guangzhou 510120
Tel: +86 (0)20 8333 7750 Ext. 3046; +86
(0)20 8333 6797 (Emergency)

No. 2 Affiliated Hospital of Guangzhou Medical College
Tel: +86 (0)20 8444 9613

No. 1 Affiliated Hospital of Guangzhou University of Traditional Chinese Medicine
Tel: +86 (0)20 3659 0957, +86 (0)20 3659 1316

No. 1 Subsidiary Hospital of Zhongshan Medical Sciences University
Tel: +86 (0)20 8777 8314

Overseas Chinese Hospital affiliated to Jinan University
Tel: +86 (0)20 8551 6025

SOS Alarm Center in Hong Kong
Tel: +852 2528 9900 (Provides medical services in Hong Kong only)

SOS Guangzhou Clinic
1/F North Tower
Ocean Pearl Building
No.19 Hua Li Rd.
Zhujiang New City, Guangzhou
Phone Number: +86 (0)20 8735-1051
Fax: +86 (0)20 8735 -2045

Office Hours: Monday to Friday 9:00 am to noon and 2:00 pm to 6:00 pm; Saturday (by appointment and emergencies only) 9:00 am to noon This clinic is run by foreign doctors who have overseas training and experience. They have a program called "one week program" in which you can become a member for a week. Consultation fee and commonly prescribed medicines such as antibiotics, cough syrup, and antihistamines are covered under the membership fee once you sign up for the one-week program. Multiple visits to the doctor during that week period are also covered.

Sun Yat Sen Memorial Hospital
107 Yanjiang Road West, Guangzhou 510120
Tel: +86 (0)20 8133-2199; +86 (0)20 8133-2469, +86 (0)20 8133-2648 (Emergency)
The urgency and the location of the patient would have to be the primary factor in making the decision to use this facility. Assurance has been given that they use disposable needles and syringes and sterilization is in evidence for those requiring such but there is no way to confirm the validity of this information. They also have an outpatient department in this hospital.

Dentists in Guangzhou:

Guangdong Provincial Dental Hospital
366 Jiang Nan Da Dao
Guangzhou 510260
Tel: +86 (0)20 8444-6867 (Director Office);
+86 (0)20 8442-7024 (Medical Dept.)
+86 (0)20 8442-7034, +86 (0)20 8443-8740 (Medical Office)

Sun Shine (Kai Yi) Dental Clinic
2 Tianhe North Road
Tel: +86 (0)20 3886 2888 Ext. 3111

Shenzhen

Shenzhen Affiliated Hospital to Beijing University
Tel: +86 (0)755 8392 3333

Shenzhen People's Hospital
Dongmen Road North
Shenzhen
Tel: +86 (0)755 2553 3018 Ext. 2553-1387
(Outpatient Dept.)

Shenzhen Red-Cross Hospital
Tel: +86 (0)755 8336 6388

Guangxi Province

Guilin

Guilin People's Hospital
70 Wenming Lu
Guilin
Guangxi 541002
Tel: +86 (0)773 282 9065, +86 (0)773 282 3767
Tel: +86 (0)773 282 5116 (Emergency)

Guizhou Province

Anshun

People's Hospital of Anshun Prefecture
22 East Hongshan Road
Anshun City
Tel: +86 (0)853 3222403

Guiyang

Attached Hospital of Guiyang Medical College
28 Guiyijie Street
Guiyang
Guizhou
Tel: +86 (0)851 6821113

Kaili

Hospital of Kaili City
418 West Beijing Road
Kaili City
Guizhou
Tel: +86 (0)855 8220700 (operator)

Zunyi

Attached Hospital of Zunyi Medical College
113 Dalian Road
Zunyi City
Tel: +86 (0)852 8622042

Hainan Province

Haikou People's Hospital
68 Desheng Sha Road
Haikou City
Hainan Province 570001
Tel: +86 (0)898 6622 3897 (Outpatient Dept. Office)
Tel: +86 (0)898 6618 9675
Tel: +86 (0)898 6622 2412 (Outpatient Dept.)

Hainan People's Hospital
Xianlie Lu, Xiuying Qu
Haikou City
Hainan Province 570011
Outpatient Dept. 8 Longhua Rd
Haikou City
Hainan Province 570001
Tel: +86 (0)898 6864 2660
Tel: +86 (0)898 6622 3287 (Outpatient Dept.)
Tel: +86 (0)898 6622 5866; +86 (0)898 6622 6666
Emergency: +86 (0)898 6222 2423

Hebei Province

People's Hospital of Hebei Province
348 He Ping Xi Lu
Xin Hua District
Shi Jia Zhuang 050011
石家庄市新华区和平西路348号
Tel: +86 (0)311 7046996 Ext. 8361/8126

Heilongjiang Province

Harbin

Provincial Hospital
82 Zhongshan Rd.
Xiangfang District

150036
Tel: +86 (0)451 566 2971

The No. 1 Hospital of Harbin
151, Diduan St
Daoli District 150010
Tel: +86 (0)451 468 3684 (Admin office)
Tel: +86 (0)451 461 4606; 461 4636

The No. 1 Hospital of Harbin Medical University

5 Youzheng St
Nangang District 150001
Tel: +86 (0)451 364 1918/360 7924/364 1563

The No. 2 Hospital of Harbin Medical University
247, Xue Fu Rd
Nangang District 150086
Tel: +86 (0)451 666 2962

Qiqihaer

The No. 1 Hospital of Qiqihaer
20 Gongyuan Lu
Longsha Dist, 161005
Tel: +86 (0)452 2425 981
Henan Province

The People's Hospital of Henan Province
7 Wei Wu Lu
Jin Shui District
Zhengzhou 450003
郑州市金水区纬五路7号
Tel: +86 (0)371 5951056, 5952183, 5580011
Fax: +86 (0)371 5964376

Hunan Province

The People's Hospital of Hunan Province
28 Dong Mao Jie
Jie Fang Xi Lu
Changsha 410002
长沙市解放西路东茅街 28号
Tel: +86 (0)731 2224611 Ext. 3333/2210

Inner Mongolia

The Affiliated Hospital to Inn Mongolia Medical College
1 Tong Dao Bei Jie
Hui Min District
Inner Mongolia 010050
内蒙古呼和浩特市回民 区通道北街1号
Tel: +86 (0)471 6965931, 6963300 Ext. 6804

Jiangsu Province

Jiangsu Provincial People's Hospital
300 Guangzhou Rd
Nanjing City
Tel: +86 (0)25-371-4511

General Hospital of Nanjing Military Base
305 Zhong Shan Dong Rd
Nanjing City
Tel: +86 (0)25 4826 808

Jiangxi Province

The People's Hospital of Jiangxi Province
152 Ai Guo Lu
Nanchang 330006
南昌市爱国路152号
Tel: +86 (0)791 6813352 Ext. 358
Tel: +86 (0)791 6813124

Jilin Province

Changchun

The No. 2 Hospital of Norman Bethune Medical University
18 Zhiqiang Street
Nanguan District
Changchun, 130041
Tel: +86 (0)431 8974612
Emergency same as above, Ext: 621

The Hospital of Changchun Chinese Medical University
20 Gongnong Road
Changchun, 130021
Tel: +86 (0)431 5955911

Yanbian

Yanbian Hospital
119 Juzi street
Yanji, 133000
Tel: +86 (0)433 2532435

Ningxia Province

The People's Hospital of Ningxia Hui Autonomous Region
Huai Yuan Lu
Xin Shi District
Yinchuan 750021
银 川 市 新 市 区 怀 远 路
Tel: +86 (0)951 2021154, 2021491 Ext. 335, 361

Qinghai Province

The People's Hospital of Qinghai Province
(The First Aid Center of Qinghai Province)
2 Gong He Lu
Xining 810007
青 海 省 西 宁 市 共 和 路2 号
Tel: +86 (0) 971 120, 8177911 Ext. 215

Shandong Province

Qingdao Municipal Hospital
1 Jiao Zhou Lu
Shi Bei District
Qingdao 266011
青 岛 市 市 北 区 胶 州 路1 号
Tel: +86 (0)532 2827191
Tel: +86 (0)531 2826437

Qianfoshan Hospital of Shandong Province
66 Jing Shi Lu
Jinan 250014
济 南 市 经 十 路66 号
Tel: +86 (0)531 2968900 Ext.2224/2082
Tel: +86 (0)531 2963647

Shanghai

General

Lifeline Shanghai is a community-based, confidential hotline providing emotional support and information to Shanghai's expatriate community.
Hotline: +86 (0)21 6279 8990

World Link Clinic (Expatriate doctors and imported vaccines)
Portman Clinic: Shanghai Center
203 W, 1376 Nanjing Xi Lu
200040
Tel: +86 (0)21 6279 7688
Appointments: +86 (0)21 6279 8678
Fax: +86 (0)21 6279 7698

Hong Qiao Clinic: Mandarine City
Unit 30, 788 Hong Xu Lu, 201103
Tel: +86 (0)21 6405-5788
Fax: +86 (0)21 6405-3587

Shanghai United Family Hospital and Clinics
1111 Xian Xia Xi Lu
Chang Ning District
Shanghai 200336 PRC
Website: http://www.shanghaiunited.com/

Medical/surgical emergencies:

Hua Dong Hospital
2nd Floor, Foreigner's Clinic
221 Yanan Xi Road
Tel: +86 (0)21 6248 4867
Tel: +86 (0)21 6248 3180 Ext. 3106

Hua Shan Hospital
15th Floor, Foreigner's Clinic
Zong He Lou
12 Wulumuqi Zhong Lu
Tel: +86 (0)21 6248-3986
Tel: +86 (0)21 6248-9999 Ext. 2531

Rui Jin Hospital, 197 Rui Jin Er Lu
Tel: +86 (0)21 6437 0045 Ext. 668101
Tel: +86 (0)21 6437 0045 Ext. 668202

The First People's Hospital
International Medical Care Center
585 Jiu Long Lu (near the Bund)
Tel: +86 (0)21 6324-3852 (24 hours)

Dental Practices in Shanghai

DDS Dental Care in Shanghai
2F/1, Tao Jiang Rd. (Dong Ping Rd.)
Tel: +86 (0)21 6466 0928
Fax: +86 (0)21 5456 2311
E-mail: cabuduo@hotmail.com

Dr Harriet Jin's Dental Surgery
Rm 17C Sun Tong Infoport Plaza
55 Huai Hai West Rd, 200030
Tel: +86 (0)21 5298 9799
Fax: +86 (0)21 5298 9799
E-mail: harrietjin@online.sh.cn

The No. 9 People's Hospital
7th Floor
Shanghai Dental Medical Center
  Cooperative Co.
(Sino-Canadian Joint venture)
Outpatient Service Building
639 Zhi-Zao-Ju Lu,
Tel: +86 (0)21 6313 3174

Maternity and Gynecology

International Peace Maternity Hospital
910 HengShan Road
Tel: +86 (0)21 6407 0434 Ext. 1105

The First Maternity and Child Hospital
536 Changle Road,
Tel: +86 (0)21 5403 5335

Pediatric Hospital
Shanghai Medical University
183 Fenglin Road, 2nd Floor
Tel: +86 (0)21 6403 7371; +86 (0)21 6404
  7129 Ext. 5009

Shanxi Province (Including Xian)

No.1 Hospital of Shanxi Medical University
85 Jie Fang Nan Lu, Taiyuan 030001
地址: 太原市解放南路85号

Tel: +86 (0)351-4044648, 4044111
  Ext.25463/26706

No. 2 College Affiliated to Xian Medical University
36 Xi Wu Lu, Xian 710004
地址: 西安市西五路36号
Tel: +86-(0)29-7273634

People's Hospital of Shaanxi Province
214 You Yi Xi Lu, Xian 710068
地址: 西安市友谊西路214号
Tel: +86-(0)29-5251331 Ext. 2283/2217,
  5241709

Sichuan Province

Chengdu

Chengdu Children's Hospital
Taishengnai Road 137
Emergency: +86 (0)28 662479

Chengdu Children's Special Hospital
The east part of Jiangjun Street
Tel: +86 (0)28 6691296

Chengdu Military Bayi Orthopaedics Hospital
Beijiaochang Houjie, Chengdu
Tel: +86 (0)28 6637492

Chengdu No.1 People's Hospital
The east part of Chunxi Road 2
Tel: +86 (0)28 6667223
Emergency: +86 (0)28 6659298

Chengdu No.2 People's Hospital
10, Qingyun Nanjie
Tel: +86 (0)28 6621522
Emergency: +86 (0)28 6740843

Chengdu No.3 People's Hospital
82, Qinglong Jie
Emergency: +86 (0)28 6638387

Hospital Attached to Chengdu Traditional Chinese Medical University
39, 12 Qiao Road
Tel: +86 (0)28 7769902

No.1 Hospital Attached to West China Medical University
37, Guoxuexiang
Emergency and Emergency +86 (0)28 5553329, 5422286
Appointment: +86 13808005795 (English, Japanese)
Medical Service: +86 (0)28 5551331(Chinese)
Office of OPD: +86 (0)28 5422290

No.2 Hospital Attached to West China Medical University
20, Section 3, Renmin Nanlu
Emergency: +86 (0)28 5501340

Sichuan International Medical Centre and Foreigners' Clinic
Tel: +86 (0)28 5422408 (English and Chinese, Monday to Friday 8:30 to 5:30)
Tel: +86 (0)28 5422777(English and Chinese)

Sichuan Province People's Hospital
1st ring road, west section 2, No. 32
Tel: +86 (0)28 7769981;
Emergency: +86 (0)28 7769262

Stomatological Hospital Attached to West China Medical University
14, Section 3, Renmin Nanlu
Tel: +86 (0)28 5553331; +86 (0)28 5501437; Emergency: +86 (0)28 5501452

Ya Fei Dental Clinic
25 Xifuhuajie (not far behind the Mao Statue), Chengdu.
Tel: +86 (0)28 6276100, +86 (0)28 6697436, +86 (0)28 6274034.
E-mail: yfdental@mail.sc.cninfo.net

Dazhu

People's Hospital of Dazhu County
West Zhongshan Street
Tel: +86 (0)23 43722184
Tel: +86 (0)23 43722184

Fengdu

People's Hospital of Fengdu County
251, Zhonghua Road
Mingshan Town
Fengdu County
Tel: +86 (0)23 70623569

Fengjie

People's Hospital of Fengjie County
61, Xinqiao Road
Fengjie County
Tel: +86 (0)23 56522704

Fuling

People's Hospital of Fuling District
2 Gaosuntang Road
Fuling District
Tel: +86 (0)23 72224460
Te: +86 (0)23 72223629 (Out-patient department).

Guangyuan

People's Hospital of Guangyuan City,
28, Jinjia-xiangzi (Jinjia Lane)
Tel: +86 (0)839 3222256
Tel: +86 (0)839 3223672 Ext. 3266

Kangding

People's Hospital of Kangding County
63, Xiangyang Street
Tel: +86 (0)836 2811445
Tel: +86 (0)836 2832445

Leshan

People's Hospital of Leshan City
76, Baita Street
Central District
Leshan
Tel: +86 (0)833 2119310, +86 (0)833 2119311
Emergency: +86 (0)833 2119328

Liangshan

First People's Hospital of Liangshan Prefecture
82 Shunjie
Xichang City
Tel: +86 (0)834 3222761, +86 (0)834 3226779
Tel: +86 (0)834 3222138

Panzhihua (Also known as JinJiang, near the border of Yunnan Province)

Central Hospital of Panzhihua City
North Dahe Road.
Tel: +86 (0)812 2223255, 2222512
Tel: +86 (0)812 2222941 Ext. 3346

Songpan

People's Hospital of Songpan County
1 Shoubei Lane South
Shuncheng Road
Jin-An Town
Tel: +86 (0)837 7232497

Urban Area

Chongqing Emergency Medical Center
1 Jiankang Road
Yuzhong District
Tel: +86 (0)23 63862747

First Attached Hospital of Chongqing Medical University
1 Youyi Road
Yuanjiagang
Tel: +86 (0) 23-68816534
Emergency: +86 (0)23 69012330.

Third People's Hospital of Chongqing City
104 Pibashan Zhengjie
Tel: +86 (0) 23 63515394

Wanzhou District (Wanxian)

Three Gorges Central Hospital of Chongqing City
165, Xincheng Road
Wanzhou District
Tel: +86 (0)23 58122821
Tel: +86 (0)23 58122622 (office)

Tianjin

General Hospital of Tianjin Medical University
154 An Shan Da
He Ping District
Tianjin 300450
天津和平区鞍山道154号

Tel: +86 (0)22 27813159

The First Center Hospital of Tianjin
24 Fu Kang Lu
Tianjin 300450
天津复康路24号
Tel: +86 (0)22 3366916

The Third Hospital of Tianjin
26 Jiang Du Lu
He Bei District
Tianjin 300250
天津河北区江都路26号
Tel: +86 (0)22 24341139

Tibet Autonomous Region

Lhasa

People's Hospital of Tibet Autonomous Region
7 North Linkuo Road
Lhasa
Tel: +86 (0)891 6332462

Tibet Autonomous Region No. 1 People's Hospital Emergency Medical Facility
This is a 24-hour facility (unlike the rest of the hospital)
18, North Lin Kuo Road, Lhasa, Tibet 850000
Emergency number: +86 (0)891 120
24 hour emergency number with an English language speaker: +86(0)891 632 2200.

Tibetan Medical Hospital of Tibet Autonomous Region
Sickward Department:
14 Buliangre Road (liangre road in Chinese)
Out-patient Department: No.10, Yutuo Road
Tel: +86 (0)891 6322351

Wuhan

No. 1 Affiliated Hospital to Hubei Medical University
238 Jie Fang Lu
Wu Chang District

Wuhan 430060
武汉市武昌区解放路238号
Tel: +86 (0)27 88041919, 88066234

No. 2 Affiliated Hospital to Hubei Medical University
169 Dong Hu Lu
Wu Chang District
Wuhan 430071
武汉武昌区东湖路169号
Tel: +86 (0)27 7312993, 7317926

Xie He Hospital Affiliated to Tong Ji Medical University
1095 Jie Fang Da Dao
Wuhan 430030
武汉汉口解放大道1277号
Tel: +86 (0)27 3646230, 3634590

Yichang Center People's Hospital
127 Yi Ling Da Dao
Yichang 443003
宜昌市夷陵大道127号
Tel: +86 (0)717 6447894, 6456947, 6457795

Xinjiang Uigur Autonomous Region

The People's Hospital of Xinjiang Uigur Autonomous Region
91 Tian Chi Lu
Urumqi 830001
乌鲁木齐市天池路91号
Tel: +86 (0)991 2822927 Ext. 3120/2209

Yunnan Province

Dali

People's Hospital of Dali Prefecture
122 South Renmin Road
Xiaguan
Tel: +86 (0)872 2125465

Jinghong

Hospital of Xishuangbanna Prefecture
17 Central Galan Road
Jinghong City
Tel: +86 (0)691 2123636 (office)

Fax: +86 (0)691 2123849

Kunming

First Attached Hospital of Kunming Medical College
153 Xichang Road
Kunming
Tel: +86 (0)871 5324888 (operator)
Emergency: +86 (0)871 5324590

First People's Hospital of Yunnan Province
172 Jinbi Road
Kunming
Tel: +86 (0)871 3634031(operator)

Lijiang

People's Hospital of Lijiang Prefecture
Fuhui Road, Dayan Town
Lijiang
Tel: +86 (0)888 5121343 (office)

Ruili

Minzu Hospital of Ruili City
1 Biancheng Street
Ruili
Tel: +86 (0)692 4141758

Zhongdian

People's Hospital of Diqing Prefecture
28 Heping Road
Zhongdian County
Tel: +86 (0)887 8222022

Zhejiang Province

Sir Run Run Show Hospital
3 Qing Chun Dong Rd
HangZhou City
Tel: +86 (0)571 8609 0073

VETERINARIANS IN CHINA

Beijing Main Veterinary Hospital
96 Huizhong Temple
Yayuncun (Asian Games Village)
Datun Anwai
Tel: +86 (0)10 64970591

Boai Small Animals Clinic
Building 11, 1st Floor
Wanquan Zhuangxiao
Haidian District Qu
Beijing, China
Tel: +86 (0)10 82616151

China Agricultural University Animal Hospital
Yuanmingyuan Xi Lu 2
North Gate of the Agricultural University
Beijing, China
Tel: +86 (0)10 6893036

Companion Animal Hospital
Dong Si Duo Fuxian
Yi Qu (Section B), Wanfujing (Prime Hotel-
  -south side)
Beijing, China
Tel: +86 (0)10 6449742

Guan Yuan Animal Hospital
Xicheng District
Siujie Hutong 4
(next to the Guanyuan Bird and Fish
  Market)
Beijing, China
Tel: +86 (0)10 66162134

Guan Sang Pet Care Center
Bei Sanhuan Zhoug Lu 7
Beijing, China
Tel: +86 (0)10 62371359

The Wuhan BeiBei Animal Hospital
Opposite Zhong Bei Cang Chu
187 Xing Hua Road
Jianghan District of Hankou
Wuhan City
Tel: +86 (0)72 65651611

List of Chambers of Commerce

Beijing

American Chamber of Commerce in Beijing
China Resource Building, Suite 1903
8 Jianguomenbei Ave
Beijing 100005
Tel: +86 (0)10 8519 1920
Fax: +86 (0)10 8519 1910
Email: amcham@amcham-china.org.cn
Website: www.amcham-china.org.cn

Australian Chamber of Commerce in Beijing
E floor, Office Tower
Beijing Hong Kong Macau Center
  (Swissotel),
2 Chaoyangmenbei Dajie
Beijing 100027
Tel: +86 (0)10 6595 9252
Fax: +86 (0)10 6595 9253
E-mail: info@austcham.org
Website: www.austcham.org

Austrian Chamber of Commerce in Hong Kong
GPO Box 8031
Central, Hong Kong
Tel: +852 3105 0152
Fax: +852 3105 9925
Email: austrocham@austrocham.com
Website: www.aa.com.hk

Belgium Chamber of Commerce in Beijing
4020 Xinhe Dasha
Sanyuanli
14, Shunyuan Street
Chaoyang District
Beijing 100027
Tel: + 86 (0)10 6465 0320
Fax: +86 (0)10 6465 2080
Email: beijing@bencham.org
Website: www.bencham.org

British Chamber of Commerce in Beijing
The British Center
Room 1001

China Life Tower
16 Chaoyangmenwai Avenue
Beijing 100020
Tel: +86 (0)10 85251111
Fax: +86 (0)10 85251100
E-mail: britcham@pek.britcham.org
Website: http://www.pek.britcham.org/

**Canada China Business Council in
Beijing**
Suite 18-2, CITIC Building,
19 Jianguomenwai Street
Beijing 100004
Tel: +86 (0)10 8526 1820/21/22
Fax: +86 (0)10 6512 6125
E-mail: ccbcbj@ccbc.com.cn
Website: www.ccbc.com

China-Britain Business Council (CBBC)
The British Center
Room 1001, China Life Tower
16 Chaoyangmenwai Avenue
Beijing 100020
Tel: +86 (0)10 8525 1111
Fax: +86 (0)10 8525 1001
Email: beijing@cbbc.org.cn
Website: www.cbbc.org

**China Council for the Promotion of
International Trade (CCPIT)
China Chamber of International
    Commerce (CCOIC)**
1 Fuxingmenwai Street
Beijing 100860
Tel: +86 (0)10 88075716
Fax: +86 (0)10 68030747
Website: http://english.ccpit.org/

**Danish Chamber of Commerce in
Beijing**
Office C412
Beijing Lufthansa Center
50 Liangmaqiao Road
Chaoyang District
Beijing 100016
Tel: +86 (0)10 6467 5748
Fax: +86 (0)10 6462 3206
E-mail: cathy@dccc.com.cn
Website: www.dccc.com.cn

European Chamber of Commerce
Lufthansa Center, Office S-123

50 Liangmaqiao Road,
Chaoyang District
Beijing 100016
Tel: +86 (0)10 6462 2065/66
Fax: +86 (0)10 6462 2067
E-mail: euccc@euccc.com.cn
Website: www.europeanchamber.com.cn

**Delegation of the European
Commission in Beijing**
15, Dong Zhi Men Wai Da Jie, San Li Tun
Beijing 100600
Tel: +86 (0)10 84548000
Fax: +86 (0)10 84548011
E-mail: Delegation-China@ec.europa.eu
Website: http://www.delchn.cec.eu.int/

**Economic representation of Flanders
in Beijing**
San Li Tun Lu, 6
CN-100600 Beijing
Tel.: +86 (0)10 6532 4964
Fax: +86 (0)10 6532 6833
E-mail: **beijing@fitagency.com**

**Economic Representation of Wallonia
Region in Beijing**
San Li Tun Lu, 6
CN-100600 Beijing
Tel.: +86 (0)10 6532 6695
Fax: +86 (0)10 6532 6696
E-mail: **awexbrubeijing@188.com**

**French Chamber of Commerce in
Beijing**
Novotel Xinqiao Beijing, Area B, 6th Floor
2 Dongjiaominxiang
Dongcheng District
Beijing 100004
Tel: +86 (0)10 65 12 17 40
Fax: +86 (0)10 65 12 14 96
E-Mail: ccifc-beijing@ccifc.org
Website: www.ccifc.org

**Delegation of German Industry &
Commerce (AHK)**
German Industry & Commerce Beijing
    Branch (GIC)
Landmark Tower 2, Unit 0811
8 North Dongsanhuan Road
Chaoyang District
100004 Beijing

Tel.: +86 (0)10 65900926 (AHK)
Fax: +86 (0)10 65906313 (AHK)
Tel.: +86 (0)10 65906151 (GIC)
Fax: +86 (0)10 65906313 (GIC)
Email: info@bj.china.ahk.de
Website: http://china.ahk.de/home/

**Italian Chamber of Commerce in
Beijing**
Unit 2606-2607, Full Tower
9, Dong San Huan Zhong Lu
Chaoyang District
Beijing 100020
Tel: +86 (0)10 85910545
Fax: +86 (0)10 85910546
E-mail: info@cameraitacina.com
Website: http://cameraitacina.com/

**Singapore Chamber of Commerce in
Beijing**
6th Floor, Office Building
Hong Kong Macau Center
2 Chaoyangmen Bei Dajie
Beijing 100027
People's Republic of China
Tel: +86 (0)10 65539786, 65014242,
65532288 ext 2143
Fax: +86 (0)10 65011518
Email: singcham@singcham.com.cn
Website: www.singcham.com.cn

**Spanish Chamber of Commerce in
Beijing**
Room 304B, Great Rock Plaza
13 Xin Zhong Xi Li
Dongcheng District
100027 Beijing
Tel.: +86(0)10 6416 9774/7323
Fax: +86(0)10 6416 1534
E-mail: info@spanishchamber-ch.com

**Swedish Chamber of Commerce in
Beijing**
Room 313, Radisson SAS Hotel
(Beijing Huang Jia Da Fan Dian)
6A, East Beisanhuan Road
Chaoyang District
Beijing 100028
Tel: +86 (0)10 5922 3388 ext. 313
Fax: +86 (0)10 6462 7454
Web site: www.swedishchamber.com.cn

E-mail: beijing@swedishchamber.com.cn

Swiss Chamber of Commerce in Beijing
Suite 100, CIS Tower
38 Liangmaqiao Lu
Chaoyang District
Beijing 100016
Tel: +86 (0)10) 6432 2020
Fax: +86 (0)10 6432 3030
E-mail: info@bei.swisscham.org
Website: www.swisscham.org

US-CHINA Business Council in Beijing
CITIC Building, Suite 10-01
19 Jianguomenwai Dajie
Beijing 100004
Tel: +86 (0)10 6592 0727
Fax: +86 (0)10 6512 5854
E-mail: info@uschina.org.cn
Website: www.uschina.org

Chengdu

**The American Chamber of Commerce
in Changdu**
606 Hongchuan Mansion
Lingshiguan Rd. Section 4,
South Renmin Rd.
Chengdu
Sichuan 610041
Tel: +86 (0)28 8524 2405
Fax: +86 (0)28 8524 8577
Email: amcham@amcham-southwest.org

**British Chamber of Commerce in
Chengdu**
1705B, 17/F
Times Plaza
2, Zongfu Road
Chengdu
Sichuan 610016
Tel: +86 (0)28 86656917
Fax: +86 (0)28 86657296
Email: info@britchamswchina.org
Website: www.britchamswchina.org

**Canada Business Development Office
in Changdu**
16/F, Chengdu Real Estate Mansion,
No. 28, Section 1,
Renminzhong Road
Chengdu,

Sichuan 610015
Tel: +86 (0)28 8627 9223
Fax: +86 (0)28 8627 9339
E-mail: bdochengdu@sina.com

China-Britain Business Council in Chengdu (CBBC)
1705B, 17/F, Block A
Times Plaza
2, Zongfu Road
Chengdu
Sichuan 610016
Tel: +86 (0)28 86656302
Fax: +86 (0)28 86657296
E-mail: enquiries@cbbc.org
Website: www.cbbc.org

European Chamber of Commerce in Chengdu
Chengdu
Sichuan Province
Tel: +86(0)28 8671 0577
Fax: +86(0)28 8666 5844
E-mail: chengdu@euccc.com.cn
Website: www.europeanchamber.com.cn

Guangzhou

The American Chamber of Commerce in Guangzhou
Main Tower, 1603
Guangdong International Hotel
339 Huanshi Donglu
Guangzhou 510098
Tel: +86 (0)20 8335 1476
Fax: +86 (0)20 8332 1642
Email: amcham@amcham-guangdong.
 org
Website: www.amcham-guangdong.org

Association of British Commerce, Guangzhou
60 Taojin Rd
Guangzhou
Tel: +86 (0)20 8359-8045

Australian Chamber of Commerce in Guangzhou
Suite E10, 2/F, Main Tower
Guangdong International Hotel
339 Huanshidong Rd.
Guangzhou 510098

Tel: +86 (0)20 2237 2866,+86 (0)20 8330
 2044
Fax: +86 (0)20 8319 0765
E-mail: mail@austcham-southchina.org
Website: www.austcham.org

Austrian Economic Chamber
Guangzhou
Tel: +86 (0)20 8666 3388, +86 (0)20 8666
 6401
Fax: +86 (0)20 8666 5312
E-mail: afecgz@163.net

British Chamber of Commerce in Guangzhou
Suite 1706, Main Tower
Guangdong International Hotel
339 Huanshi-dong Rd
Guangzhou, 510098
Tel: +86 (0)20 8331 5013, +86 (0)20 8331
 3120
Fax: +86 (0)20 8331 5016
E-mail: manager@britchamgd.com
Website: www.can.britcham.org/

Canadian Business Forum, Guangdong
Suite 801
China Hotel
Liuhua Rd.
Guangzhou
Tel: +86 (0)20 8669 5148; +86 (0)20 8666
 0569

Canada China Business Council
Suite 801, Office Tower China Hotel
Liu Hua Lu
Guangzhou, 510015
Tel: +86 (0)20 8666 0569
Fax: +86 (0)20 8667 2401
E-mail: ccbcgz@ccbc.com.cn

Danish Chamber of Commerce in Guangzhou
c/o ROYAL DANISH CONSULATE GENERAL
China Hotel Office Tower, Suite 1578 Liu
 Hua Lu
Guangzhou 510015
Tel: +86 (0)20 8666 0795 ext.15
Fax: +86 (0)20 8667 0315
E-mail: dccsc@dccsc.net
Website: www.dccsc.net

Economic Representation of Flanders in Guangzhou
c/o Consulate-General of Belgium in Guangzhou,
Room 1601-1602A
Office Tower,
Citic Plaza,
233, Tian He Bei Lu
CN-510613 Guangzhou
Tel.: +86 (0)20 38770463, +86 (0)20 38770493
Fax: +86 (0)20 38770462
E-mail: guangzhou@fitagency.com

Economic Representation of Wallonia Region in Guangzhou
c/o Consulate-General of Belgium in Guangzhou
Room 1601
Office Tower
Citic Plaza,
233 Tianhe Bei Lu
CN-510613 Guangzhou
Tel.: +86 (0)20 3877 1768
Fax: +86 (0)20 3877 1483
E-mail: awexgz@pub.guangzhou.gd.cn

European Chamber of Commerce in Guangzhou
Guangzhou 510000
Guangdong Province
Tel: +86 (0)20 8758 0479
Fax: +86 (0)20 6121 1006
E-mail: prd@euccc.com.cn
Website: www.europeanchamber.com.cn

French Chamber of Commerce and Industry in Guangzhou
2/F, 64 Shamian St.
Guangzhou 510130
Tel: +86 (0)20 8121 6818
Fax: +86 (0)20 8121 6228
E-mail: ccifc-guangzhou@ccifc.org
Website: www.ccifc.org

German Industry and Commerce Chamber (GIC) in Guangzhou
Suite 2915
Metro Plaza
Tianhe-bei Rd
Guangzhou, 510075

Tel: +86 (0)20 8755 2353
Fax: +86 (0)20 8755 1889
E-mail: info@ahk.org.hk
Website: http://www.china.ahk.de/

China-Italy Chamber of Commerce, Guangzhou
CITIC Plaza, 233 Tianhe-Bei Rd
Guangzhou 510613
Tel: +86 (0)20 3877 0892
Fax: +86 (0)20 3877 0893
E-mail: infoguangdong@cameraitacina.com
Website: www.cameraitacina.com

Italian Institute for Foreign Trade
Suite 1361, Office Tower China Hotel
Liuhua Rd
Guangzhou 510015
Tel: +86 (0)20 8667 0013; +86 (0)20 8666 3566
Fax: +86 (0)20 8667 2573

Korea Trade Promotion Corporation
Suite 1010-11
Main Tower
Guangdong International Hotel
339 Huanshi-dong Rd.
Guangzhou 510098
Tel: +86 (0)20 8334 0052, +86 (0)20 8334 0170
Fax: +86 (0)20 8335 1142

New Zealand Development Association
C950 Office Tower China Hotel
Liu Hua Road
Guangzhou 510015
Tel: +86 (0)20 8667 0253
Fax: +86 (0)20 8666 6420

International Enterprise Singapore
Suite 2501
CITIC Plaza
233 Tianhe-Bei Rd
Guangzhou 510613
Tel: +86 (0)20 3891 1911
Fax: +86 (0)20 3891 1772
E-mail: guangzhou@iesingapore.gov.sg
Website: www.iesingapore.com

Singapore Chamber of Commerce
Tel: +86 (0)20 8850 8118
E-mail: chamber@singapore-club.org
Website: www.singcham.com.cn

Spanish Chamber of Commerce in Guangzhou
Room 30-D, A Tower
Guangdong International Hotel
339 Huan Shi Dong Rd.
Yue Xiu District
Guangzhou 510098
Tel.: +86(0)20 2237 2862
Fax: +86(0)20 2237 2864
E-mail: guangdong@
  spanishchamber-ch.com
Website: www.spanishchamber.ch.com

Swedish Trade Council
Suite 1306, Main Tower
Guangdong International Hotel
339 Huanshi-dong Rd.
510098
Tel: +86 (0)20 8331 6019
Fax: +86 (0)20 8330 2939
Website: www.swedishchamber.com.cn

Hangzhou

China-Britian Business Council in Hangzhou (CBBC)
A-809, Zhejiang World Trade Center
122 Shuguang Road
Hangzhou
Zhejiang 310007
Tel: +86 (0)571 87631069
Fax: +86 (0)571 87630961
Email: hangzhou@cbbc.org.cn
Website: www.cbbc.org

Nanjing

Canada Business Development Office in Nanjing
Suite D, 24th Floor, Chun Feng Mansion
No. 37 Hua Qiao Road
Nanjing 210029
Tel: +86 (0)25 8471 2286
Fax: +86 (0)25 8471 2286

China-Britain Business Council in Nanjing (CBBC)
Rm 2514-2515
50 Zhong Hua Road
Nanjing 210001
Tel: +86 (0)25 52311740
Fax: +86 (0)25 52233773
Email: nanjing@cbbc.org.cn
Website: www.cbbc.org

European Chamber of Commerce in Nanjing
C/o Xuanwu Hotel
4F 193 Zhong Yang Road
Nanjing 210009
E-mail: nanjing@euccc.com.cn
Website: www.europeanchamber.com.cn

Qingdao

China-Britain Business Council in Qingdao
Room 503, 5th Floor
121 Yan An San Road
Qingdao 266071
Tel: +86 (0)532 83869772
Fax: +86 (0)532 83869329
Email: qingdao@cbbc.org.cn
Website: www.cbbc.org

Shanghai

American Chamber of Commerce in Shanghai
Shanghai Center, #568
1376 Nanjing Xilu
Shanghai 200040
Tel: +86 (0)21 6279 7119
Fax: +86 (0)21 6279 7643
Email: info@amcham-shanghai.org
Website: www.amcham-shanghai.org

Australian Chamber of Commerce in Shanghai
Suite 6709, Apollo Building
1440 Yan 'An Middle Road
Shanghai 200040
Tel: +86 (0)21 6248 8301/ 2496/ 5989
Fax: +86 (0)21 6248 5580
Email: admin@austchamshanghai.com
Website: www.austchamshanghai.com

Belgium Chamber of Commerce in Shanghai
Tel: +86 (0)21 5403 8177 ext 118, 117
Fax: +86 (0)21 5403 8167
Email: office-sh@bencham.org
Website: www.bencham.org

British Chamber of Commerce in Shanghai
Suite 1703 Westgate Tower
1038 Nanjing Xi Lu
Shanghai 200041
Tel: +86 (0)21 6218 5022
Fax: +86 (0)21 6218 5066
Website: www.sha.britcham.org

Canada China Business Council in Shanghai
Suite 912, Central Plaza,
227 Huang Pi Bei Lu
Shanghai 200003
Tel: +86 (0)21 6359 8908/09
Fax: +86 (0)10 6375 9361
E-mail: ccbcsh@ccbc.om.cn

China-Britain Business Council in Shanghai
Unit 1701-2, Westgate Tower
1038 Nanjing Road W
Shanghai 200041
Tel: +86 (0)21 6218 5183
Fax: +86 (0)21 6218 5193
Email: shanghai@cbbc.org.cn
Website: www.cbbc.org

Danish Chamber of Commerce in Shanghai
Tian An Center
338 Nanjing Road West
Shanghai 200003
Tel: +86 138 1811 4020
Fax: +86 (0)21 6359 3592
E-mail: mail@dccc-shanghai.com
Website: www.dccc-shanghai.com

European Chamber of Commerce in Shanghai
Unit 2204, Shui On Plaza
333 Huai Hai Zhong Road
Shanghai 200021
Tel: +86 (21) 6385 2023
Fax: +86 (21) 6385 2381

E-mail: shanghai@euccc.com.cn
Website: www.europeanchamber.com.cn

Economic Representation of Flanders in Shanghai
Wu Yi Road, 127
CN-200050 Shanghai
Tel.: +86 (0)21 6437 8467
Fax: +86 (0)21 6437 7574
E-mail: shanghai@fitagency.com

Economic Representation of Wallonia Region in Shanghai
Wu Yi Road, 127
CN-200050 Shanghai
Tel.: +86 (0)21 6437 9234
Fax: +86 (0)21 6437 7083
E-mail: awexsh@188.com

Economic Representation of Brussels Capital Region in Shanghai
Wu Yi Road, 127
CN-200050 Shanghai
Tel.: +86 (0)21 6437 5224
Fax: +86 (0)21 6437 6541
E-mail: mail@brussels-china.com

French Chamber of Commerce in Shanghai
Mayfair Tower,
83 Fu Min Road, 2e floor,
Shanghai 200040
Tel: +86 (0)21 6132 7100
Fax: +86 (0)21 6132 7101
E-Mail: ccifc-shanghai@ccifc.org
Website: www.ccifc.org

Delegation of German Industry & Commerce (AHK)
German Industry & Commerce Shanghai Branch (GIC)
29/F Pos Plaza
1600 Century Avenue
Pudong
Shanghai 200122
Tel.: +86 (0)21 50812266 (AHK)
Fax: +86 (0)21 50812009 (AHK)
Tel.: +86 (0)21 68758536 (GIC)
Fax: +86 (0)21 68758573 (GIC)
Email: office(at)sh.china.ahk.de
Website: http://china.ahk.de

Italian Chamber of Commerce in Shanghai
Suite 3605, The Center
989 Changle Road
Shanghai 200031
Tel: +86 (0)21 54075181
Fax: +86 (0)21 54075182
E-mail: infoshanghai@cameraitacina.com
Website: http://cameraitacina.com/

Spanish Chamber of Commerce in Shanghai
Room 514, No.885 Renmin Road
Huaihai Zhonghua Tower
Huangpu District
Shanghai 200010
Tel.: +86(0)21 6326 4177
Fax: +86(0)21 6326 4082
E-mail: shanghai@
   spanishchamber-ch.com
Website: www.spanishchamber.ch.com

Swedish Chamber of Commerce in Shanghai
c/o Beijing Scandinavian Furniture Co.
   Ltd
3908B, Nanzheng Building
580 Nanjing West Road
Shanghai 200041
Tel: +86 (0)21 6217 0838
Fax: +86 (0)21 6217 0562
Web site: www.swedishchamber.com.cn
E-mail: shanghai@swedishchamber.com.
   cn

Swiss Chamber of Commerce in Shanghai
Room 1710-1711
1388 Shaan Xi North Road
Shanghai 200060
Tel: +86 (0)21 6149 8207
Fax: +86 (0)21 6149 8132
Email: info@sha.swisscham.org
Website: www.swisscham.org

US-CHINA Business Council in Shanghai
1701 Beijing West Road, Room 1301
Shanghai 200040
Tel: +86 (0)21 6288 3840
Fax: +86 (0)21 6288 3841

E-mail: info@uschina.org.cn
Website: www.uschina.org

Shenyang

Canada Business Development Office in Shenyang
B-704, 21st Century Tower
Century Road, Hunan New District
Shenyang 110179
Tel: +86 (0)24 2374 6008
Fax: +86 (0)24 2374 6009
E-mail: bdoshenyang@sina.com
Website: www.ccbc.com

China-Britain Business Council in Shenyang
Room 901, Tower 2, Shenyang City Plaza,
206 Nanjing North Street,
Heping District
Shenyang 110001
Tel: +86 (0)24 23341600
Fax: +86 (0)24 23341858
Email: lisa.liu@cbbc.org.cn
Website: www.cbbc.org

European Chamber of Commerce in Shenyang
Shenyang
Tel: +86 (24) 8681 1888
Fax: +86 (24) 81077521
E-mail: shenyang@euccc.com.cn
Website: www.europeanchamber.com.cn

Shenzhen

Canada Business Development Office in Shenzhen
3/F, C-1
International Science and Technology
   Business Platform
Southern District of Shenzhen
High-Tech Industrial Park
Shenzhen 518057
Tel: +86 (0)755) 2671 2368
Fax: +86 (0)755) 2671 2166
E-mail: bdoshenzhen@sina.com

China-Britain Business Council in Shenzhen
Room 1121, Tower A, International
   Chamber of Commerce

Fuhua Yi Lu, Futian District
Shenzhen 518048
Tel: +86 (0)755 8219 8148
Fax: +86 (0)755 8219 3159
Email: shenzhen@cbbc.org.cn
Website: www.cbbc.org

Italian Chamber of Commerce in Shenzhen
Room 318, Comprehensive Building
South District
Shenzhen High Tech Park
Shenzhen 518057
Tel: +86 (0)755 26017768
Fax: +86 (0)755 26017798
E-mail: infoguangdong@cameraitacina.
  com
Website: http://cameraitacina.com/

Tianjin

The American Chamber of Commerce
Hyatt Regency, #402
Tianjin No.219 Jiefang North Road
Tianjin 300042
Tel: +86 (0)22 2312 2517 ext.402
Fax: +86 (0)22 2312 2519
Email: secretary@amchamtianjin.org
Website: www.amchamtianjin.org

European Chamber of Commerce in Tianjin
Tel: +86(22) 23520011
Fax: +86(22) 23531011
E-mail: tianjin@euccc.com.cn
Website: www.europeanchamber.com.cn

Wuhan

China-Britain Business Council in Wuhan
Room 1203, Tower
New World International Trade Center
568 Jianshe Avenue
Wuhan 430022
Tel: +86 (0)27 8577 0989
Fax: +86 (0)27 8577 0991
Email: wuhan@cbbc.org.cn
Website: www.cbbc.org

List of Embassies and Consulates in China

Beijing

Embassy of the Islamic State of Afghanistan
8 Tung Chih Men Wia
Chao Yang District, Beijing
Tel: +86 (0)10 6532 1532
Fax: +86 (0)10 653 226603
E-mail: afgemb_beijing@yahoo.com

Embassy of the Republic of Albania
28, Guang Hua Lu
Beijing
Tel: +86 (0)10 6532 1120
Fax: +86 (0)10 6532 5451

Embassy of the Democratic People's Republic of Algeria
7, San Li Tun Lu
Beijing
Tel: +86 (0)10 6532 1231

Embassy of the Republic of Angola
1-13-1 Ta Yuan Diplomatic Office Building
Beijing
Tel: +86 (0)10 6532 6968
Fax: +86 (0)10 6532 6969

Embassy of the Republic of Argentina
11, Dong Wu Jie, San Li Tun
Beijing
Tel: +86 (0)10 6532 1406
Fax: +86 (0)10 6532 2319

Embassy of Armenia
4-1-61, Tayuan Diplomatic Apartments
Beijing 100600
Tel: +86 (0)10 65325677
Fax: +86 (0)10 65325654

Embassy of Australia
21 Dong Zhi Men Wai Da Jie
San Li Tun
Beijing
Tel: +86 (0)10 6532 2331
Fax: +86 (0)10 6532 4349
E-mail: pubaff.beijing@dfat.gov.au
Austrade (Commercial Office)

Tel: +86 (0)10 6532 6726 and +86 (0)10
6532 6731
Website: www.austemb.org.cn

Embassy of the Republic of Austria
5, Dong Wu Jie
Xiu Shui Nan Jie
Jian Guo Men Wai
Beijing
Tel: +86 (0)10 6532 2061
Fax: +86 (0)10 6532 1505
Tel: +86 (0)10 6532 1777
Fax: +86 (0)10 6532 1149
Website: http://www.aussenministerium.
  at/peking
E-mail: peking-ob@bmeia.gv.at

Embassy of the Republic of Azerbaijan
Qijiayuan Diplomatic Compound
Villa B-3
Beijing 100600
Tel: +86 (0)10 6532 4614
Fax: +86 (0)10 6532 4615
Website: http://www.azerbembassy.org.
  cn/
E-mail: mailbox@azerbembassy.org.cn

Embassy of the State of Bahrain
312- 313, Third Floor, Lufthansa Center
  (Office Building)
50 Chao Yang District
Beijing 100016
Tel: +86 (0)10 64635574
Fax: +86 (0)10 64635504

**Embassy of the People's Republic of
Bangladesh**
42, Guang Hua Lu
Beijing China
Tel: +86 (0)10 6532 2521
Fax: +86 (0)10 6532 4346
Website: http://bangladeshembassy.com.
  cn/

Embassy of the Republic of Belarus
2-10-1, Ta Yuan Diplomatic Office
  Building
Beijing, China, 100600
Tel: +86 (0)10 6532 6426/1691
Fax: +86 (0)10 6532 6417
E-mail: china@belembassy.org

Embassy of Belgium
6, San Li Tun Lu
Beijing
Tel: +86 (0)10 6532 1736
Fax: +86 (0)10 6532 5097
E-mail: Beijing@diplobel.org
Website: www.diplomatie.be/beijing/

Embassy of the Republic of Benin
38, Guang Hua Lu
Beijing
Tel: +86 (0)10 6532 2741
Fax: +86 (0)10 65325103

Embassy of the Republic of Bolivia
2-3-2, Ta Yuan Diplomatic Office Building
Beijing
Tel: +86 (0)10 6532 3074/3076
Fax: +86 (0)10 6532 4686
E-mail: embolch@public3.bta.net.cn

**Embassy of Bosnia and Herzegovina
in China**
1-5-1 Ta Yuan Diplomatic Office Building
Bejing 100600
Tel: +86 (0)10 6532 6587/ +86 (0)10 6532
  0185
Fax: +86 (0)10 6532 6418
E-mail: ambbhdip@public.bta.net.cn

Embassy of the Republic of Botswana
1-8-1, 1-8-2, Ta Yuan Diplomatic Office
  Building
Beijing
Tel: +86 (0)10 6532 5751
Fax: +86 (0)10 6532 5713

**Embassy of the Federative Republic of
Brazil**
27, Guang Hua Lu
Beijing
Tel: +86 (0)10 6532 3883/2881
Fax: +86 (0)10 6532 2751
E-mail: info@brazil.org.cn
Website: www.brazil.org.cn

Embassy of the Brunei Darussalam
1-91, San Li Tun Office Building
Beijing
Tel: +86 (0)10 6532 4094
Fax: +86 (0)10 6532 4097
E-mail: beb@public.bta.net.cn

Embassy of the Republic of Bulgaria
4, Xiu Shui Bei Jie
Jian Guo Men Wai
Beijing
Tel: +86 (0)10 6532 1946
Commercial Office: +86 (0)10 6532 4925
Fax: +86 (0)10 6532 2826
E-mail: bulemb@public.bta.net.cn
Website: http://www.bulgaria.bg/Asia/
Beijing/en/default.htm

Embassy of the Republic of Burundi
25, Guang Hua Lu
Beijing
Tel: +86 (0)10 6532 1801
Fax: +86 (0)10 6532 2381

Royal Embassy of Cambodia
9, Dong Zhi Men Wai Da Jie
Beijing 100600
Tel: +86 (0)10 6532 1889
Fax: +86 (0)10 6532 3507
E-mail: cambassybeijing@yahoo.com

Embassy of the Republic of Cameroon
7, Dong Wu Jie, San Li Tun
Beijing
Tel: +86 (0)10 6532 1828
Fax: +86 (0)10 6532 1761
Date of Establishment of Diplomatic
  Relations: March 26, 1971

Embassy of Canada
19, Dong Zhi Men Wai Da Jie
Beijing
Tel: +86 (0)10 6532 3536/3031
Fax: +86 (0)10 6532 4072/ 4311
E-mail: bejing@international.gc.ca
Website: www.beijing.gc.ca

Embassy of the Republic of Chad
21, Guang Hua Lu
Beijing
Tel: +86 (0)10 6532 1296/4830
Fax: +86 (0)10 6532 3638

Embassy of the Republic of Chile
1, Dong Si Jie, San Li Tun
Beijing
Tel: +86 (0)10 6532 1641
Fax: +86 (0)10 6532 3170

Embassy of the Republic of Colombia
No. 34, Guang Hua Lu
Beijing
Tel: +86 (0)10 532 3377/3166
E-mail: embajada.beijing@sprintcol.
  sprint.com

Embassy of the Republic of the Congo
No. 7, Dong Si Jie, San Li Tun
Beijing
Tel: +86 (0)10 6532 1658

Embassy of the Republic of Cote d'Ivoire
No. 9, Bei Xiao Jie, San Li Tun
Beijing
Tel: +86 (0)10 6532 1482
Fax: +86 (0)10 6532 2407
Date of Establishment of Diplomatic
  Relations: March 2, 1983

Embassy of the Republic of Croatia
2-1-31, San Li Tun Diplomatic Apartments
Beijing
Tel: +86 (0)10 6532 6241
Fax: +86 (0)10 6532 6257
E-mail: vrhpek@public.bta.net.cn

Embassy of the Republic of Cuba
1, Xiu Shui Nan Jie, Jian Guo Men Wai
Beijing
Tel: +86 (0)10 6532 6656/1714
Fax: +86 (0)10 6532 2870/6532
Commercial Office:
Tel. +86 (0)10 6532 2516
Fax: +86 (0)10 6532 2129
E-mail: informacion1@embchina.minrex.
  gov.cu

Embassy of the Republic of Cyprus
2-13-2, Ta Yuan Diplomatic Office Bldg
14 Liang Ma He Nan Lu
Chao yang District
Beijing 100600
Tel: +86 (0)10 6532 5057
Fax: +86 (0)10 6532 5060
E-mail: cyembpek@public3.bta.net.cn

Embassy of the Czech Republic
Ri Tan Lu, Jian Guo Men Wai
Beijing
Tel: +86 (0)10 6532 6902

Fax: +86 (0)10 6532 5653
Website: http://www.mzv.cz/wwwo/
    default.asp?idj=2&amb=60

**Embassy of the Democratic People's
Republic of Korea**
11, Ri Tan Bei Lu, Jian Guo Men Wai
Beijing 100600
Tel: +86 (0)10 6532 1186
Commercial Office: +86 (0)10 6532 4308

Royal Danish Embassy
1 Dong Wu Jie, San Li Tun
Beijing, China
Tel: +86 (0)10 6532 9900
Fax: +86 (0)10 6532 2439/9999
Website: http://www.ambbeijing.um.dk
E-mail: bjsamb@um.dk

**Embassy of the Republic of Djibouti in
Beijing**
1-1-122 Ta Yuan Diplomatic Compound
Chaoyang District
Beijing 100600
Tel: +86 (0)10 65327857, 65329309
Fax: +86 (0)10 65327858

Embassy of the Dominican Republic
3-2-62 Tanyuan Gongyu Diplomatic
    Compund
Beijing 100600
Tel: +86 (0)10 853 22423

Embassy of the Republic of Ecuador
11-21, Jian Guo Men Wai
Beijing
Tel: +86 (0)10 6532 4371/3849
Fax: +86 (0)10 6532 4371

Embassy of the Arab Republic of Egypt
2, Ri Tan Dong Lu
Beijing
Tel: +86 (0)10 6532 1825
Fax: +86 (0)10 6532 5365
Commercial Office: +86 (0)10 6532 1920
E-mail: eg_emb_bj@yahoo.com

**Embassy of the Republic of Equatorial
Guinea**
No. 2, Dong Si Jie, San Li Tun
Beijing, China
Tel: +86 (0)10 6532 3679
Fax: +86 (0)10 6532 3805/0438

Embassy of the State of Eritrea
1-4-2, Ta Yuan Diplomatic Office Building
Beijing
Tel: +86 (0)10 6532 6534
Fax: +86 (0)10 6532 6532

**Embassy of the Federal Democratic
Republic of Ethiopia**
No. 3, Xiu Shui Nan Jie
Beijing
Tel: +86 (0)10 6532 5258/5318
Fax: +86 (0)10 6532 5591
E-mail: ethiochina@ethiopiaemb.org.cn
Website: www.ethiopiaemb.org.cn

Embassy of the Republic of Fiji
1-15-2 Ta Yuan Diplomatic Building
14 Liang Ma He Nan Lu,
SanLiTun, Chaoyang District
Beijing 100600
Tel: +86 (0)10 6532 7305
Fax: +86 (0)10 6532 7253
E-mail: info@fijiembassy.org.cn
Website: www.fijiembassy.org.cn

Embassy of the Republic of Finland
1-10-1 Ta Yuan Office Building
Beijing
Tel: +86 (0)10 6532 1817/8541
Fax: +86 (0)10 6532 1884/8547
Commercial Office: +86 (0)10 6467 8084
Fax: +86 (0)10 6467 8082
E-mail: finemb@public3.bta.net.cn

Embassy of the Republic of France
3 Dong San Jie, San Li Tun
Beijing
Tel: +86 (0)10 6532 1331
Fax: +86 (0)10 6532 4841
Commercial Office: +86 (0)10 6501 4866/
    4870
Website: www.ambafrance-cn.org

Embassy of the Republic of Gabon
36, Guang Hua Lu
Beijing
Tel: +86 (0)10 6532 2810
Fax: +86 (0)10 6532 2621

Embassy of Georgia
LA 03-02, Section A,
Liangmaqiao Diplomatic Compound

Tel: +86 (0)10 65327518, 65327525
Fax: +86 (0)10 65327519
E-mail: geobeijing@gmail.com

Embassy of the Federal Republic of Germany
17, Dong Zhi Men Wai Da Jie
Chaoyang District
Beijing
Tel: +86 (0)10 85329000
Fax: +86 (0)10 65325336
E-mail: embassy@peki.diplo.de
Commercial Office: +86 (0)10 6532 5556/5560

Embassy of the Republic of Ghana
8, San Li Tun Lu
Beijing
Tel: +86 (0)10 6532 1319/1544
Fax: +86 (0)10 6532 3602

Embassy of the Hellenic Republic of Greece
19, Guang Hua Lu
Beijing
Tel: +86 (0)10 6532 1317
Fax: +86 (0)10 6532 1277
E-mail: gremb.pek@mfa.gr
Website: http://www.grpressbeijing.com

Embassy of Grenada in Beijing
T3-2-52, Ta Yuan Diplomatic Office Building
Tel: +86 (0)10 65321208/1209
Fax: +86 (0)10 65321015

Embassy of the Republic of Guinea-Bissau in Beijing
2-2-101, Ta Yuan Diplomatic Compound
Tel: +86 (0)10 65327393
Fax: +86 (0)10 65327106

Embassy of the Cooperative Republic of Guyana
1, Xiu Shui Dong Jie
Jian Guo Men Wai
Beijing
Tel: +86 (0)10 6532 1337
Fax: +86 (0)10 6532 5741

Embassy of the Republic of Hungary
10 Dong Zhi Men Wai Da Jie
Beijing

Tel: +86 (0)10 6532 0665
Fax: +86 (0)10 6532 2719
Commercial Office: +86 (0)10 6532 3182
Fax: +86 (0)10 6532 5131
E-mail: consular_office@pek.kum.hu

Embassy of the Republic of Iceland
Landmark Tower 1
802, 8 Dongsanhuan Bei Lu
Beijing 100004
Tel: +86 (0)10 6532 6881
Fax: +86 (0)10 6532 6883
E-mail: icemb.beijing@utn.stjr.is
Website: http://www.iceland. org/cn/english/

Embassy of the Republic of India
1 Ri Tan Dong Lu
100600 Beijing, China
Tel: +86 (0)10 6532 1908/1856
Fax: +86 (0)10 6532 4684
E-mail: webmaster@indianembassy.org. cn
Website: http://www.indianembassy.org. cn/

Embassy of the Republic of Indonesia
Office Building B
San Li Tun
Beijing 100600
Tel: +86 (0)10 6532 5488
E-mail: set.indonesia.kbri@deplu.go.id

Embassy of the Islamic Republic of Iran
13, Dong Liu Jie
San Li Tun
Beijing 100600
Tel: +86 (0)10 6532 2040/4871
Fax: +86 (0)10 65321403
E-mail: information@iranembassyinchina. org

Embassy of the Republic of Iraq
25, Xiu Shui Bei Jie
Jian Guo Men Wai
Beijing
Tel: +86 (0)10 65323385, 65321873, 65320731
Fax: +86 (0)10 65321596, 65320733

Embassy of the Republic of Ireland
3, Ri Tan Dong Lu
Beijing
Tel: +86 (0)10 65322691, 65322914
Fax: +86 (0)10 6532 6857
E-mail: beijing@dfa.ie
Website: http://www.embassyofireland.
  cn/

Embassy of Israel
West Wing Office, CWTC
1 Jian Guo Men Wai Da Jie
Beijing 100600
Tel: +86 (0)10 85320500, 85320662
Fax: +86 (0)10 85320555, 85320613
Website: http://beijing.mfa.gov.il

Embassy of the Republic of Italy
No. 2 Dong Er Jie
San Li Tun
Beijing
Tel: +86 (0)10 85327600
Fax: +86 (0)10 65324676
E-mail: ambasciata.pechino@esteri.it
Website: http://www.ambitaba.
  sk/Ambasciata_Pechino/

Embassy of Jamaica in Beijing
Jian Guo Men Wai Diplomatic Compound
1 Xiu Shui Street, Room 6-2-72
Beijing 100600
Tel: +86 (0)10 65320667, 65320670-1
Fax: +86 (0)10 65320669
E-mail: embassy@jamaicagov.cn
Website: http://www.jamaicagov.cn/

Embassy of Japan
7, Ri Tan Lu, Jian Guo Men Wai
Beijing
Tel: +86 (0)10 6532 2361
Fax: +86 (0)10 65324625
E-mail: ryoji@eoj.cn
Website: http://www.cn.emb-japan.
  go.jp/index_e.htm

Embassy of the Hashemite Kingdom of Jordan
5, Dong Liu Jie
San Li Tun
Beijing 100600
Tel: +86 (0)10 6532 3906
Fax: +86 (0)10 6532 3283

Embassy of the Republic of Kazakhstan
9, Dong Liu Jie
San Li Tun
Beijing
Tel: +86 (0)10 6532 6182
Fax: +86 (0)10 6532 6183
E-mail: doors@public3.bta.net.cn
Website: http://www.kazembchina.org/

Embassy of the Republic of Kenya
4, Xi Liu Jie
San Li Tun
Beijing
Tel: +86 (0)10 6532 3381
Fax: +86 (0)10 6532 1770
E-mail: kenrepbj@hotmail.com

Embassy of the State of Kuwait
23, Guang Hua Lu
Beijing
Tel: +86 (0)10 6532 2216
Fax: +86 (0)10 65321607

Embassy of the Kyrgyz Republic
2-4-1, Ta Yuan Diplomatic Office Building
Beijing
Tel: +86 (0)10 6532 6458
Fax: +86 (0)10 6532 6459

Embassy of the Laos People's Democratic Republic
11, Dong Si Jie, San Li Tun
Beijing
Tel: +86 (0)10 6532 1224
Fax: +86 (0)10 6532 6748

Embassy of the Republic of Latvia in Beijing
71 Greenland Garden
Greenland Road 1A
Chaoyang District
Beijing 100016
Tel: +86 (0)10 64333863
Fax: +86 (0)10 64333810
E-mail: embassy.china@mfa.gov.lv
Website: http://www.latvianembassy.org.
  cn/en/

Embassy of Lebanon
51, Dong Liu Jie, San Li Tun
Beijing

Tel: +86 (0)10 6532 1560
Fax: +86 (0)10 6532 2770
E-mail: Lebanon@public.bta.net.cn

Embassy of the Kingdom of Lesotho
2-3-13, San Li Tun Diplomatic Compound
Beijing
Tel: +86 (0)10 6532 6842
Fax: +86 (0)10 6532 6845

Embassy of the Republic of Liberia in Beijing
Room 013, Gold Island Diplomatic
  Compound
1 Xi Ba He Nan Lu
Beijing 100028
Tel: +86 (0)10 64403007
Fax: +86 (0)10 64403918

Embassy of the People's Bureau of the Great Socialist People's Libyan Arab Jamahiriya
3, Dong Liu Jie, San Li Tun
Beijing 100600
Tel: +86 (0)10 6532 3666
Fax: +86 (0)10 6532 3391

Embassy of the Republic of Lithuania
8-2-12, Ta Yuan Diplomatic Office
  Building
Beijing
Tel: +86 (0)10 6532 4421/84518520
Fax: +86 (0)10 6532 4421/84514442
E-mail: emlituan@public3.bta.net.cn;
  amb.cn@urm.lt

Embassy of the Grand-Duchy of Luxembourg
21, Nei Wu Bu Jie
Beijing
Tel: +86 (0)10 6513 5937
Fax: +86 (0)10 6513 7268
E-mail: pekin.amb@mae.etat.lu

Embassy of the Republic of Macedonia
5-2-22 San Li Tun Diplomatic Apartments
Beijing
Tel: +86 (0)10 6532 6282/7846
Fax: +86 (0)10 6532 6756/7847
E-mail: macdebas@public3.bta.net.cn
Website: http://www.
  macedonianembassy.com.cn/

Embassy of the Republic of Madagascar
3, San Li Tun Dong Jie
Beijing
Tel: +86 (0)10 6532 1353
Fax: +86 (0)10 6532 2102

Embassy of Malaysia
2, Liang Ma Qiao Bei Jie
Chaoyang District
Beijing 100600
Tel: +86 (0)10 6532 2531/2/3
Fax: +986 (0)10 6532 5032
E-mail: mwbjing@kln.gov.my
Website: http://www.kln.gov.
  my/perwakilan/beijing

Embassy of the Republic of Mali
8, Dong Si Jie, San Li Tun
Beijing
Tel: +86 (0)10 65321704, 65325530
Fax: +86 (0)10 6532 1618

Embassy of the Republic of Malta
1-51, Diplomatic Office Building
San Li Tun
Beijing
Tel: +86 (0)10 6532 3114
Fax: +86 (0)10 6532 6125
E-mail: maltaembassy.beijing@gov.mt

Embassy of the Republic of the Marshall Islands
2-14-1, Ta Yuan Diplomatic Office
  Building
Beijing
Tel: +86 (0)10 6532 5904
Fax: +86 (0)10 6532 4679

Embassy of the Islamic Republic of Mauritania
9, Dong San Jie
San Li Tun
Beijing
Tel: +86 (0)10 6532 1346
Fax: +86 (0)10 6532 1685

Embassy of the Republic of Mauritius in Beijing
202 Dong Wai Diplomatic Office Building
23, Dong Zhi Men Wai Da Jie
Beijing 100600

Tel: +86 (0)10 65325695/5696/5698
Fax: +86 (0)10 65325706
E-mail: mebj@public.bta.net.cn

Embassy of Mexico
5, Dong Wu Jie
San Li Tun
Beijing
Tel: +86 (0)10 65322574/2070/1947
Fax: +86 (0)10 65323744
E-mail: embmxchn@public.bta.net.cn

Embassy of the Republic of Moldova in Beijing
2-9-1, Ta Yuan Office Building
14 Liang Ma He Nan Lu
Chaoyang District
Beijing 100600
Tel: +86 (0)10 65325494
Fax: +86 (0)10 65325379

Embassy of Mongolia
2 Xiu Shui Bei Jie
Jian Guo Men Wai
Beijing
Tel: +86 (0)10 6532 1203
Fax: +86 (0)10 6532 5045
Commercial Office: +86 (0)10 6532 1952
E-mail: mail@mongolembassychina.org
Website: http://www.mongolembassychina.org/

Embassy of the Kingdom of Morocco
16, San Li Tun Lu
Beijing
Tel: +86 (0)10 65321489, 65321796
Fax: +86 (0)10 6532 1453

Embassy of the Republic of Mozambique
1-7-2, Ta Yuan Diplomatic Office Building
14, Liang Ma He Nan Lu
Beijing 100600
Tel: +86 (0)10 6532 3664
Fax: +86 (0)10 6532 5189
E-mail: embamoc@embmoz.org

Embassy of the Union of Myanmar in Beijing
6, Dong Zhi Men Wai Street
Chaoyang District
Beijing 100600

Tel: +86 (0)10 65320351/0359
Fax: +86 (0)10 65320408
E-mail: myanmarconsular@yahoo.com
Website: http://www.myanmarembassy.com/

Embassy of the Republic of Namibia
1-13-2, Ta Yuan Diplomatic Office Building
Beijing
Tel: +86 (0)10 6532 4810
Fax: +86 (0)10 6532 4549
E-mail: namemb@eastnet.com.cn

Royal Nepalese Embassy
1, Xi Liu Jie
San Li Tun Lu
Beijing
Tel: +86 (0)10 6532 3251
Fax: +86 (0)10 65323251
E-mail: info@nepalembassy.org.cn
Website: www.nepalembassy.org.cn

Royal Netherlands Embassy
4, Liang Ma He Nan Lu
Beijing
Tel: +86 (0)10 6532 1131
Fax: +86 (0)10 6532 4689
E-mail: pek@minbuza.nl
Website: http://www.hollandinchina.org/index_cn.htm

Embassy of New Zealand
1 Dong Er Jie, Ri Tan Lu
Beijing
Tel: +86 (0)10 6532 2731
Fax: +86 (0)10 6532 4317
E-mail: enquiries@nzembassy.cn
Website: http://www.nzembassy.com/china

Embassy of the Republic of Niger in Beijing
1-21, San Li Tun Apartment
Beijing 100600
Tel: +86 (0)10 65324279
Fax: +86 (0)10 65327041

Embassy of the Federal Republic of Nigeria
2, Dong Wu Jie, San Li Tun
Beijing

Tel: +86 (0)10 6532 3631
Fax: +86 (0)10 6532 1650
Website: http://www.nigeriaembassy.cn/

Royal Norwegian Embassy
1 Dong Yi Jie, San Li Tun
Beijing
Tel: +86 (0)10 6532 2261
Fax: +86 (0)10 6532 2392
Commercial Office: +86 (0)10 6532 2262
Fax: +86 (0)10 6532 2398
E-mail: emb.beijing@mfa.no
Website: http://www.norway.cn/

Embassy of the Sultanate of Oman
6, Liang Ma He Nan Lu
Beijing
Tel: +86 (0)10 6532 3692
Fax: +86 (0)10 6532 7185

Embassy of the Islamic Republic of Pakistan
1, Dong Zhi Men Wai Da Jie
Beijing
Tel: +86 (0)10 6532 2504/2072
Fax: +86 (0)10 6532 2715
Commercial Office: +86 (0)10 6532 2581

Embassy of the State of Palestine
2, Dong San Jie, San Li Tun
Beijing
Tel: +86 (0)10 6532 3327
Fax: +86 (0)10 65323241

Embassy of Papua New Guinea
2-11-2, Ta Yuan Diplomatic Office
  Building
Beijing
Tel: +86 (0)10 6532 4312
Fax: +86 (0)10 6532 5483
E-mail: kundu_beijing@pngembassy.
  org.cn
Website: http://en.pngembassy.org.cn/

Embassy of the Republic of Peru
2-82 San Li Tun Diplomatic Office
  Building
Beijing
Tel: +86 (0)10 6532 4658
Fax: +86 (0)10 6532 2178
E-mail: lpekin@public.bta.net.cn

Embassy of the Republic of the Philippines
23, Xiu Shui Bei Jie, Jian Guo Men Wai
Beijing
Tel: +86 (0)10 6532 2518/1872
Fax: +86 (0)10 65323761
E-mail: main@philembassy-china.org
Website: http://www.chuguo.cn/
  common/embassy/philippines.htm

Embassy of the Republic of Poland
1 Ri Tan Lu
Jian Guo Men Wai
Beijing
Tel: +86 (0)10 6532 1235
Fax: +86 (0)10 6532 1745
Commercial Office: Tel. +86 (0)10 6532
  1888
Fax: +86 (0)10 6532 4958
E-mail: polska@public2.bta.net.cn
Website: http://www.polecom.com.cn

Embassy of the Republic of Portugal
2-15-1/2 Ta Yuan Diplomatic Office
  Building
Beijing
Tel: +86 (0)10 6532 3497
Fax: +86 (0)10 6532 4637
Commercial Office: +86 (0)10 6532 6745
Fax: +86 (0)10 6532 6746
E-mail: embport@public2.bta.net.cn

Embassy of the State of Qatar
2-9-2, Ta Yuan Diplomatic Office Building
Beijing
Tel: +86 (0)10 6532 2231
Fax: +86 (0)10 65325274/5122

Embassy of the Republic of South Korea
4/f China World Tower
1 Jian Guo Men Wai Da Jie
Beijing
Tel: +86 (0)10 6505 2608
Fax: +86 (0)10 6505 3067
E-mail: webmaster@koreanembassy.cn
Website: http://www.koreaemb.org.cn/

Embassy of Romania
Ri Tan Lu Dong Er Jie
Beijing
Tel: +86 (0)10 6532 3442

Fax: +86 (0)10 6532 5728
E-mail: ambasada@roamb.link263.com

Embassy of the Russian Federation
4 Dong Zhi Men Bei Zhong Jie
Beijing
Tel: +86 (0)10 6532 2051
Fax: +86 (0)10 6532 4853
Commercial Office: +86 (0)10 6532 2201
E-mail: embassy@russia.org.cn
Website: http://www.russia.org.cn/

Embassy of the Republic of Rwanda
30, Xiu Shui Bei Jie
Beijing
Tel: +86 (0)10 6532 2193
Fax: +86 (0)10 6532 2006

Royal Embassy of Saudi Arabia
1, Bei Xiao Jie, San Li Tun
Beijing
Tel: +86 (0)10 6532 4825
Fax: +86 (0)10 6532 5324

Embassy of the Republic of Senegal in Beijing
305, Dong Wai Diplomatic Office Buiding
23, Dong Zhi Men Wai Da Jie
Beijing 100600
Tel: +86 (0)10 65325035, 65323798
Fax: +86 (0)10 65327330, 65322693

Embassy of the Republic of Serbia in Beijing
1, Dong Liu Jie
San Li Tun
Beijing 100600
Tel: +86 (0)10 65323516/1693/5413/3016
Fax: +86 (0)10 65321207
E-mail: yuamba@public.bta.net.cn
Website: http://www.embserbia.cn

Embassy of the Republic of Sierra Leone
7, Dong Zhi Men Wai Da Jie
Beijing
Tel: +86 (0)10 6532 1222
Fax: +86 (0)10 6532 3752
E-mail: slembbj@public3.bta.net.cn

Embassy of the Republic of Singapore
1, Xiu Shui Bei Jie
Jian Guo Men Wai
Beijing
Tel: +86 (0)10 6532 1115
Fax: +86 (0)10 6532 9405
E-mail: singemb_bej@sgmfa.gov.sg
Website: http://www.mfa.gov.sg/beijing/

Embassy of the Slovak Republic
Ri Tan Lu, Jian Guo Men Wai
Beijing
Tel: +86 (0)10 6532 1531
Fax: +86 (0)10 6532 4814

Embassy of the Republic of Slovenia
57, Block F
Ya Qu Yuan, King's Garden Villas
18, Xiao Yun Road
Chao Yang District
Beijing 100600
Tel: +86 (0)10 64681030, 64681154
Fax: +86 (0)10 64681040

Embassy of the Republic of Somalia
2, San Li Tun Lu
Beijing
Tel: +86 (0)10 65321651, 65320717
Fax: +82 (0)10 6532 1752
E-mail: somaliaemb.beij@yahoo.com

Embassy of South Africa
5, Dong Zhi Men Wai Da Jie
Beijing 100600
Tel: +86 (0)10 65320171
Fax: +86 (0)10 65327139
E-mail: safrican@163bj.com

Embassy of Spain
9 San Li Tun Lu
Beijing
Tel: 6532 1986
Fax: +86 (0)10 6532 3401
Commercial Section: +86 (0)10 6532 2072
Fax: +86 (0)10 6532 1128
E-mail: embesp@public.bta.net.cn
Website: http://www.mae.
 es/embajadas/pekin

Embassy of the Democratic Socialist Republic of Sri Lanka
3, Jian Hua Lu
Jian Guo Men Wai
Beijing
Tel: +86 (0)10 6532 1861

Fax: +86 (0)10 6532 5426
E-mail: lkembj@public3.bta.net.cn
Website: http://www.slemb.com/

Embassy of the Republic of Sudan
1, Don Er Jie
San Li Tun
Beijing
Tel: +86 (0)10 6532 3715
Fax: +86 (0)10 65321280
E-mail: mail@sudanembassychina.com
Website: www.sudanembassychina.com

Embassy of the Republic of Suriname in Beijing
2-2-22, Jianguomenwai Diplomatic
  Compound
Beijing 100600
Tel: +86 (0)10 65322939/2938
Fax: +86 (0)10 65322941
E-mail: surembchina@hotmail.com

Embassy of Sweden
3, Dong Zhi Men Wai Da Jie
Beijing
Tel: +86 (0)10 6532 9790
Fax: +86 (0)10 6532 5008
Commercial Section:
Fax: +86 (0)10 6532 3803
E-mail: ambassaden.peking@foreign.
  ministry.se
Website: http://www.swedemb-cn.org/

Embassy of Switzerland
3, Dong Wu Jie
San Li Tun
Beijing
Tel: +86 (0)10 6532 2736
Fax: +86 (0)10 6532 4353
E-mail: vertretung@bei.rep.admin.ch

Embassy of the Syrian Arab Republic
6, Dong Si Jie
San Li Tun
Beijing
Tel: +86 (0)10 6532 1372
Fax: +86 (0)10 6532 1575
E-mail: sy@syria.org.cn
Website: http://www.syria.org.cn/

Embassy of the Republic of Tajikistan in Beijing
1-4, Section A, Liangmaqiao Diplomatic
  Compound
Beijing 100600
Tel: +86 (0)10 65322598
Fax: +86 (0)10 65323039
E-mail: tjkemb@public2.bta.net.cn

Embassy of the United Republic of Tanzania
8, Liang Ma He Nan Lu
San Li Tun
Beijing
Tel: +86 (0)10 6532 1491
Fax: +86 (0)10 65324351/1695
E-mail: tanrep@tanzaniaembassy.org.cn
Website: http://www.tanzaniaembassy.
  org.cn/eindex.asp

Royal Thai Embassy
40, Guang Hua Lu
Beijing
Tel. +86 (0)10 65321749
Fax: +86 (0)10 65321748
E-mail: thaibej@public.bta.net.cn

Embassy of the Democratic Republic of Timor-Leste in Beijing
Room 156, Gold Island Diplomatic
  Compound
1, Xibahe Nan Lu
Beijing 100028
Tel: +86 (0)10 64403072/3079
Fax: +86 (0)10 64403071
E-mail: rdtlemb_beijing@yahoo.com
Website: http://www.timor-leste.gov.tl

Embassy of the Republic of Togo
11, Dong Zhi Men Wai Da Jie
Beijing
Tel: +86 (0)10 6532 2202
Fax: +86 (0)10 6532 5884

Embassy of the Kingdom of Tonga in Beijing
Suite 3002, Embassy House
Dong Zhi Men Wai Xiao Jie
Beijing 100600
Tel: +86 (0)10 84499757
Fax: +86 (0)10 84499758

Embassy of the Tunisian Republic
1, San Li Tun Dong Jie
Beijing
Tel: +86 (0)10 6532 65325818
Fax: +86 (0)10 65325044
E-mail: at_beijing@netchina.com.cn

Embassy of the Republic of Turkey
9, Dong Wu Jie, San Li Tun
Beijing
Tel: +86 (0)10 65321715
Fax: +86 (0)10 6532 5480
E-mail: embassy@turkey.org.cn
Website: http://www.turkey.org.cn/

Embassy of Turkmenistan
King's Garden Villa D-1
18 Xiaoyun Lu
Beijing
Tel: +86 (0)10 6532 6975/6976
Fax: +86 (0)10 6532 2269
E-mail: embturkmen@netchina.com.cn

Embassy of the Republic of Uganda
5, San Li Tun Dong Jie
Beijing
Tel: +86 (0)10 6532 1708
Fax: +86 (0)10 6532 2242
E-mail: info@ugandaembassycn.org

Embassy of Ukraine
11, Dong Liu Jie
San Li Tun
Beijing
Tel: +86 (0)10 6532 6359
Fax: +86 (0)10 6532 6765
Commercial Section: +86 (0)10 6532 4013
E-mail: ukrembcn@public3.bta.net.cn
Website: http://www.ukremb.cn/eng/

Embassy of the United Arab Emirates
1-9-1, Ta Yuan Diplomatic Office Building
Beijing
Tel: +86 (0)10 65327650/7651/7653
Fax: +86 (0)10 65327652
E-mail: info@uaeemb.com

**Embassy of the United Kingdom of
Great Britain and Northern Ireland**
11, Guang Hua Lu
Beijing
Tel: +86 (0)10 51924000

Fax: +86 (0)10 6532 1937
E-mail: commercialmail@peking.mail.fco.
gov.uk
Website: http://www.uk.cn/

**Embassy of the United States of
America**
3, Xiu Shui Bei Jie, Jian Guo Men Wai
Beijing
Tel: +86 (0)10 6532 3831 and +86 (0)10
6532 3431
E-mail: AmCitBeijing@state.gov
Website: http://beijing.usembassy-china.
org.cn

Embassy of the Republic of Uruguay
2-7-2, Ta Yuan Diplomatic Office Building
Beijing
Tel: +86 (0)10 6532 4445
Fax: +86 (0)10 6532 7375
E-mail: urubei@public.bta.net.cn

Embassy of the Republic of Uzbekistan
2-1-92, Ta Yuan Diplomatic Compound
Beijing
Tel: +86 (0)10 65326305, 65322551
Fax: +86 (0)10 6532 6304
E-mail: Embassy@uzbekistan.cn
Website: http://www.uzbekistan.cn

Embassy of Vanuatu
3-1-11 San Li Tun
Diplomatic Compound
Beijing
Tel: +86 (0)10 6532 0337
Fax: +86 (0)10 6532 0336
Email: vanuatuembassybj@yahoo.com.cn

Embassy of the Republic of Venezuela
14, San Li Tun Lu
Beijing
Tel: +86 (0)10 6532 1295
Fax: +86 (0)10 6532 3817
E-mail: embvenez@public.bta.net.cn
Website: http://www.venezuela.org.cn

**Embassy of the Socialist Republic of
Vietnam**
32, Guang Hua Lu
Jian Guo Men Wai
Beijing
Tel: +86 (0)10 6532 1155

Fax: +86 (0)10 6532 5720
Commercial Section: +86 (0)10 6532 5415

Embassy of the Republic of Yemen
5, Dong San Jie
San Li Tun
Beijing
Tel: +86 (0)10 6532 1558
Fax: +86 (0)10 65327997
E-mail: info@embassyofyemen.net
Website: http://www.embassyofyemen.
   net

Embassy of the Republic of Zaire
6, Dong Wu Jie
San Li Tun
Beijing
Tel: +86 (0)10 6532 2713

Embassy of the Republic of Zambia
5, Dong Si Jie
San Li Tun
Beijing
Tel: +86 (0)10 6532 1554
Fax: +86 (0)10 6532 1891

Embassy of the Republic of Zimbabwe
7, Dong San Jie
San Li Tun
Beijing
Tel: +86 (0)10 6532 3795
Fax: +86 (0)10 6532 5383

Chengdu

France Consulate-General Chengdu
30th Floor
Tianfu Time Square
2, Zong Fu Lu
Chengdu
Sichuan Province 610016
Tel: +86 (0)28 66666060, 66666103
E-mail: chancellerie@consulfrance_
   chengdu.org
Website: http://www.consulfrance-
   chengdu.org/

**Consulate General of the Federal
Republic of Germany in Chengdu**
6th Floor, Western Tower
19, 4th Section
Renmin Nan Lu

Chengdu
Sichuan Province 610000
Tel: +86 (0)28 85280800
Fax: +86 (0)28 85268308
E-mail: zreg@cheng.diplo.de

Pakistan Consulate General Chengdu
8th Floor, Western Tower
19, 4th Section, Renmin Nan Lu
Chengdu
Sichuan Province 610041

**Republic of South Korea Consulate
General Chengdu**
19F Paradise Oasis Mansion
2, Xia Nan Da Jie
Chengdu
Sichuan Province 610000
Tel: +86 (0)28 86165800
Fax: +86 (0)28 86165789
E-mail: schong95@mofat.go.kr
Website: http://www.mofat.
   go.kr/fe/e_a001/e_cnch/

Singapore Consulate General Chengdu
1st Floor, Guancheng Square
308, Shuncheng Da Jie
Chengdu
Sichuan Province 610000

**Royal Thai Consulate-General in
Chengdu**
Kempinski Hotel, 2nd Floor, Office
   Building
42 Renmin Nan Lu, 4th Section
Chengdu
Sichuan Province 610000
Tel: +86 (0)28 85180688, 85192668
Fax: +86 (0)28 85125928

**Consulate General of the United States
of America in Chengdu**
Ling Shi Guan Lu
Chengdu
Sichuan Province 610041
Tel: +86 (0)28 85583992, 85589642
Fax: +86 (0)28 85583520
E-mail: consularchengdu@state.gov
Website: http://chengdu.usconsulate.
   gov/

Chongqing

Consulate General of the Kingdom of Cambodia in Chongqing
1902, Building A
9 Yanghe Lu, JiangBei District
Chongqing 401120
Tel: +86 (0)23 89116415
Fax: +86 (0)23 89111369

Canada Consulate General Chongqing
Chongqing Suite 1705
Metropolitan Tower
Wu Yi Road
Yu Zhong District
Chongqing
Tel: +86 (0)23 6373 8007
Fax: +86 (0)23 6373 8026
E-mail: chonq@international.gc.ca
Website: http://geo.international.gc.ca/
asia/china/locations/chong
qing/default-en.asp#1

Denmark Consulate General Chongqing
1 Metropolitan Tower, 31/F
68 Zou Rong Lu, Yuzhong District
Chongqing 400010
Tel: +86 (0)23 63726600, 63725280
Fax: +86 (0)23 63725160
E-mail: chongqing@dtcchina.dk
Website: http://www.dtcchina.
um.dk/en/menu/Omos/Kontakos/

Japan Consulate General Chongqing
37 F, Metropolitan Tower
68 Zou Rong Lu, Yuzhong District
Chongqing 400010
Tel: +86 (0)23 63733585
Fax: +86 (0)23 63733589
Website: http://www.chongqing.cn.emb-
japan.go.jp/index_c.htm

Consulate General of the United Kingdom of Great Britain and Northern Ireland in Chongqing
28F, Metropolitan Tower, Zou Rong Lu
Yuzhong District
Chongqing 400010
Tel: +86 (0)23 63691500
Fax: +86 (0)23 63691525
E-mail: chongqing.consular@fco.gov.uk

Dalian

Consulate General of Japan in Shenyang (Dalian Office)
3F, Senmao Building
147 Zhongshan Lu
Xigang District, Dalian
Liaoning Province 116011
Tel: +86 (0)411 83704077
Fax: +86 (0)411 83704066
E-mail: ryojikan@dljapan.com
Website: http://www.dalian.cn.emb-
japan.go.jp/ch/l

Guangxi

Consulate General of the Kingdom of Cambodia in Nanning
2F, Nanfeng Tower
85, Minzu Avenue, Nanning
Guangxi Province 530000
Tel: +86 (0)771 5889892, 5889893
Fax: +86 (0)771 5888522

Consulate Office of the Kingdom of Thailand in Nanning
Room 2212, Guilin Tower
1, Wen Xin Lu, Nanning
Guangxi Province 530000
Tel: +86 (0)771 5506698
Fax: +86 (0)771 5506628
E-mail: thainng@mf.go.th

Consulate General of Socialist Republic of Vietnam in Nanning
1F, Investment Plaza
109 Minzu Dadao, Nanning
Guangxi Province 530000
Tel: +86 (0)771 5510561
Fax: +86 (0)771 5534738

Guangzhou

Australian Consulate General in Guangzhou
12/F, Development Centre
3 Linjiang Road, Zhujiang New City,
Guangzhou.
Tel: +86 (0)20 3814 0111
Fax: +86 (0)20 3814 0112
E-mail: guangzhou.consular@dfat.gov.au

Website: http://www.guangzhou.china.
embassy.gov.au

Belgian Consulate General in Guangzhou
Room 1601-02A, CITIC Plaza
233, Tianhe North Rd
Guangzhou 510613
Tel: +86 (0)20 38770188
Fax: +86 (0)20 38770288

Cambodia Consulate- General in Guangzhou
Suite 8114, Garden Tower, Garden Hotel
Huanshi-dong Rd.
Guangzhou 510064
Tel: +86 (0)20 8387 9005, 8333 8999
Fax: +86 (0)20 8387 9006
E-mail: Cambodia@public.guangzhou.
gd.cn

Canada Consulate General in Guangzhou
Suite 801, Office Tower
China Hotel, Liuhua Rd
Guangzhou 510015
Tel: +86 (0)20 8666 0569
Fax: +86 (0)20 8667 2401
E-mail: ganzu.consular-consulaire@
international.gc.ca
Website: http://www.beijing.
gc.ca/guangzhou/en/

Cuba Consulate General in Guangzhou
Room 1004, East Tower
Huapu Plaza
13, Huaming Rd
Zhu Jiang New City
Guangzhou 510635
Tel: +86 (0)20 22382603/04
Fax: +86 (0)20 22382605
E-mail: cgeneral@cubaconsuladogz.com
Website: http://embacuba.cubaminrex.
cu/Default.aspx?tabid=1378

Danish Consulate General in Guangzhou
Suite 1578, Office Tower
China Hotel, Liuhua Rd
Guangzhou 510015
Tel: +86 (0)20 8666 0795
Fax: +86 (0)20 8667 0315
E-mail: cangkl@um.dk

Website: http://www.gkguangzhou.
um.dk/da

Finland Consulate General in Guangzhou
Suites 3309-3312
CITIC Plaza
233 Tianhe-Bei Rd
Guangzhou 510613
Tel: +86 (0)20 3877 0188
Fax: +86 (0)20 3877 0288
E-mail: sanomat.kan@formin.fi
Website: http://www.finland.cn/

French Consulate General in Guangzhou
Suite l801, Main Tower
Guangdong International Hotel
339 Huanshi-dong Rd
Guangzhou 510098
Tel: +86 (0)20 8330 3405, 8331 0909
(Economic)
Fax: +86 (0)20 8331 3437
E-mail: info@consulfrance-canton.org
Website: http://www.ambafrance-cn.org

German Consulate General in Guangzhou
19/F, Main Tower
Guangdong International Hotel
339 Huanshi-dong Rd
Guangzhou 510098
Tel: +86 (0)20 8330 6533
Fax: +86 (0)20 8331 7033
E-mail: info@kanton.diplo.de
Website: http://www.kanton.diplo.de

Indonesia Consulate General in Guangzhou
Suites 1201-1223 West Wing
Dongfang Hotel
Guangzhou 510016
Tel: +86 (0)20 8601 8772 / 8790 / 8850 /
8870
Fax: +86 (0)20 8601 8773
E-mail: kjriguangzhou@yahoo.com
Website: http://www.indonesianembassy-
china.com/EN/guangzhou.htm

Italy Consulate General in Guangzhou
Suite 5207, CITIC Plaza
233 Tianhe-Bei Rd
Guangzhou 510613
Tel: +86 (0)20 3877 0556 Ext. 7/8/9

Fax: +86 (0)20 3877 0270
E-mail: itconsgz@gitic.com.cn
Website: http://www.itconsgz.org.cn

Japan Consulate General in Guangzhou
1/F Garden Tower
Garden Hotel, Huanshi-dong Rd
Guangzhou 510064
Tel: +86 (0)20 8334 3009, 8399 2345 (visa appointments)
Fax: +86 (0)20 8333 8972
E-mail: ryojikan@public.guangzhou.gd.cn
Website: http://www.guangzhou.cn.emb-japan.go.jp/cgjp_cn/

Malaysian Consulate General
Suite 1915-1918
CITIC Plaza
233 Tianhe-Bei Rd
Guangzhou 510613
Tel: +86 (0)20 8739 5660, 3877 0766/0763
Fax: +86 (0)20 8739 5669
E-mail: mwgzhou@public.guangzhou.gd.cn

Mexican Consulate General
Room 02-03, 14 Floor
Metro Plaza, Tianhe North Rd
Guangzhou 510620
Tel.: +86 (0)20 22220981
Fax: +86 (0)20 22221006

Consulate General of the Kingdom of Nepal in Guangzhou
Room 905, 9/F
Third Building of Dongjun Square
836, Dongfeng Dong Lu
Guangzhou, 510080
Tel: +86 (0)20 87672448, 87662197, 87664560
Fax: +86 (0)20 87672523

Netherlands Consulate General in Guangzhou
Suite 705 Main Tower
Guangdong International Hotel
339 Huanshi-dong Rd
Guangzhou 510098
Tel: +86 (0)20 8330 2067
Fax: +86 (0)20 8330 3601
E-mail: nedcons@gitic.com.cn

Website: http://www.hollandinchina.org/cn/cg/guangzhou.htm

Consulate General of New Zealand in Guangzhou
Room 1160, Commercial Mansion
China Hotel
Guangzhou 510015
Tel: +86 (0)20 86670253
Fax: +86 (0)20 86666420

Philippine Consulate General in Guangzhou
Suites 709-711, Main Tower
Guangdong International Hotel
339 Huanshi-dong Rd
Guangzhou 510098
Tel: +86 (0)20 81886968
Fax: +86 (0)20 81862041
E-mail: gzphcggz@public1.guangzhou.gd.cn
Website: http://pcggz.bizhosting.com

Poland Consulate General in Guangzhou
63 Shamian St.
Guangzhou 510130
Tel: +86 (0)20 8121 9993, 8121 8991
Fax: +86 (0)20 8121 9995
E-mail: plcogeca@public.guangzhou.gd.cn (General)
Website: http://www.consulateguangzhou.com/english/main_english.htm

Consulate General of Republic of Korea in Guangzhou
18/F West Tower
Yangcheng International Trade Centre
Tiyu-dong Rd.
Guangzhou
Tel: +86 (0)20 3887 0555 Ext. 102
Fax: +86 (0)20 3887 0923
E-mail: guangzhou@mofat.go.kr
Website: http://www.mofat.go.kr/mission/emb/embassy_en.mof?si_dcode=CN-GU

Singapore Consulate General in Guangzhou
Suite 3318, CITIC Plaza

233 Tianhe-Bei Rd
Guangzhou 510613
Tel: +86 (0)20 38912345
Fax: +86 (0)20 38912933, 38912131 (for visa)
Website: http://www.mfa.gov. sg/xiamenchi/

Swedish Consulate General in Guangzhou
1002B-1003 CITIC Plaza
233 Tianhe-Bei Rd
Guangzhou 510098
Tel: +86 (0)20 3891 2383
Fax: +86 (0)20 3891 2100
E-mail: generalkonsulat.kanton@foreign. ministry.se
Website: www.swedenabroad. com/guangzhou

Consulate General of Switzerland in Guangzhou
Room 811 – 812
Commercial Mansion
Garden Hotel
Guangzhou 510133
Tel: +86 (0)20 83338999-811, 8338999- 812
Fax: +86 (0)20 83877447

Thai Consulate General in Guangzhou
M07, Garden Hotel
368 Huanshi Dong Lu
Guangzhou 510064
Tel: +86 (0)20 83804277, 83849937, 83338989 - 10-19
Fax: +86 (0)20 83889959, 83889567

Consulate General of the UK of Great Britain and Northern Ireland in Guangzhou
7/F (Trade & Investment and Public Affairs Sections)
2/F (Consular and Visa Sections)
Main Tower, Guangdong International Hotel
339 Huanshi-dong Rd
Guangzhou 510098
Tel: +86 (0)20 8314 3000, 8335 1354/1316 (Cultural & Education)

Fax: +86 (0)20 8333 6485, 8331 2799 (Consular Enquiries)
Consular Enquiries: guangzhou. consular@fco.gov.uk
Visa Enquiries: guangzhou.visas@fco. gov.uk
Website: http://www.uk.cn/gz/english/ index.asp

USA Consulate General in Guangzhou
1 Shamian-Nan St
Guangzhou 510133
Tel: +86 (0)20 8121 8000, 81218418 (American Citizen Services)
Fax: +86(0)20 8121 9001
Website: http://guangzhou.usembassy- china.org.cn/

Vietnam Consulate-General in Guangzhou
North Section
2/F Tower B
Landmark Hotel
Qiaoguang Rd
Guangzhou 510115
Tel: +86 (0)20 8330 5911/ 5910
Fax: +86 (0)20 8330 5915
E-mail: tlsqvn@mx2.gd.cei.gov.cn

Hohhot

Consulate General of Mongolia in Hohhot
Unit 1, Building 5
Wulan Residential Area
Saihan District
Hohhot 010020
Tel: +86 (0)471 4923819, 4303266/254
Fax: +86 (0)471 4303250

Kunming

Royal Consulate General of Cambodia in Kunming
20/F, Jinquan Hotel
93 Renmin Dong Lu
Kunming
Tel: +86 (0)871 3317320
Fax: +86 (0)871 3316220

Consulate General of Lao People's Democratic Republic in Kunming
1/F Main Tower
Camellia Hotel
96 Dong Feng Dong Lu
Kunming
Tel: +86 (0)871 3176623/4
Fax: +86 (0)871 3178556

Consulate General of Malaysia in Kunming
Room 401-405
Sakura Hotel
29 Dongfeng Lu
Kunming
Tel: +86 (0)871 3165888/6241/6242
Fax: +86 (0)871 3113503

Consulate General of the Union of Myanmar in Kunming
2/F, Main Tower
Camellia Hotel
96 Dong Feng Road, E.
Kunming
Tel: +86 (0)871 3163000/6215
Fax: +86 (0)871 3176309

Royal Thai Consulate General in Kunming
1/F, South Building
Kunming Hotel
145 Dong Feng Dong Lu
Kunming
Tel: +86 (0)871 3168916/3149296
Fax: +86 (0)871 3166891

Consulate General of Socialist Republic of Vietnam in Kunming
1/F, Jiaxing Hotel
529 Beijing Lu
Kunming
Tel: +86 (0)871 3183092
Fax: +86 (0)871 3183085

Lhasa

Royal Nepalese Consulate General in Lhasa
Chancery: No.13 Norbulingka Lu
Lhasa
Tel: +86 (0)891 6830609
Fax: +86 (0)891 6836890

Qingdao

Consulate General of the Republic of South Korea in Qingdao
Chancery: No.17, Hong Kong Dong Lu
Laoshan District
Qingdao
Tel: +86 (0)532 88976001
Fax: +86 (0)532 88976005
E-mail: qdconsul@mofat.go.kr
Website: www.qdcon.org.cn

Shanghai

Argentina Consulate-General in Shanghai
4F West Tower
Sun Plaza
88 Xianxia Lu
Shanghai
Tel: +86 (0)21 62780300
Fax: +86 (0)21 62958539
E-mail: consuargensh@online.sh.cn
Website: http://www.consuargensh.
com/chinese/

Australian Consulate-General Shanghai
Level 22
CITIC Square
1168 Nanjing Xi Lu
Shanghai 200041
Tel: +86 (0)21 52925500
Fax: +86 (0)21 52925511
E-Mail: acgshang@public.sta.net.cn
Website: www.shanghai.china.embassy.
gov.au

Austrian Consulate-General in Shanghai
3A, Qihua Tower
1375 Huaihai Zhong Lu
Shanghai
Tel: +86 (0)21 64740268
Fax: +86 (0)21 64741554

Consulate General of the Kingdom of Belgium in Shanghai
127 Wuyi Lu
Shanghai
Tel: +86 (0)21 64376579
Fax: +86 (0)21 64377041

E-mail: shanghai@diplobel.org
Website: http://www.diplobel.
org/shanghai/

The Consulate General of the Republic of Bulgaria in Shanghai
7K Hongqiao Business Center
2272 Hongqiao Lu
Shanghai 200336
Tel: +86 (0)21 62376183
Fax: +86 (0)21 62376189

Consulate General of the Federative Republic of Brazil in Shanghai
10F, Qihua Tower
1375 Huaihai Zhong Lu
Shanghai
Tel: +86 (0)21 64370110
Fax: +86 (0)21 64370160
E-mail: consbrasxangai@consbrasxangai.
com
Website: http://consbrasxangai.com/

British Consulate General in Shanghai
Suite 301, Shanghai Center
1376 Nanjing Xi Lu
Shanghai
Tel: +86 (0)21 62798103
Fax: +86 (0)21 62798254
E-mail: britishconsulate.shanghai@fco.
gov.uk
Website: http://www.uk.cn/bj/index.
asp?city=4

Royal Consulate General of Cambodia in Shanghai
Room 901-902
Hua Sheng Building
400 Hankou Lu
Shanghai
Tel: +86 (0)21 63600949
Fax: +86 (0)21 63611437
E-mail: tangjx@online.sh.cn

Consulate General of Canada in Shanghai
Suite 604
Shanghai Center
1376 Nanjing Xi Lu
Shanghai
Tel: +86 (0)21 62798400
Fax: +86 (0)21 62798401

E-mail: shngi@international.gc.ca
Website: www.shanghai.gc.ca

Consulate General of the Republic of Chile in Shanghai
Room 305, Equatorial Hotel Shanghai
65 Yan'an Xi Lu
Shanghai
Tel: +86 (0)21 62498000
Fax: +86 (0)21 62498333

Consulate General of the Republic of Cuba in Shanghai
5F, New Town Mansion
55 Loushanguan Lu
Shanghai
Tel: +86 (0)21 62753078
Fax: +86 (0)21 62753147

Consulate General of the Czech Republic in Shanghai
Room 808, New Town Center
83 Loushanguan Lu
Shanghai
Tel: +86 (0)21 62369925/62369926
Fax: +86 (0)21 62369920
E-mail: shanghai@embassy.mvz.cz
Website: http://www.mzv.cz/wwwo/
default.asp?idj=15&amb=101

Consulate General of the Kingdom of Denmark in Shanghai
Room 701, Shanghai International Trade Center
2201 Yan'an Xi Lu
Shanghai
Tel: +86 (021 62090500
Fax: +86 (0)21 62090504
E-mail: shagk@um.dk
Website: http://www.gkshanghai.
um.dk/da

Consulate General of the Arab Republic of Egypt in Shanghai
19A/B, Qihua Tower
1375 Huaihai Zhong Lu
Shanghai
Tel: +86 (0)21
64331020/64330622/64330502
Fax: +86 (0)21 64330049

Consulate General of the Republic of Finland in Shanghai
2501-05, CITIC Square,
1168 Nanjing Xi Lu
Shanghai
Tel: +86 (0)21 52929900
Fax: +86 (0)21 52929880
E-mail: sanomat.sng@formin.fi
Web page: www.finland.cn

Consulate General of the Republic of France in Shanghai
2 F, Hai Tong Securities Tower
689 Guang Dong Lu
Shanghai
Tel: +86 (0)21 61032200
Fax: +86 (0)21 63411055
E-mail: info@consulfrance-shanghai.org
Website: http://www.consulfrance-shanghai.org

Consulate General of the Federal Republic of Germany in Shanghai
118 Yongfu Lu
Shanghai
Tel: +86 (0)21 34010106
Fax: +86 (0)21 64714448
Website: http://www.shanghai.diplo.de/Vertretung/shanghai/zh/Startseite.html

Greece Consulate-General in Shanghai
Suite 3501-02
Shanghai Centure Plaza
989 Changle Lu
Shanghai
Tel: +86 (0)21 54670505
Fax: +86 (0)21 54670202
E-mail: greekconsulate@126.com

Consulate General of the Republic of Hungary
Room 2811, Haitong Securities Tower
689 Guangdong Lu
Shanghai
Tel: +86 (0)21 63410564/63410764
Fax: +86 (0)21 62410574
Website: http://www.huemb.org.cn/english/index_e.html

Consulate General of the Republic of India in Shanghai
Room 1008, Shanghai International Trade Center
2201 Yan'an Xi Lu
Shanghai
Tel: +86 (0)21 62758882/62758885/62758886
Fax: +86 (0)21 62758881
E-mail: cgisha@public.sta.net.cn
Website: http://www.indianconsulate.org.cn/

Consulate General of the Islamic Republic of Iran in Shanghai
17 Fuxing Rd. (W)
Shanghai 200030
Tel: +86 (0)21 64332997
Fax: +86 (0)21 64336826

Consulate General of Ireland in Shanghai
Room 700A, Shanghai Center
1376 Nanjing Xi Lu
Shanghai
Tel: +86 (0)2162798729
Fax: +86 (0)21 62798739
E-mail: shanghai@dfa.iet
Website: http://embassyofireland.cn/Ireland/consulate.htm

Israel Consulate-General in Shanghai
Room 703, New Town Mansion
55 Loushanguan Lu
Shanghai
Tel: +86 (0)21 62098008
Fax: +86 (0)21 62098010
Website:http://shanghai.mfa.gov.il/mfm/web/main/missionhome.asp?MissionID=106

Consulate General of the Republic of Italy in Shanghai
11A, 11B, Qihua Tower
1375 Huaihai Zhong Lu
Shanghai
Tel: +86 (0)21 64716980
Fax: +86 (0)21 64716977

Honorary Consul of Jamaica to Shanghai
16F, Zhongda Square

989 Dongfang Lu
Shanghai
Tel: +86 (0)21 58313553
Fax: +98 (0)21 68763299
E-mail: gs_intl@163.net
Website: http://www.jamaicagov.cn/cn/
embassy.asp

Consulate General of Japan in Shanghai
8 Wanshan Lu
Shanghai
Tel: +86 (0)21 52574766
Fax: +86 (0)21 62788988
Website: http://www.shanghai.cn.emb-
japan.go.jp/cn/index_cn.htm

General Consulate of Luxembourg in Shanghai
4th Floor
12 Zhongshan Dong Yi Lu
Shanghai 200002
Tel: + 86 (0)21 6339 0400
Fax: +86 (0)21 6339 0433
E-mail: shanghai.cg@mae.etat.lu

Consulate General of Malaysia in Shanghai
Room 1101, CITIC Square
1168 Nanjing Xi Lu
Shanghai
Tel: +86 (0)21 52925424
Fax: +86 (0)21 52925951

Consulate General of the United States of Mexico in Shanghai
9A, 9B, Qihua Tower
1375 Huaihai Zhong Lu
Shanghai
Tel: +86 (0)21 64373451
Fax: +86 (0)21 64370336

Honorary Consul of Monaco to Shanghai
1 Longdong Ave.
Pudong New District
Shanghai
Tel: +86 (0)21 58332199
Fax: +86 (0)21 58331577

Royal Nepalese Honorary Consul to Shanghai
28F, No.2 Lane
1040 Caoyang Lu
Shanghai
Tel: +86 (0)21 52661811
Fax: +86 (0)21 52661819

Consulate General of the Kingdom of the Netherlands in Shanghai
4F, East Tower, Sun Plaza
88 Xianxia Lu
Shanghai
Tel: +86 (0)21 62099076
Fax: +86 (0)21 62099079

Consulate General of New Zealand in Shanghai
15F, Qihua Tower
Huaihai Zhong Lu
Shanghai
Tel: +86 (0)21 64711127
Fax: +86 (0)21 64310226

Royal Norwegian Consulate General in Shanghai
Room 321
Zhongshan Dong Yi Lu
Shanghai
Tel: +86 (0)21 63239988
Fax: +86 (0)21 63233938
E-mail: cons.gen.shanghai@mfa.no
Website: http://www.norway.org.cn/
shanghai/welcome/welcome.htm

Consulate General of the Islamic Republic of Pakistan
Suite O
7F Hongqiao Business Center
2272 Hongqiao Lu
Shanghai
Tel: +86 (0)21 62377000
Fax: +86 (0)21 62377066
E-mail: pakrepshanghai@yahoo.com
Website: http://www.
pakconsulateshanghai.org.
cn/cn/index/

Consulate General of the Republic of Peru in Shanghai
Suite 2705, Kerry Center
1515 Nanjing Xi Lu

Shanghai
Tel: +86 (0)21 52985900
Fax: +86 (0)21 52985905
E-mail: conperu@conpersh.com
Website: http://www.conpersh.com/

Consulate General of the Republic of Philippines in Shanghai
Suite 368, Shanghai Center
1376 Nanjing Xi Lu
Shanghai
Tel: +86 (0)21 62798337
Fax: +86 (0)21 62798332
E-mail: pcg@philcongenshanghai.org
Website: http://www.philcongenshanghai.org/

Consulate General of the Republic of Poland in Shanghai
618 Jianguo Xi Lu
Xuhui District
Shanghai
Tel: +86 (0)21 64339288
Fax: +86 (0)21 64330417
E-mail: cgpl@polandshanghai.org
Website: http://www.polandshanghai.org/default.htm

Consulate General of the Republic of Korea in Shanghai
Room 402, Shanghai International Trade Center
2200 Yan'an Xi Lu
Shanghai
Tel: +86 (0)21 62196420
Fax: +86 (0)21 62196918

Consulate General of Romania in Shanghai
Room 305, West Tower, Sun Plaza
Xianxia Lu
Shanghai
Tel: +86 (0)21 62701146
Fax: +86 (0)21 62085105

Consulate General of the Russian Federation in Shanghai
20 Huangpu Lu
Shanghai
Tel: +86 (0)21 63248383/63242628
Fax: +86 (0)21 63069982
E-mail: gkshanghai@mail.ru

Website: http://www.russia.org.cn/eng/

Consulate General of the Republic of Singapore in Shanghai
89 Wanshan Lu
Shanghai
Tel: +86 (0)21 62785566
Fax: +86 (0)21 62956038
E-mail: singcg_sha@sgmfa.gov.sg
Website: http://www.mfa.gov.sg/shanghai/

Consulate General of Slovak Republic in Shanghai
4B Qihua Tower
Huaihai Zhong Lu
Shanghai
Tel: +86 (0)21 64314205
Fax: +86 (0)21 64713604

Consulate General of Republic of South Africa in Shanghai
Room 2706, the Bund Center
220 Yan'an Zhong Lu
Shanghai
Tel: +86 (0)21 53594977
Fax: +86 (0)21 63352980
E-mail: sacgmkt@yahoo.com

Consulate General of Spain in Shanghai
12 Zhongshan Dong Yi Lu
Shanghai
Tel: +86 (0)21 63213543
Fax: +86 (0)21 63211396

Consulate General of the Kingdom of Sweden in Shanghai
Room 1530-1541, Shanghai Central Plaza
381 Huaihai Zhong Lu
Shanghai
Tel: +86 (0)21 63916767
Fax: +86 (0)21 63915067
E-mail: generalkonsulat.shanghai@foreign.ministry.se
Website: http://www.swedenabroad.com/Start____19591.aspx

Consulate General of the Swiss Confederation in Shanghai
Room 302, 22F, Building A
Far East International Plaza

88 Xianxia Lu
Shanghai
Tel: +86 (0)21 62700519-21
Fax: +86 (0)21 62700522
E-mail: Vertretung@sha.rep.admin.ch
Website: http://www.eda.admin.ch/
china_beishan/c/home.html

Royal Thai Consulate General in Shanghai
3F, No.7 Zhongshan Dong Yi Lu
Shanghai
Tel: +86 (0)21
63234095/63219371/63219406
Fax: +86 (0)21 63234140
Website: http://www.thaishanghai.com/
chinese/c_index.html

Consulate General of the Republic of Turkey in Shanghai
13F, Qihua Tower
1375 Huaihai Zhong Lu
Shanghai
Tel: +86 (0)21 64746838
Fax: +86 (0)21 62785272
E-mail: tcsanghaybsk@163.com

Consulate General of Ukraine in Shanghai
Room 502, Sun Plaza West Tower
88 Xianxia Lu
Shanghai
Tel: +86 (0)21 62953195/62953196
Fax: +86 (0)21 62953171
E-mail: ukrconsh@sh163.net
Website: http://www.ukrconsh.com.cn/
index.asp

Consulate General of the United States of America in Shanghai
1469 Huaihai Zhong Lu
Shanghai
Tel: +86 (0)21 64336880
Fax: +86 (0)21 64334122
Website: http://www.usembassy-china.org.
cn/shanghai/index-c.html

Consulate General of the Oriental Republic of Uruguay
Room 2403, Hong Kong New World
Tower
300 Huaihai Zhong Lu

Shanghai
Tel: +86 (0)21 63353927
Fax: +86 (0)21 63353741

Shenyang

Consulate General of the Democratic People's Republic of Korea in Shenyang
1 Huanghe Ave
Huanggu District
Shenyang
Tel: +86 (0)24 86852742
Fax: +86 (0)24 86855432

Consulate General of Japan in Shenyang
50 14th Wei Lu
Heping District
Shenyang
Tel: +86 (0)24 23227490
Fax: +86 (0)24 23222394
E-mail: sykohou@mail.sy.ln.cn
Website: http://www.shenyang.cn.emb-
japan.go.jp/cn/

Consulate General of the Republic of Korea in Shenyang
37 South 13th Wei Lu
Heping District
Shenyang
Tel: +86 (0)24 23853388
Fax: +86 (0)21 23855170

Consulate General of the Russia Federation in Shenyang
31 South 13th Wei Lu
Heping District
Shenyang
Tel: +86 (0)24 23223927
Fax: +86 (0)24 23223907
E-mail: ruscons@mail.sy.ln.cn
Website: http://www.russia.org.cn/eng/

US Consulate General in Shenyang
Consulate General of the United States
of America
52 14th Wei Lu
Heping District
Shenyang
Tel: +86 (0)24 23220804
Fax: +86 (0)24 23222374

Website: http://shenyang.usembassy-
china.org.cn/

Wuhan

**Consulate General of the Republic of
France in Wuhan**
Room 809, Wuhan International Trade
  Center
566 Jianshe Dadao
Hankou
Wuhan
Tel: +86 (0)27 85778403/85778405/85778
  406/85778423
Fax: +86 (0)27 85778426
E-mail: chancellerie@consulfrance-
wuhan.org
Website: http://www.ambafrance-cn.org

Xiamen

**Consulate General of the Republic of
the Philippines in Xiamen**
Lingxiang Li, Lianhua Xincun
Xiamen
Tel: +86 (0)592 5130355/51303662

**Consulate General of the Republic of
Singapore in Xiamen**
Unit 05-07/08
The Bank Center
189 Xiahe Lu
Xiamen
Tel: +86 (0)592 2684691
Fax: +86 (0)592 2684694
E-mail: singcg_xmn@sgmfa.gov.sg
Website: http://www.mfa.gov.
  sg/xiamenchi/

Xian

Royal Thailand Consulate Office in Xian
4th Floor, Yu Lang International Building
77, Jie Fang Lu
Xian

List of International Schools in China

International Schools in Beijing

**Australian International School
Beijing**
7 Louzizhuang Road
Chaoyang District;
Beijing 100018
Tel.: +86 (0)10 84394315-6
Fax: +86 (0)10 84391583
E-mail: enquiries@aisb.cn
Website: www.aisb.cn

Beijing City International School
77 Baiziwan Nan Er Road
Beijing 100022
Tel: +86 (0)10 8771 7171
Fax: +86 (0)10 8771 7778
E-mail: info@bcis.cn
Website: http://www.bcis.cn

British International School in Beijing
17, Area 4
An Zhen Xi Li
Chaoyang District
Beijing 100029
Tel: +86 (0)10 6443 3151
Fax: +86 (0)10 6443 3156
E-mail: admissions@biss.com.cn
Website: www.biss.com.cn

British School of Beijing
E-mail: info@britishschool.org.cn
Website: www.britishschool.org.cn

Shunyi Campus
Cuizhu Xin Cun, Linyin Road
Tianzhu Town, Shunyi District
Beijing 101312
Tel: +86 (0)10 6458 0884
Fax: +86 (0)10 6458 0509

Sanlitun Campus
5 Xiliujie, Sanlitun Road
Chaoyang District
Beijing 100027
Tel: +86 (0)10 8532 3088
Fax: +86 (0)10 8532 3089

Dulwich College International Beijing
Dulwich College Beijing is a franchise of the famous English public school that has its main site in Dulwich, London. There is a Dulwich College in Shanghai and plans exist for possible branches in Suzhou and south China. Famous students include many prominent figures including Anand Panyarachun (twice Prime Minster of Thailand), Peter Lilly (Former British Shadow Chancellor) among many other influential public figures.
89 Capital Airport Road
Legend Garden Villas
Shunyi District
Beijing 101300
Tel: +86 (0)10 6454 9000
Fax: +86 (0)10 6454 9001
E-mail: admissions@dcbeijing.cn
Website: www.dcbeijing.cn

Eton International School
(Not related to the famous Eton
  College in the UK)
Palm Springs International Apartments
8 Chaoyang Park South Road
Chaoyang District
Beijing 100026
Tel: +86 (0)10 6539 7171
Fax: +86 (0)10 6539 8817
E-mail: info@etonkids.com
Website: www.etonkids.com

International School of Beijing
– Shunyi
10 An Hua Street
Shunyi District
Beijing 101300
Tel: +86 (0)10 8149 2345
Fax: +86 (0)10 8046 2001
E-mail: isb-info@isb.bj.edu.cn
Website: www.isb.bj.edu.cn

Harrow School International Beijing
Harrow School Beijing is a franchise of the famous English public school that has its original site at Harrow-on-the-hill, in the UK. Former students have included former British Prime Minister Winston Churchill, inventor of photography Fox Talbot, and the first Prime Minister of India, Pundit

Nehru, among many renowned politicians and leaders of industry.
5, 4th Block
Anzhenxili
Chao Yang District
Beijing 100029
Tel: +86 (0)10 6444 8900
Fax: +86 (0)10 6445 3870
E-mail: enquiries@harrowbeijing.cn
Website: www.harrowbeijing.cn

The International Children's House
English Montessori Kindergarten
China World Trade Center
North Lodge
1 Jian Guo Men Wai Avenue
Beijing 100004
Phone: +86 (0)10 6505-3869, 6505-2288
  Ext.81299
Fax: +86 (0)10 6505-1237
E-mail: info@montessoribeijing.com
Website: www.montessoribeijing.com

Western Academy of Beijing
PO Box 8547
10 Lai Guang Ying Dong Lu
Chao Yang District
Beijing 100103
Tel: +86 (0)10 8456 4155
Fax: +86 (0)10 6437 5935
E-mail: hr@westernacademy.com
Website: www.wab.edu

Yew Chung International School
Honglingjin Park, No 5 Houbalizhuang
Chaoyang District
Beijing 100025
Tel: +86 (0)10 8583 3731
Fax: +86 (0)10 8583 2734
E-mail: bisinq@ycef.com
Website: www.ycef.com

International Schools in Chengdu

Chengdu International School
Chengdu International School
99 Shuxi Lu
Zhong Hai International Community
Chengdu
Sichuan 611731
P.R. China
Tel: +86 (0)28 8608 1162
Fax: +86 (0)28 8759 2265

Website: www.iscchengdu.org

QSI International School of Chengdu
American Garden
188 South 3rd Ring Road
Chengdu
Sichuan 610000
Fax: +86 (0)28 8519 8393
Tel: +86 (0)28 8519 8393
E-mail: chengdu@qsi.org

International Schools in Dongguan (Guangdong)

Dongguan HSKAMA International School
HSKAMA International School
Chashan Dongguan City,
Guangdong Province
Tel: +86 (0)769 8686 2669/8686 2648
Fax: +86 (0)769 8686 2881
E-mail: hkkama@126.com
Website: http://www.hskama.com/

QSI International School in Dongguan
Block A2 Dongcheng Center
Dongguan, Guangdong
Fax: +86 (0)769 2230 0130, +86 (0)769 8507 7978
Tel: +86 (0)769 2230 0131, +86 (0)769 8535 4999
E-mail: dongguang@qsi.org

International Schools in Guangzhou

American International School of Guangzhou
Box 212, Ti Yu Dong Post Office
Guangzhou 5106(0)20
Tel: +86 (0)20 8735 3393
Fax: +86 (0)20 8735 3339
E-mail: info@aisgz.edu.cn
Website: www.aisgz.edu.cn

British School of Guangzhou
937 Binjiang East Road
Guangzhou
Guangdong Province
Tel: +86 (0)20 3430 5886
Fax: +86 (0)20 3430 5887
E-mail: info@bsg.org.cn
Website: www.bsg.org.cn

Guangzhou Grace Academy
Riverside Garden, Guangzhou
Guangdong
Tel: +86 (0)20 8450 0180
Fax: +86 (0)20 8450 0190
E-mail: ggagga@pub.gz.gd.cn
Website: http://www.ggagga.net/

Guangzhou Nanhu International School
55, Huayang Street
Tiyu Dong Road
TianHe District
Guangzhou 510620
Tel: +86 (0)20 38866952/ 38863606
Fax: +86 38863680
E-mail: admissions@gnischina.com
Website: www.gnischina.com

Utahloy International School
6 km Sha Tai Highway
Jin Bao Gang
Tong He
Guangzhou 510515
Tel: +86 (0)20 8770 3919/3917
Fax: +86 (0)20 8779 1696
E-mail: uis@utahloy.com
Website: www.utahloy.com

International Schools in Nanjing

British School of Nanjing
1 Jinling Hotel Road
Jiangsu Province
Nanjing 211100
Tel: +86 (0)25 5210 8987
Fax: +86 (0)25 5210 2385
E-mail: info@bsn.org.cn
Website: www.bsn.org.cn

Nanjing International School
Xian Lin College and University Town
Nanjing 210046
Tel: +86 (0)25 8589 9111
Fax: +86 (0)25 8589 9222
E-mail: enquiries@nanjing-school.com
Website: http://www.nanjing-school.com

International Schools in Shanghai

British International School of Shanghai

600 Cambridge Forest New Town
2729 Hunan Road
Pudong
Shanghai 201315
Tel: +86 (0)21 5812 7455
Fax: +86 (0)21 5812 7465
E-mail: principal@bisshanghai.com
Website: www.bisshanghai.com

Concordia International School (PK-12)

999 Ming Yue Road
JinQiao
Pudong
Shanghai 201206
US style teaching curriculum with a
   Christian emphasis
Estimated tuition and fees
   US$12,700–$21,300
Tel: +86 (0)21 5899 0380
Fax: +86 (0)21 5899 1685
E-mail: roberth@ciss.com.cn
Website: www.ciss.com.cn

Dulwich College International – Shanghai (Nursery–Year 9)

Recently opened new Main Campus which currently admits students up to Year 9. The school will eventually provide a complete Secondary Education. The Early Years students attend the DUCKS Campus just across the street from the new Main Campus. Dulwich College Shanghai is a franchise of the famous English public school with its main site in Dulwich, London. Former students include the famous author P.G. Wodehouse, Former Governor of the Bank of England Sir Eddie George, and many British actors (including Chiwetel Ejiofor) and politicians (Including Rt Hon Peter Lilley MP and Anand Panyarachun, who was twice Prime Minister of Thailand).
266 LanAn Road
JinQiao, Pudong
Shanghai 201206
Tel: +86 (0)21 5899 9910
Website: www.dulwichcollege.cn
E-mail: info@dulwichcollege.cn
Estimated tuition: US$2,600–$21,400

Deutsche Schule Shanghai (German School of Shanghai)

Together with the French School (EFS) the German School Shanghai (DSS) has built a new and innovative "Eurocampus" for about 1,000 students near HongQiao Airport.
German School of Shanghai
30 Zhu Guang Lu, Lane 399
Shanghai 201702, China
Tel: +86 (0)21 3976 0555
E-mail: info@ds-shanghai.org.cn
Website: www.ds-shanghai.org.cn

Ecole Francaise de Shanghai (3 yr–18 yr) (French School of Shanghai)

Located near Hong Qiao airport, the Shanghai French school shares its campus with the Shanghai German School.
30 Zhu Guang Lu, Lane 399
Shanghai 201702
Tel: +86 (0)21 3976 0555
Fax: +86 (0)21 3976 0577
Estimated tuition: US$3,000–US$12,000
Website: http://ef.shanghai.online.fr/
E-mail: rm.marchais@ef-shanghai.com

Shanghai American School – Puxi Campus (PK–12)

258 Jin Feng Lu
Zhudi Town, Minhang District
Shanghai 201107
Tel: +86 (0)21 6221 1445
Fax: +86 (0)21 6221 1269
E-mail: info@saschina.org
Websites: www.saschina.org
Puxi Elementary School: www.saschina.
   org/es
Puxi Middle School: www.saschina.
   org/sams
Puxi High School: www.saschina.org/hs
Accepts English-speaking students
Estimated tuition and fees
   US$11,500–$22,800

Shanghai American School – PuDongCampus (PK-8)
Shanghai Links Executive Community
San Jia Gang, Pudong
Shanghai 201201
Tel: +86 (0)21 6221 1445
Fax: +86 (0)21 5897 0011
E-mail: info@saschina.org
Pudong School: http://www.saschina.
  org/pudong/
Accepts English-speaking students
Estimated tuition and fees
  US$11,500–$22,800

Shanghai Community International Schools (PK–12)
Web-Site: www.scischina.org
E-mail: info@scischina.org

Pudong campus
800 Xiuyan Road
Kangqiao, Pudong
Shanghai 201315
Tel: +86 (0)21 5812 9888
Fax: +86 (0)21 5812 9000

HongQiao Campus
1161 Hongqiao Road
Shanghai 200051
US-based educational program in a small
  school environment.
Estimated tuition and fees
  US$8,000-$20,000
Tel: +86 (0)21 6261 4338
Fax: +86 (0)21 6261 4639

Shanghai Japanese School
3185 Hongmei Road, Hong Qiao
Japanese nationals only
Fees: approx. 80,000 Japanese yen per
month.
The school has over 700 Japanese
students.
Tuition fees for primary and middle school
are RMB 1,200 per month.
Tel: +86 (0)21 6401 2747
Fax: +86 (0)21 6401 2747

Shanghai Korean School
2999 Qi Xin Road
Korean nationals only

Shanghai Livingston American School (PK–12)
Curriculum and instruction are modeled
on the California public school system.
Estimated tuition: US$11,000– $18,500
580 GanXi Rd
ChangNing District
Shanghai 200336
Tel: +86 (0)21 6238 3511/5218 8372
Fax: +86 (0)21 5218 0390
Website: www.laschina.org
E-mail: info@laschina.org

Shanghai Rego International School
189 Dongzha Road
Minhang District
Shanghai 201100
Tel: +86 (0)21 6492 3431
Fax: +86 (0)21 6498 5072
E-mail: info@srisrego.com
Website: www.srisrego.com

Shanghai Singapore International School
301, Zhujian Road
MinHang District
Shanghai 201107
Tel: +86 (0)21 62219288
Fax: +86 (0)21 62219188
Website: www.ssis.cn

Sino-Canada High School
1 Liannan Rd
Luxu Town Wujiang
Suzhou, Jiangsu Province
215211
Tel: +86 (0)512 63262288
Fax: +86 (0)512 63262255
E-mail: info@sinocanada.cn
Website: www.sinocanada.cn

SMIC Private School (PK-12)
Semiconductor Manufacturing International Cooperation School
169 Qing-Tong Road
Pudong 201203
Tel: +86 (0)21 5855 4588, ext.230
Website: www.smic-school.cn
E-mail: Gregory_Jones@smicschool.com
English and Chinese track courses.
Currently has more then 500 students
  and 90 faculty members.

Estimated tuition: US$6,000– $9,000

Western International School of Shanghai – International School (American Curriculum)
555 Lian Min Road
Xujing Town, Qing Pu District
Shanghai 201702
Tel: +86 (0)21 6976 6388, 6976 6969
Fax: +86 (0)21 6976 6833
E-mail: admission@wiss.cn
Website: www.wiss.cn

International Schools in Shenzhen

Shekou International School
Jing Shan Villas, Nan Hai Road
Shekou, Shenzhen
Guangdong Province 518067
Te: +86 (0)755 2669 3669
Fax: +86 (0)755 2667 4099
E-mail: sis@sis.org.cn
E-mail: admissions@sis.org.cn
Website: www.sis.org.cn

QSI International School of Shenzhen (Shekou)
2nd Floor, Bitao Building
8 Tai Zi Road, Shekou
Shenzhen, Guangdong, 518069
Tel: +86 (0)755 2667 6030/ +86 (0)755 2667 6031
E-mail: Shenzhen@qsi.org
E-mail: Shekou@qsi.org

International Schools in Suzhou

Dulwich College International Suzhou
Opened in August 2007 with a registered 200 students, Dulwich College Suzhou is a franchise of the famous English public school with its main site in Dulwich, London. Former students include the famous author P.G. Wodehouse, Former Governor of the Bank of England Sir Eddie George, and many British actors (Including Chiwetel Ejiofor) and politicians.
360 Gangtian Road
Suzhou Industrial Park
Suzhou, Jiangsu Province
215021
Tel: +86 (0)512 67619073
Fax: +86 (0)512 67619083

E-mail: info@dcsuzhou.cn
Website: www.dulwichcollege.cn
Estimated tuition: US$2,600–$21,400

Suzhou Eton House International School
70 Jinshan Road
New District
Suzhou 215011
Tel: +86 (0)512 68255939
E-mail: enquiry@etonhouse-sz.com
Website: www.etonhouse-sz.com

Suzhou Singapore International School
82 Xing Han Street
Suzhou Industrial Park
Suzhou, Jiangsu 215021
Tel: +86 (0)512 676 10082
Fax: +86 (0)512 676 17699
E-mail: ssis@ssis-suzhou.com
Website: www.ssis-suzhou.com

International Schools in Tianjin

Teda International School
9 Xiao Yuan St.
TEDA
Tianjin
E-mail: tjtis@starinfo.net.cn
Website: www.tedainternationalschool. net

Tianjin International School
1 Meiyuan Road
Huayuan New Technology and Industrial Garden
Nankai District
Tianjin 300384
Tel: +86 (0)22 8371 0900
Fax: +86 (0)22 8371 0300
Website: www.tiseagles.com

The International School in Tianjin
Wei Shan Road Shuang Gang
Jin Nan Economic Development Zone
Jin Nan District
Tianjin 300350
Tel: +86 (0)22 2859 2001
Fax: +86 (0)22 2859 2007
E-mail: tist@public.tpt.tj.cn
Website: www.tistschool.org

Tianjin Rego International School
31 Zijin Shan Road
Hexi District
Tianjin
Tel: +86 (0)22 2334 3375
Fax: +86 (0)22 2353 3932
E-mail: info@regoschool.org
Website: www.regoschool.org

Other International Schools in China

Ningbo International School
Zhangshi, Zhenhai District
Ningbo
Zhejiang Province 315200
E-mail: johnturner@nbis.net.cn
Website: www.nbis.net.cn

Qingdao MTI International School
Children's Club
3rd Floor Children's Activity Center
6 Dong Hai Xi Road
Qingdao 266071
E-mail: qmis@qmischina.com
Website: www.qmischina.com

QSI International School in ChongQing
Chongqing University West Road
University Town, Shapingba
Chongqing 401331
Tel: +86 (0)23 65620109
Fax: +86 (0)23 65620105
E-mail: chongqing@qsi.org

QSI International School of Zhuhai
2 Longxing St.105 Gongbei
Zhuhai 51902
Tel: +86 (0)756 8156134
Fax: +86 (0)756 8189021
E-mail: Zhuhai@qsi.org

Xian Hi-Tech International School
Xi'an Hi Tech International School
New Industrial Park of Xi'an Hi-Tech
  Development Zone
Xi'an, Shaanxi
710119
E-mail: kevinblissett@etonhouse-xian.
  com
Website: www.etonhouse-xian.com

Law Firms in China

Law Firms in Beijing

Adamas Law Firm
Shenku Yard, Ritan Park
Chaoyang District PRC
100020 Beijing
Tel: +86 (0)10 8563 1202
Fax: +86 (0)10 8561 2433
Website: www.adamas-asia.com

Allen & Overy
Suite 522, China World Tower 2
1 Jian Guo Men Wai Avenue
Beijing 100004
Tel: +86 (0)10 6505 8800
Fax: +86 (0)10 6505 6677
Website: www.allenovery.com

Anderson & Anderson LLP
In Association with Zhonglun W&D Law
  Firm
Suite 701 Dachong Commercial Building
32 Xiaoyun Road
Chaoyang District
100005 Beijing
Tel: +86 (0)20 8386-3433
Fax: +86 (0)10 6463-1591
Website: www.anallp.net

Andrews Kurth LLP
Room 2007, Capital Mansion
6 Xinyuan Nanlu
Chaoyang District
100004 Beijing
Tel: +86 (0)10 8486 2699
Fax: +86 (0)10 8486 8565
Website: www.andrewskurth.com

Baker Botts L.L.P.
7-5-32 Qijiayuan Diplomatic Compound
9 Jianguomenwai Dajie
Beijing 100600
Tel: +86 (0)10 8532 7900
Fax: +86 (0)10 8532 7999
Website: www.bakerbotts.com

Baker & Daniels LLP
Room 1919, Tower 2
China World Trade Center
1 JianGuoMenWai Avenue

Beijing 100004
Tel: +86 (0)10 6505 7733
Fax: +86 (0)10 6505 8730
Website: www.bakerdaniels.com

Beiten Burkhardt
Suite 3130, 31st Floor, South Office Tower
Beijing Kerry Center
1 Guang Hua Road
Chao Yang District
Beijing 100020
Tel: +86 (0)10 8529 81 10
Fax: +86 (0)10 8529 81 23
Website: www.bblaw.com

Birindelli e Associates
Beijing Kerry Center
South Office Tower
Unit 3120, 1
Guanghua Road
Chaoyang District
Beijing 100020
Tel: +86 (0)10 8529 8111
Fax: +86 (0)10 8529 8112
Website: www.bea-law.com

Blake, Cassels & Graydon LLP
7 Dong Sanhuan Zhonglu
Suite 901, Office Tower A
Beijing Fortune Plaza
Chaoyang District
Beijing 100020
Tel: +86 (0)10 6530 9010
Fax: +86 (0)10 6530 9008
Website: www.blakes.com

Chadbourne & Parke LLP
Beijing Fortune Center
Room 902
Tower A, 7 Dongsanhuan Zhonglu
Chayoyang District
100020 Beijing
Tel: +86 (0)10 6530 8846
Fax: +86 (0)10 6530 8849
Website: www.chadbourne.com

Chang Tsi & Partners
Attorneys at Law and IP Attorneys
8th Floor Tower A
Hundred Island Park
Bei Zhan Bei Jie Street
Xicheng District

Beijing 100044
(Main Office)
Tel: +86 (0)10 8836 9999
Fax: +86 (0)10 8836 9996
Website: www.ctw.com.cn

Cleary Gottlieb Steen & Hamilton LLP
Twin Towers – West
12 B Jianguomen Wai Da Jie
Chaoyang District
100022 Beijing
Tel: +86 (0)10 5920 1000
Website: www.clearygottlieb.com

Clifford Chance LLP
3326 China World Tower 1
1 Jianguomenwai Dajie
Beijing 100004
Tel: +86 (0)10 6505 9018
Fax: +86 (0)10 6505 9028
Website: www.cliffordchance.com

C&M (China) Law Offices
CTS Tower, Suite 1610
2 Bei Sanhuan East Road
Beijing 100028
(Main Office)
Tel: +86 (0)10 64686688; 64685454
Fax: +86 (0)10 64612507; 64571392
E-mail: cmlo@cmlo.com.cn
Website: www.sinosino.com

Dewey Ballantine LLP
1 Jianguomenwai Avenue
Suite 1626
China World Trade Center
Beijing 100004
Tel: + 86 (0)10 6505 9486
Fax: + 86 (0)10 6505 0086

DLA Piper UK LLP
20th Floor, South Tower
Beijing Kerry Center
1 Guanghua Road
Chaoyang District
Beijing 100020
Tel: +86 (0)10 6561-1788
Fax: +86 (0)10 6561-5158
Website: www.dlapiper.com

Duan & Duan Lawyers
Suite 3506

Beijing Fortune Center
Middle Road East 3rd Ring
Beijing

Garvey Schubert Barer
820 South Tower
Beijing Kerry Center
1 Guang Hua Road
Chaoyang District
Beijing 100020
Tel: +86 (0)10 8529 9880
Fax: +86 (0)10 8529 9881
Website: www.GSBlaw.com

Heller Ehrman
Solicitors and International Lawyers
Suite 718, China World Tower 1
1 Jianguomenwai Avenue
Beijing 100004
Tel: +86 (0)10 5866 9738
Fax: +86 (0)10 5866 9739
Website: www.hellerehrman.com

Herbert Smith LLP
Units 1410-1415 China World Tower 1
1 Jianguomenwai Avenue
Beijing 100004
Tel: +86 (0)10 6505 6512
Fax: + 86 (0)10 6505 6516
Website: www.herbertsmith.com

Hogan & Hartson LLP
10th Floor, South Tower
Beijing Kerry Center
1 Guanghua Road
100020 Beijing
Tel: +86 (0)10 6598 8600
Fax: +86 (0)10 8529 7408
Website: www.hhlaw.com

Holland & Knight LLP
1206, 12th Floor, West Tower
Twin Towers
B-12 Jianguomenwai Avenue
Chaoyang District
100027 Beijing 100022
Tel: +86 (0)10 65661968; +86 (0)10 656
    61278
Fax: +86 (0)10 656 61258
Website: www.hklaw.com

Hunton & Williams LLP
517-520 South Office Tower
Beijing Kerry Center
1 Guanghua Road
Chaoyang District
Beijing 100020
Tel: +86 (0)10 5863 7500
Fax: +86 (0)10 5863 7591
Website: www.hunton.com

Johnson Stokes & Master
Suite 2918-2924, China World Tower 1
1 Jian Guo Men Wai Avenue
Beijing 100004
Tel: +86 (0)10 6505 2202
Fax: +86 (0)10 6505 2225
Website: www.jsm.com

Jones Day
3201 China World Tower 1
1 Jianguomenwai Avenue
Beijing 100004
Tel: +86 (0)10 5866 1111
Fax: +86 (0)10 5866 1122
Website: www.jonesday.com

Jun He Law Offices
China Resources Building
20th Floor
8 Jianguomenbei Avenue
Beijing 100005
(Main Office)
Tel: +86 (0)10 8519 1300
Fax: +86 (0)10 8519 1350
Website: www.junhe.com

Kingsound & Partners
11/Fl., Block B
KingSound International Center
116 Zizhuyuan Road
Haidian District
Beijing 100089
(Main Office)
Tel: +86 (0)10 5893 0011
Fax: +86 (0)10 5893 0022
Website: www.kingsound-ip.com.cn

King & Wood
40th Floor, Office Tower A
Beijing Fortune Plaza
7 Dongsanhuan Zhonglu
Chaoyang District

Beijing 100020
(Main Office)
Tel: +86 (0)10 5878 5588
Fax: +86 (0)10 5878 5599
Website: www.kingandwood.com

Kirkpatrick & Lockhart Preston Gates Ellis LLP
Suite 711-712, Tower W1
Oriental Plaza
1 East Chang An Avenue
100738 Beijing
Tel: +86 (0)10 8518 8528
Fax: +86 (0)10 8518 9299
Website: www.klgates.com

Kun Lun Law Firm
Suite A508, Nanxincang International
   Tower
A22 Dongsi Shitiao
Dongcheng, Beijing
Tel: +86 (0)10 64096455
Fax: +86 (0)10 64096437
E-mail: beijing@kunlunlaw.com
Website: www.kunlunlaw.com

LeBoeuf, Lamb, Greene & MacRae LLP
A Limited Liability Partnership
including Professional Corporations
Formerly LeBoeuf, Lamb, Leiby & MacRae
Room B8, 21st Floor, Hanwei Plaza
7 Guanghau Road
Chaoyang District
Beijing 10004
Tel: +86 (0)10 6561 0422
Fax: +86 (0)10 6561 0425
Website: www.llgm.com

Lehman, Lee & Xu
(International Law & Practice Group)
China Lawyers, Patent & Trademark
   Agents
10-2 Liangmaqiao Diplomatic
   Compound
22 Dongfang East Road
Chaoyang District
Beijing 100600
(Main Office)
Tel: +86 (0)10 8532 1919
Fax: +86 (0)10 8532 1999
Website: www.lehmanlaw.com

Liu, Shen & Associates
Hanhai Plaza (1+1 Plaza)
10th Floor, 10 Caihefang Road
Haidian District
Beijing 100080
(Main Office)
Tel: +86 (0)10 6268 0066
Fax: +86 (0)10 6268 1818
Website: www.liu-shen.com

Lovells
Level 2
Office Tower C2
The Towers, Oriental Plaza
1 East Chang An Avenue
Dongcheng District
Beijing 100738
Tel: +86 (0)10 8518 4000
Fax: +86 (0)10 8518 1656
Website: www.lovells.com

Milbank, Tweed, Hadley & McCloy LLP
Twin Towers (East)
B 12 Jiangoumenwai Avenue
10th Floor, Suites 29-31
Beijing 100022
Tel: +86 (0)10 5123 5120
Fax: +86 (0)10 5123 5191
Website: www.milbank.com

Morgan, Lewis & Bockius LLP
Beijing Kerry Center North Tower
Suite 2005, 20th Floor
1 Guang Hua Road
Chaoyang District
Beijing 100020
Tel: +86 (0)10 5876 3500
Fax: +86 (0)10 5876 3501
Website: www.morganlewis.com

Morrison & Foerster LLP
Suite 3408
China World Tower 2
1 Jian Guo Men Wai Avenue
100004 Beijing
Tel: +86 (0)10 6505 9090
Fax: +86 (0)10 6505 9091
Website: www.mofo.com.cn

O'Melveny & Myers LLP
31F, China World Tower 1
1 Jianguomenwai Avenue

Beijing 100004
Tel: +86 (0)10 6535 4200
Fax: +86 (0)10 6535 4201
Website: www.omm.com

Paul, Hastings, Janofsky & Walker
Suite 1101, China World Tower 1
1 Jian Guo Men Wai Avenue
Beijing 100004
Tel: +86 (0)10 6535 5300
Fax: +86 (0)10 6505 3459
Website: www.paulhastings.com/offices_
  beijing.aspx

**Paul, Weiss, Rifkind, Wharton &
Garrison LLP**
Unit 3601, Fortune Plaza Office
Tower A, No. 7 Dong Sanhuan Zhonglu
Chao Yang District
Beijing 100020
Tel: +86 (0)10 5828 6300
Fax: +86 (0)10 6530 9070/9080
Website: www.paulweiss.com

Shearman & Sterling LLP
12th Floor East Tower, Twin Towers
B-12 Jianguomenwai Dajie
Beijing 100022
Tel: +86 (0)10 5922 8000
Fax: +86 (0)10 6563 6000
Website: www.shearman.com

Simpson Thacher & Bartlett LLP
29/F China Merchants Tower
118, Jianguo Road
Chaoyang District
Beijing 100022
Tel: +86 (0)10 8567 2999
Fax: +86 (0)10 8567 2988

**Skadden, Arps, Slate, Meagher & Flom
LLP**
East Wing Office, Level 4
China World Trade Center
1 Jian Guo Men Wai Avenue
100004 Beijing
Tel: +86 (0)10 6505 5511
Fax: +86 (0)10 6505 5522
Website: www.skadden.com

Squire, Sanders & Dempsey L.L.P.
25th Floor, North Tower

Suite 2501
Beijing Kerry Center
1 Guang Hua Road
Chaoyang District
Beijing 100020
Tel: +86 (0)10 8529 6998
Fax: +86 (0)10 8529 8088
Website: www.ssd.com

Sullivan & Cromwell LLP
Suite 501, China World Trade Center
1 Jianguo Menwei Avenue
Beijing 100004
Tel: +86 (0)10 5923 5900
Fax: +86 (0)10 5923 5950
Website: www.sullcrom.com

TransAsia Lawyers
Suite 2218, China World Tower 1
1 Jianguomenwai Avenue
Beijing 100004
(Main Office)
Tel: +86 (0)10 6505 8188
Fax: +86 (0)10 6505 8198
Website: www.transasialawyers.com

Vinson & Elkins LLP
20/F, Beijing Silver Tower
2, Dong San Huan Bei Lu
Chaoyang District
Beijing 100027
Tel: +86 (0)10 6410 6300
Fax: +86 (0)10 6410 6360
Website: www.velaw.com

Vivien Chan & Co.
Solicitors & Notaries
Agents for Trade Marks & Patents
China-Appointed Attesting Officer
Changan Tower
Suite 508
10 East Changan Street
Beijing 100006
Tel: +86 (0)10 6522 7069
Fax: +86 (0)10 6522 6967
Website: www.vcclawservices.com

Wang & Wang
A Limited Liability Partnership
B1207, Huixin Plaza
8 Beishihuan Zhong Road
Chaoyang District

Beijing 100101
Tel: +86 (0)10 6493 3139
Fax: +86 (0)10 6499 3036
Website: www.wangandwang.com

White & Case
Limited Liability Partnership
Beijing International Club Office Tower
9th Fl., 21 Jian Guo Men Wai Street
Beijing 100020
Tel: +86 (0)10 8532 9800
Fax: +86 (0)10 6532 6720
Website: www.whitecase.com

Wilmer Cutler Pickering Hale and Dorr LLP
1206 North Tower
Beijing Kerry Center
1 Guanghua Road
Beijing 100020
Tel: +86 (0)10 8529 7588
Fax: +86 (0)10 8529 7566
Website: www.wilmerhale.com

Wright & Kou
Full Tower, Suite 908
9 East Third Ring Road
Chaoyang District
Beijing 100020
(Main Office)
Tel: +86 (0)10 8591 0295
Fax: +86 (0)10 8591 0297

Law Firms in Chengdu

Chengdu Public Notary office
35 Dong Cheng Gen Xia St
Chengdu, Sichuan
Tel: +86 (0)28 86696320

King & Wood Lawyers
22/F, City Tower
86 Section One
Renminnanlu
Chengdu 610016
Tel: +86 (0)28 8620 3818
Fax: +86 (0)28 8620 3819/3820

Law Firms in Chongqing

King & Wood Lawyers
Room 2, 18th Floor

Metropolitan Tower
68 Zourong Road
Chongqing 400010
Tel: +86 (0)23 6371 5199
Fax: +86 (0)23 6371 5399

Law Firms in Dalian

Jun He Lawyers
International Finance Tower
Suite F, 16th Floor
15 Remin Road
Dalian 116001
Tel: +86 (0)411 8250 7578
Fax: +86 (0)411 8250 7579
E-mail: junhedl@junhe.com

Law Firms in Guangzhou

Adamas Law Firm
c/o Wang Jing & Co. Law Firm
Room 1402, 14/F, South Tower
World Trade Center
371-375 Huan Shi Dong Road
Guangzhou 510095
Tel: +86 (0)20 8778 0330
Fax: +86 (0)20 8778 1800
E-mail: guangzhou@adamas-asia.com

Anderson & Anderson LLP
In Association with Guangdong Hong An
   Xin Law Firm
Suite 3901, 39th Floor
Profit Tower
76 West Huangpu Avenue
Tianhe District
Guangzhou 510623
Tel: +86 (0)20 3839 2008
Fax: +86 (0)20 3839 2009
Website: www.anallp.net

C & I Partners
Unit A, 11/F International Trade Centre
1 Linhe Xi Road, Guangzhou 510820
Tel: +86 (0)20 3878 3750
Fax: +86 (0)20 3878 3066

David Y Y Fung & Co
Unit B, 15/F Guangdong International
   Hotel
Tower A
339 Huan Shi Dong Road

Guangzhou 510098
Tel: +86 (0)20 83311000 / 83311622 /
83311657
Fax: +86 (0)208331 1135

Guangdong Huanyu Law Firm
Rm 2216, CITIC Plaza
233 North Tianhe Road
Guangzhou 510620
Tel: +86 (0)20 3891 2641
Fax: +86 (0)20 3891 2645

Guangzhou Overseas Chinese Law Office
472 Dongfeng Dong Road
Guangzhou 510050
Tel: +86 (0)20 8383 1026
Fax: +86 (0)20 8386 4920

Guangzhou Yuexiu District Notary Public Office
1/F, 3/F, Jiguan Office Building
483, Huifu East Rd
Yuexiu, Guangzhou
Tel: +86 (0)20 8317 8376

Guang Zhi Zhou Law Office
5/F, Huayu Building, 113 Xiao Bei Road
Guangzhou 510030
Tel: +86 (0)20 8355 4168
Fax: +86 (0)20 8356 0753

King & Wood Law Firm
54/F CITIC Plaza
233 Tianhe Road North
Guangzhou 510613
Tel: +86 (0)20 3891 1000
Fax: +86 (0)20 3891 2082/2083.

Kun Lun Law Firm
Suite 1906, China Mayors Plaza
189 Tianhe Bei Road
Guangzhou
Tel: +86 (0)20 87556180
Fax: +86 (0)20 87551834
E-mail: kllaw@kunlunlaw.com
Website: www.kunlunlaw.com

Lehman, Lee & Xu
Suite 418-2
Goldlion Digital Network Center
138 Tiyu Road East
Tianhe District

Guangzhou 510620
Tel: +86 (020) 8511 8683
Fax: +86 (020) 3878-1801
E-mail: guangzhou@lehmanlaw.com

Stephenson Harwood & Lo
Jeremy Sargent (British Consulate
    General Honorary Legal Adviser)
1907 Peace World Plaza
362-366 Huanshi Road East
Guangzhou 510060
Tel: +86 (0)20 8387 8965
Fax: +86 (0)20 8386 3119

Trust Law Firm
21-22F, Guangdong Holding Tower
555 Dongfeng Road
Guangzhou 510050
Tel: +86 (0)20 8385 5488 8385 7615
Fax: +86 (0)208385 1444

Wang Jing & Co. Law Firm
14/F, South Tower
World Trade Centre
371-375 Huan Shi Dong Road
Guangzhou 510095
Tel: +86 (0)20 8760 0082
Fax: +86 (0)20 8778 4482

Law Firms in Hainan

Jun He Lawyers
Nanyang Building
Suite 1107
Binhai Avenue
Haikou
Hainan 570105
Tel: +86 (0)898 6851 2544
Fax: +86 (0)898 6851 3514
E-mail: junhehn@junhe.com

Law Firms in Hangzhou

King & Wood
Room 810-812
Jiahua International Business Center
15 Hangda Road Hangzhou
Zhejiang Province 310007
Tel: +86 (0)571 8993 5988
Fax: +86 (0)571 8993 5989

Law Firms in Qingdao

Baker & Daniels LLP
4/F, Office Tower
Crowne Plaza Qingdao
76 Hong Kong Middle Road
266071 Qingdao
Tel: +86 (0)532 575 1051
Fax: +86 (0)532 575 1055
Website: www.bakerdaniels.com.cn

Law Firms in Shanghai

Adamas Law Firm
Suite 608 Dynasty Business Centre
457 Urumqi Road North
Jing An District
Shanghai 200040
Tel: +86 (0)21 6249 0302
Fax: +86 (0)21 6249 0501
E-mail: shanghai@adamas-asia.com

Allen & Overy, Shanghai Office
18th Floor, Bank of Shanghai Tower
168 Yin Cheng Middle Road
Pudong
Shanghai 200120
Tel: +86 (0)21 3896 5000
Fax: +86 (0)21 3896 5050
Website: www.allenovery.com

Anderson & Anderson LLP
Room 111, Guo Lin Business Center
233 Rushan Road
Pudong New District
Shanghai
Tel: +86 (0)21 5081 5956
Fax: +86 (0)21 5081 6125
Website: www.anallp.net

**Beiten Burkhardt
Rechtsanwälte (German
    Attorneys-at-Law)**
Suite 3503, 35th Floor
The Center
989 Chang Le Road
Xuhui District
Shanghai 200031
Tel: +86 (0)21 5407 5557
Fax: +86 (0)21 5407 5559
Website: www.bblaw.com

Birindelli e Associates
Shanghai Kerry Center
Unit 506
1515 Nanjing West Road
Shanghai 200040
(Main Office)
Tel: +86 (0)21 5298 5060
Fax: +86 (0)21 5298 5061
Website: www.bea-law.com

Clifford Chance LLP
40/F Bund Center
222 Yan An East Road
Shanghai 200002
Tel: +86 (0)21 6335 1855
Fax: +86 (0)21 6335 0337
Website: www.CliffordChance.com

DLA Piper UK LLP
Level 28, Suites 2807 - 2810
Bank of China Tower
200 Yin Cheng Middle Road
Pudong New Area
Shanghai 200120
Tel: +86 (0)21 5037 2726
Fax: +86 (0)21 5037 2268
Website: www.dlapiper.com

Duan & Duan
Shartex Plaza
Suite 1700
88 Zun Yi Nan Road
200336 Shanghai
(Main Office)
Tel: +86 (0)21 6219 1103
Fax: +86 (0)21 6275 2273
Website: www.duanduan.com

Herbert Smith LLP
Herbert has a formal alliance with the
    leading
German firm Gleiss Lutz and
the leading Dutch and Belgian firm
    Stibbe.
38/F Bund Center, 222 Yan An Road East
Shanghai 200002
Tel: +86 (0)21 6335 1144
Fax: +86 (0)21 6335 1145
Website: www.herbertsmith.com

Hogan & Hartson LLP
Raffles City, Suite 3006

268 Xi Zang Zhong Road
200001 Shanghai
Tel: +86 (0)21 6340 4666
Fax: +86 (0)21 6340 4999
Website: www.hhlaw.com

Jin Mao Law Firm
18/F & 21/F Universal Mansion
168 Yu Yuan Road
Shanghai 200040
(Main Office)
Tel: +86 (0)21 6249 6040
Fax: +86 (0)21 6249 5611
Website: www.jinmao.com.cn

Johnson Stokes & Master
Suite 2501-2504
Plaza 66
1266, Nanjing Road West
Shanghai 200040
Tel: +86 (0)21 6288 0688
Fax: +86 (0)21 6288 0131
Website: www.jsm.com

Jones Day
30th Floor
Shanghai Kerry Centre
1515 Nanjing Road West
Shanghai 200040
Tel: +86 (0)21 2201 8000
Fax: +86 (0)21 5298 6569
Website: www.jonesday.com

Jun He Lawyers
Shanghai Kerry Center
32nd Floor
1515 Nanjing Road West
Shanghai 200040
Tel: +86 (0)21 5298 5488
Fax: +86 (0)21 5298 5492
E-mail: junhesh@junhe.com

King & Wood Lawyers
28-29/F, Huai Hai Plaza
1045 Huai Hai Road (M)
Shanghai 200031
Tel: +86 (0)21 2412 6000
Fax: +86 20 2412 6150

Kun Lun Law Firm
Suite F, 13th Floor
Hua Min Empire Plaza

728 Yan An Xi Road
Shanghai
Tel: +86 (0)21 62113098
Fax: +86 (0)21 62112108

Lehman, Lee & Xu
(International Law & Practice Group)
China Lawyers
Patent & Trademark Agents
Suite 209-210
Kerry Centre
1515 West Nanjing Road
Shanghai 200040
Tel: +86 (0)21 5298 5252
Fax: +86 (0)21 6288 2699
Website: www.lehmanlaw.com

Lovells
11th Floor
Shanghai Kerry Centre
1515 Nanjing West Road
Shanghai 200040
Tel: +86 (0)21 6279 3155
Fax: + 86 (0)21 6279 2695
Website: www.lovells.com

Morrison & Foerster LLP
Bund Center
Suite 3803
No. 222 Yan An Road
Huangpu District
Shanghai 200002
Tel: +86 (0)21 6335 2290
Fax: +86 (0)21 6335 2291
Website: www.mofo.com.cn

O'Melveny & Myers LLP
Plaza 66, Tower 1
37th Floor
1266 Nanjing Road West
Shanghai 200040
Tel: +86 (0)21 2307 7000
Fax: +86 (0)21 2307 7300
Website: www.omm.com

Paul, Hastings, Janofsky & Walker LLP
2301 Hong Kong New World Tower
300 Huai Hai Middle Road
200021 Shanghai
Tel: +86 (0)21 6103 2900
Fax: +86 (0)21 6103 2990

Website: www.paulhastings.com/offices_
shanghai.aspx

Squire, Sanders & Dempsey L.L.P.
Suite 1207, 12th Floor
Shanghai Kerry Centre
1515 Nanjing Road West
Shanghai 200040
Tel: +86 (0)21 6103 6300
Fax: +86 (0)21 6103 6363
Website: www.ssd.com

TransAsia Lawyers
Unit 1101 Platinum
233 Tai Cang Road
Shanghai 200020
Tel: +86 (0)21 6141 0998
Fax: +86 (0)21 6141 0995
Website: www.transasialawyers.com

Vivien Chan & Co.
The Headquarters Building
Suite 1002
168 Central Tibet Road
Shanghai 200001
Tel: +86 (0)21 6387 9222
Fax: +86 (0)21 6387 9111
Website: www.vcclawservices.com

Wang & Wang
A Limited Liability Partnership
580 Nan Jing West Road 2308
Shanghai 200041
Tel: +86 (0)21 523 40739
Fax: +86 (0)21 523 40672
Website: www.wangandwang.com

White & Case
Limited Liability Partnership
(0)218 Shanghai Bund
12 Building
12 Zhongshan Dong Yi Road
Shanghai 200002
Tel: +86 (0)21 6321 2200
Fax: +86 (0)21 6323-9252
Website: www.whitecase.com

Win and Sun Law Firm
11F, Tongsheng Tower
458 Fushan Road
Shanghai 200042
Tel: +86 (0)21 50819091

Fax: +86 (0)21 50819091
Website: www.winandsun.com
E-mail: info@winandsun.com

Law Firms in Shenzhen

Anderson & Anderson LLP
In Association with Jun Ze Jun Law Firm
Suite 34D, Noble Centre
1006 3rd Fu Zhong Road
Futian District
Shenzhen 518026
Tel: +86 (0)20 8386-3433
Fax: +86 (0)755 8298 7171
Website: www.anallp.net

Guangdong Kingdom Law Firm
18/F CEC Information Tower
Xinwen Road 1st, Fu Tian District
Shenzhen 518034
Tel: +86 (0)755 82947336
Fax: +86-(0)755 82947500
Website: www.law12.com

Guangdong Zhiming Law Firm
Rm 1319, 13th Floor
Xincheng Building
1027 Shennan Zhong Road
Shenzhen 518031
Fax: +86 (0)755 2495818
Tel: +86 (0)755 2495818, +86 (0)755
    2061602, +86 (0)755 2061920
E-mail: wangltf@public.szonline.net
Website: www.zhiminglawyer.com

Jun He Lawyers
Shenzhen Development Bank Tower
Suite 15-C, 5047 East Shennan Road
Shenzhen 518001
Tel: +86 (0)755 2587 0765
Fax: +86 (0)755 2587 0780
E-mail: junhesz@junhe.com

King & Wood Lawyers
47/F, Shun Hing Square
Di Wang Commercial Centre
5002 Shennan Road East
Shenzhen 518008
Tel: +86 (0)755 8212 5533/5599
Fax: +86 (0)755 8212 5580/5590

Kun Lun Law Firm
Suite 25C, Special Zone Press Tower
6008 Shennan Road
Shenzhen
Tel: +86 (0)755 83515955
Fax: +86 (0)755 83515277
Website: www.kunlunlaw.com

Lehman, Lee & Xu
(International Law & Practice Group)
China Lawyers, Patent & Trademark
  Agents
Suite 810 Excellence Times Square
4068 Yitian Road
Futian District
Shenzhen 518048
Tel: +86 (0)755 2399 6188
Fax: +86 (0)755 8209 6738
Website: www.lehmanlaw.com

Sylvester & Associates Co. Ltd
103, Hai Jing Ge, Nanhai Garden
Xing Nan Road
Nanshan District
Shenzhen 518054
Tel: +86 (0)755 2686 7423/ 2607 2150/
  2607 2250
Fax: +86 (0)755 2643 1049
Website: www.sylvester-associates.com

Win and Sun Law Firm
Floor21, Industrial Bank Building
4013 Shennan Road
Guangdong Province
Shenzhen 518048
Tel: +86 (0)755 83026386/ 83026389
Fax: +86 (0)755 83026828/ 83026990
Website: www.winandsun.com
E-mail: info@winandsun.com

Law Firms in Xian

King & Wood
Room 333, 3rd Floor
Hyatt Regency Xian
158 Dong Da Street
Xi'an
Shaanxi 710001
Tel: +86 (0)29 8769 1499
Fax: +86 (0)29 8769 1377

Relocation Companies in China

AGS Four Winds
www.agsfourwings.com
Has offices in major cities on the
  mainland
5/F Len Shing Industrial Centre
4, A Kung Ngam Village Road
Shaukeiwan
Hong Kong
Tel: +852 2 885 9666
Fax: +852 2 567 7594
E-mail: enquiries-hongkong@
  agsfourwinds.com

Allied Pickfords
www.alliedpickfords.com.cn
Allied Pickfords Beijing Office
812, Building A
The Spaces International Center
Chaoyang District
Beijing 100020
Tel: +86 (0)10 5870 1133
Fax: +86 (0)10 5870 0818
Email: enquiry@alliedpickfords.com.cn

Allied Pickfords Shanghai Office
Room 801
268 Zhongshan Nan Road
New Resources Plaza
Shanghai 200010
Tel: +86 (0)21 6332 3322
Fax: +86 (0)21 6332 2998
Email: enquiry@alliedpickfords.com.cn

Asia Pacific Access
www.apachina.com
(HQ in Beijing, offices in Shanghai and
  Guangzhou)
Beijing Ancient Observatory
Jianguomen Bridge South-West Corner
Beijing 100005
Tel: +86 (0)10 6512 9996
Fax: +86 (0)10 8561 8756
E-mail: info@apachina.com

Asian Express
www.aemovers.com.hk
Has offices in all major cities on the
  mainland
Asian Express Hong Kong (China HQ)
26th Floor Two Chinachem Plaza
68 Connaught Road Central

Two Chinachem Plaza
Hong Kong
Tel: +852 2893-1000
Fax: +852 2311-3036
E-mail: hongkong@aemovers.com.hk

Asian Tigers K.C. Dat (China) Ltd
www.asiantigersgroup.com
CHINA HQ (Beijing)
Room 302, Grand Rock Plaza
13 Xinzhongxili,
Dongcheng District
Beijing 100027
Tel: +86 (0)10 6415 1188
Fax: +86 (0)10 6417 9579
E-mail: general.pek@asiantigers-china.
 com

Baltrans International Moving
www.bim.com.hk
BALtrans International Cargo Ltd (Beijing)
B11, 16/F, Han Wei Plaza
7 Guang Hua Road
Chao Yang District
Beijing 100004
Tel: +86 (0)10 65614171
Fax: +86 (0)10 65614170
E-mail: baltrans@95777.com

BALtrans International Moving (Hong
 Kong)
Unit 1510, 15/F
Ocean Center
5 Canton Road
Tsim Sha Tsui
Kowloon, Hong Kong
Tel: +852 2756 2882
Fax: +852 2759 9772/ 2148 6712
E-mail: contact@bim.com.hk

BALtrans International Moving (Shanghai)
Block A, 5/Fl
C & E Building,
1898 Tian Shan Road
Shanghai, 200051.
Tel: +86 (0)21 62281933
Fax: +86 (0)21 62293933
E-mail: balshb@online.sh.cn

Beijing Airfreight Forwarding
Company
Xibinhe Lu
Anwai
Beijing

Tel: +86 (0)10 422 5670

Beijing Friendship Packing and
Transportation Company
5 Xiliu Jie Sanlitun
Beijing
Tel: +86 (0)10-532-4375/532-4827

China Brother Co.
www.brotherchina.com.cn
Tel: +86 (0)10-80753488
Fax: +86 (0)10 81733388
E-mail: wht@brotherchina.com.cn

Columbia International Removals
www.columbia-removals.com.hk
Specializes in international & local
household removals, fine art services,
office relocation, household items
& documents storage, total logistics
solutions
Room 2213 Hong Kong Plaza
188 Connaught Road West
Hong Kong
Tel: +852 2547-6228
Fax: +852 2858-2418
E-mail: info@columbia-removals.com.hk

Crown Relocations
www.crownrelo.com
Have warehouses and offices in 8 satellite
cities in China (and Hong Kong), all of
which have connections to any city or
town within Greater China.

Crown Relocations Beijing Office
Room 201, West Tower
Golden Bridge Bldg.
A1 Jianguomenwai Dajie
Beijing 100020
Tel: +86 (0)10-65850640
Fax: +86 (0)10-65850648

Crown Relocations Hong Kong (China
 HQ)
Crown Worldwide Building
9-11 Yuen On Street
Siu Lek Yuen
Shatin, N.T.
Hong Kong
Tel: +852 2636 8388
Fax: +852 2637 1677
Email: china@crownrelo.com

Elite8 China (Relocation experts around Shanghai and Beijing)
www.elite8china.com.cn
16F, Hua Min Empire Plaza
726 Yan'An West Road
Shanghai 200050
Tel: +86 (0)21 6211 8911x888
Fax: +86 (0)21 6211 2707**King's Mover International (KMI)**
www.kingsmoverintl.com
King's Mover International (CHINA HQ)
1, Huatianyuan, Xiba,
Dongbaxiang, Chaoyang District,
Beijing 100018
Toll Free: 800 810 0898
Tel: + 86 (0)10 8432 7267
Fax: + 86 (0)10 8432 7263
Email: kmi@kingsmoverintl.com

King's Mover International (Shanghai)
Room 1615, Building 1, Tianbaohuating,
775, Siping Road
Hongkou District,
Shanghai 200092
Toll Free: 800 810 0898
Tel: +86 (0)21 65756707
Fax: +86 (0)21 65083425
Email: shanghai@kingsmoverintl.com

Kuehne & Nagel Global Relocation
www.kuehne-nagel.com
Kuehne & Nagel Beijing Office
26 Xiaoyun Road
Beijing, Chaoyang District
Beijing 100016
Tel: +86 (0)10 84580908
Fax: +86 (0)10 84585315
info.beijing@kuehne-nagel.com

Kuehne + Nagel Hong Kong (**Asia Pacific HQ**)
38 Gloucester Road
Wanchai
Hong Kong
Tel: +852 2823 7688
Fax: +852 2527 8396
E-mail: info.hongkong@kuehne-nagel.com

Links Relocations
www.linksrelo.com
Links Relocation Hong Kong Office
Rm. A-C, 11/F, Champion Building,
287-291 Des Voeux Road

Central, Hong Kong
Tel: +852 2366 6700
Fax: +852 2366 6400
Email: links@linksrelo.com

Links Relocation Shanghai Office
Rm. 3309, 3rd Floor, East Wing,
Harbour Building
1 Feng He Road,
Pu Dong, Shanghai,
China 200120
Tel: +86 (0)21 5882 2282
Fax: +86 (0)21 5882 2810
Email: shanghai@linksrelo.com

Overseas Moving Network International (OMNI)
Santa Fe Relocation Services Co. Ltd.
www.santaferelo.com
Santa Fe Relocation Beijing Office
2, Street No. 8
Beijing Airport Logistics Zone
Beijing 101300
Tel: +86 (0)10 6947 0688
Fax: +86 (0)10 6947 0699
E-mail: beijing@santafe.com.cn

Santa Fe Relocation Guangzhou Office
Room 1307-9
West Tower
Guangzhou International Commercial Centre
Ti Yu Dong Road
Guangzhou 510620
Tel: +86 (0)20 3887 0630
Fax: +86 (0)20 3887 0629
E-mail: guangzhou@santafe.com.cn

Santa Fe Relocation Hong Kong Office
18/F, C.C. Wu Building
302-8 Hennessy Road
Wanchai, Hong Kong
Tel: +852 2574 6204
Fax: +852 2834 5380
E-mail: sales@santafe.com.hk

Santa Fe Relocation Shanghai Office
5th Floor
Tian Hong Building
80 Xian Xia Road
Shanghai 200336
Tel: +86 (0)21 6233 9700
Fax: +86 (0)21 6233 9005
E-mail: shanghai@santafe.com.cn

Primacy Relocation
www.primacy.com
Primacy Shanghai Office
20F, The Centre
989 Changle Rd.
Shanghai 200031
Tel: +86 (0)21 5117 5858
Fax: +86 (0)21 5116 6899
E-mail: Info.Asia@primacy.com

Primacy Hong Kong Office
Suites 609-610
100 Queens Rd. Central
Hong Kong
Tel: +852 3470 0001
Fax: +852 3470 0030
E-mail: Info.Asia@primacy.com

Relocasia
www.relocasia.com
Relocasia Hong Kong Office
F2, 13F
Gee Tung Cheong Ind Building
4 Fung Yip Street
Chai Wan
Hong Kong
Tel: +852 2976 9969
Fax: +852 2976 9947
E-mail: enquiry@relocasia.com

Relocasia Shanghai Office
16th Floor
258 Wei Hai Road
South Wing
Merchant Plaza
Shanghai
Tel: +86 (0)21 5228 3076
Fax: +86 (0)21 5228 3061
E-mail: enquiry@relocasia.com

Sinotrans Global Freight
www.sinotrans.com
Sinotrans Beijing Head Office
Sinotrans Plaza
Xizhimen North St.
Beijing 100044
(Sea Freight) Tel: +86 (0)10 465 2354
(Rail Freight) Tel: +86 (0)10 381 4440
(Air Cargo) Tel: +86 (0)10 501 1014
(Exhibition Transport) Tel: +86 (0)10 467 1713

Contact Details for Airlines in China – Passenger

Air China
IATA Code: CA
Corporate website: www.airchina.com. cn
Corporate HQ (Beijing)
Beijing international post office
PO BOX 100600-6606
Beijing 100600
Global Sales Hotline: +86 4008 100 999
Tel: +86 (0)10 6459 5912
Fax: +86 (0)10 8479 8686

Air Macau
IATA Code: NX
Corporate website: www.airmacau. com.mo
Air Macau Beijing Office
8/F, 22 Jian Guo Men Wai Da Jie
CVIK
Beijing
Tel: +86 (0)10 6515 8988
Tel: +86 (0)10 6515 9398
Fax: +86 (0)10 6515 9979

Air Macau Guangzhou Office
Room 220, Comprehensive Business Building
Airport Logistic Zone, West Side, North Exit Avenue
Baiyun International Airport
Guangzhou 510470
Tel: +86 (0)20 3607 0399
Fax: +86 (0)20 3607 0265

Air Macau Shanghai Office
Rm 302, Shanghai International Equatorial Hotel
65 Yan An Road West Shanghai PRC
Tel: +86 (0)21 6248 1110
Fax: +86 (0)21 6248 7870

Air Macau Shenzhen Office
Room 1101, Hualian Bldg.
2008 Shennan Middle Road, Futian
Shenzhen 51828
Tel: +86 (0)755 2777-3728/3738
Fax: +86 (0)755 2777 0787

**Cathay Pacific Airways (IATA Code: CX)/
Dragonair (IATA Code: KA)
(Dragon is a subsidiary of Cathay
   Pacific Airways)
Cathay Pacific Airways Corporate
   website: www.cathaypacific.com
Dragonair Corporate website: www.
   dragonair.com**
Cathay Pacific Airways/Dragonair
   – Beijing Office
28/F, East Tower, Twin Towers
B-12 Jianguomenwai Avenue
Chaoyang District
Beijing 100022
Tel: 400-88-10288 (within China only)
Tel: +86 (0)10) 6459 0038
Tel: 10800-852-1888 (China Netcom
   Group)
Tel: 10800-152-1888 (China Telecom
   Group)
Fax: +86 (0)10 5905 7730

Cathay Pacific Airways/Dragonair
   – Guangzhou Office
M02, Garden Hotel,
368 Huanshi Dong Lu,
Guangzhou
Tel: 400-88-10288 (within China only)
Fax: +86 (0)20 8383 8478

Cathay Pacific Hong Kong (CorporateHQ)
10/F, Peninsula Office Tower
18 Middle Road
Tsim Sha Tsui, Kowloon
Hong Kong
Tel: +852 2747 1888
Fax: +852 2560 1411

Dragonair Hong Kong (Corporate HQ)
Unit 4601-05, 46/F
Cosco Tower
183 Queen's Road
Central
Hong Kong
Tel: +852 3193-3888
Fax: +852 3193 3889

Cathay Pacific Airways/Dragonair
   – Shanghai Office
Room 2101-2104
Shanghai Square Office Tower

138 Huai Hai Zhong Road
Shanghai
Tel: 40088-10288 (within China only)
Tel: +86 (0)21 6375 6375
Fax: +86 (0)21 6375 6700

**China Eastern Airlines
IATA Code: MU
Corporate website: www.ce-air.com**
Shanghai International Airport Co., Ltd.
900 Qihang Road
Pudong Airport
Shanghai 201202

**China Southern Airlines
IATA Code: CZ
Corporate website: www.cs-air.com**
Bai Yun Airport,
International Affairs Dept.,
Guangzhou City,
510406
Tel: +86 (0)20 8668 2000

**East Star Airlines
IATA Code: 8C
Corporate website: www.eaststar-air.
   com**
Wuhan, Hubei
People's Republic of China
Tel hotline: +86 (0)27 95151

**Hainan Airlines
IATA Code: HU
Corporate website: www.hnair.com**
A-6th floor of HNA Development
   Building
29 Haixiu Road, Haikou
Hainan Island
Tel: +86 (0)898 66739684/ 66739224
Fax: +86 (0) 898 66739634

**Heli Express Ltd
Corporate website: www.heliexpress.
   com**
Room 1603
16/F China Merchants Tower
Shun Tak Centre
200 Connaught Road Central
Hong Kong
Tel: +852 2108 9988
Fax: +852 2108 9938

Hong Kong Airlines
IATA Code: HX
Corporate website: www.hkairlines.com
L2, CNAC House
12 Tung Fai Road,
HK International Airport
Lantau
Hong Kong
Tel: +852 2559 1966
Fax: +852 2215 3028

Hong Kong Express Airways
IATA Code: UO
Corporate website: www.hongkongexpress.com
7th Floor, One Citygate
20 Tat Tung Road,
Tung Chung, Lantau,
Hong Kong
Tel: +852 3151 1888

Juneyao Airlines
IATA Code: HO
Corporate website: www.juneyaoairlines.com
Tel: +86 (0)21 51116511
24 Hour hotline: 4007006000 (within China only)

Lucky Air
IATA Code: 8L
Corporate website: www.luckyair.net
Kunming, Yunan

Okay Airways
IATA Code: BK
Corporate website: www.okair.net
Tianjin Binhai International Airport
Tianjin 300300
Tel: +86 (0)22 6032 5500
Fax: +86 (0)22 6032 5575

Shandong Airlines
IATA Code: SC
Corporate website: www.shangdongair.com.cn
11ᵗʰ floor, Shandong Aviation Mansion
5746 Er Huan East Road
Lixia District
Jinan Shandong 250014
Tel: +86 (0)531 96777

Shanghai Airlines
IATA Code: FM
Corporate website: www.shanghai-air.com
212 Jiangning Road,
Shanghai 200041
Tel: +86 (0)21 6835 5528

Shenzhen Airlines
IATA Code: ZH
Corporate website: www2.shenzhenair.com
Baoan International Airport,
Shenzhen 518128
Tel +86 (0)755 2777 1999
Fax: +86 (0)755 777 7242

Sichuan Airlines
IATA Code: 3U
Corporate website: www.scal.com.cn
Number 11 Sector
2 Renmin Nan Lu
Chengdu, Sichuan
Tel: +86 (0)28 8665 4858 /86657163

Spring Airlines
IATA Code: 9S
Corporate website: www.china-sss.com
1558 Ding Xi Road
Shanghai 200050
24 hour service line: +86 (0)21 6252 0000
Fax: +86 (0) 21 6252 3734

United Eagle Airlines
IATA Code: EU
Corporate website: www.ueair.com
Floor 6, South West China
Aeronautical Devices Company
Shuang Liu International Airport
Cheng Du
Tel: +86 (0)28 6666 8888
Tel: +86 (0)28 6600 6333
Fax +86 (0)28 8570 6199

VIVA Macau Airlines
IATA Code: ZG
Corporate website: www.flyvivamacau.com
Alm Dr. Carlos D' Assumpcao,
181-187 Edf. Jardim Brilhantismo
9 Andar

Macau
Tel: +853 2871 8880
Fax: +853 2871 8803
E-mail: inquiry@flyvivamacau.com

Xiamen Airlines
IATA Code: MF
Corporate website: www.xiamenair. com.cn
22 Dailao Road,
Xiamen, 361006

Contact Details for International Airlines in China

Aeroflot Russian Airlines
IATA Code: SU
Corporate website: www.aeroflot.ru

Aeroflot – Beijing Office
2 Chao Yanf Men Bei Da Jie,
Beijing 100027
Tel: +86 (0)10 6501 2563
Fax: +86 (0)10 6594 1869

Aeroflot – Hong Kong Office
Suite 2918, 29 Floor Shui on Centre,
6-8 Harbour Road,
Wanchai, Hong Kong
Tel: +852 2537 2611
Fax: +852 2537 2614
E-mail: sales@aeroflot.com.hk

Aeroflot- Shanghai Office
SUITE 203 A, Shanghai Centre
1376, Nanjing Xi Road
Shanghai
Tel: +86 (0)21 62798033
Fax: +86 (0)21 62798035
E-mail: shatosu@aeroflot.ru

Aerosvit – Ukrainian Airlines
IATA Code: W
Corporate website: www.aerosvit.ua

Aerosvit Beijing Office
Room922/924, Towercrest Plaza
3 Maizidian Xilu, Chao Yang District
Beijing 100016
Tel: +86 (0)10 8458 0909
Fax: +86 (0)10 8458 0910

Aerosvit Shanghai Office
Room 508A, Shanghai Center,
1376 Nanjingxilu
Shanghai 200040
Tel: +86 (0)21 62798181/62798182
Fax: +86 (0)21 62798182
E-mail: shaoffice@aerosvit.com

Air Asia
IATA Code: AK
Corporate website: www.airasia.com
1st Floor
International Trade Building,

338, Hubingnan Road,
Xiamen
Call AirAsia's China Call Centre Number:
  +86 (0)592 516 7777

Air Astana
IATA Code: KC
Corporate website: www.airastana.com
Air Astana Beijing Office
Office 517,
50 Liangmaqiao Road
Chaoyang District,
Beijing, 100016 (Kempinski Hotel,Beijing
  Lufthansa Center)
Tel: +86 (0)1064651030/ 64665067
E-mail: beijing@airastana.com

Air Canada
IATA Code: AC
Corporate website: www.aircanada.
  com

Air Canada Beijing Office
C201 Beijing Lufthansa Centre
50 Liangmaqiao Road
Beijing 100016
Tel: +86 (0)10 6468 2001
Fax: +86 (0)10 6463 0576

Air Canada Hong Kong
Room 1612, Tower One
New World Tower
18 Queens Road, Central
Hong Kong
Tel: +852 2867 8111
Fax: +852 2868 4919

Air Canada Shanghai Office
Room 3901, United Plaza
1468 Nan Jing Rd West
Shanghai 200040
Tel: +86 (0)21 6279 2999
Fax: +86 (0)21 6247 2982

Air France
IATA Code: AF
Air France China
  – General/Reservations
Tel: 4008 808 808 (within China)
Fax: +86 (0)20 3878 5225
Corporate website (China): http://
  www.airfrance.com.cn/

Air France – Beijing Office
Kuntai International Mansion

Building 1, 16/F Room 1606-1611
12A Chao Yang Men Wai Dajie
Beijing 100020
Tel: +86 (0)10 5922 0808
Fax: +86 (0)10 5879 7628

Air France – Guangzhou office
13F Gao Sheng Building
109 Ti Yu West Road
Tian He District
Guangzhou 510620
Tel: +86 (0)20 3879 5730
Fax: +86 (0)20 3878 5200

Air France – Hong Kong Office
18/F Vicwood Plaza
199 Des Voeux Road
Central, Hong Kong
Tel: +852- 2501 9433
Fax: +852- 2581 9665

Air France – Shanghai Office
Ciro's Plaza Room 3901B
No. 388 Nanjing Xi Lu
Shanghai 200003
Tel: +86 (0)21 6334 5633
Fax: +86 (0)21 6334 5703

Air India
IATA Code: AI
Corporate website: www.airindia.in

Air India – Shanghai Office
1008/1009 (P) Kerry Centre
1515 Nanjin G West
Shanghai
Tel: +86 (0)21 2598 5698
Fax: +86 (0)21 5298 6798

Air India – Hong Kong Office
Room 2901-2
29th Floor, Vickwood Plaza
199 Des Voeux Road
Hong Kong
Tel : +852 2522 4772 / +852 2522 1176
Fax : +852 2868 0132 / +852 2522 2261

Air Mauritius
IATA Code: MK
Cororate website: www.airmauritius.
  com

Air Mauritius Beijing Office
Room 509A, 5/F, Kelun Building

12 Guanghua Street
Chaoyang District
Beijing 100020
Tel: +86 (0)10 6581 2968
Fax: +86 (0)10 6581 5908
E-mail: bjsmkpax@tam.com.hk

Air Mauritius Guangzhou Office
Room 2506, North Tower
World Trade Center
371-375 Huan Shi Dong Lu
Guangzhou
Tel: +86 (0)20 8762 1393
Fax: +86 (0)20 8762 1323
E-mail: canmkpax@tam.com.hk

Air Mauritius Hong Kong office
Room 1901A
19/F Far East Finance Centre
16 Harcourt Road
Admiralty
Hong Kong
Tel: +852 2523 1114
Fax: +852 2525 0910
E-mail: mkhongkong@airmauritius.com.
  hk

Air Mauritius Shanghai Office
Room 1810, 18/F
Haitong Securities Tower 689
Guangdong Road
Shanghai 200001
Tel: +86 (0)21 6341 0672
Fax: +86 (0)21 6341 0648
E-mail: shamkpax@tam.com.hk

Air New Zealand Limited
IATA Code: NZ
Corporate website: www.
  airnewzealand.com

Air New Zealand Hong Kong Office
Suite 1701
Jardine House
1 Connaught Place
Central
Hong Kong
Tel: +852 2862 8988
Fax: +852 2862 8989
Email: hkgreservations@airnz.co.nz

Air New Zealand Shanghai Office
Unit 4005, 40/F

CITIC Square
1168 Nanjing Road West
Shanghai 200041
Tel: +86 (0)21 5292 8755
Fax: +86 (0)21 5292 8775
Email: shareservations@airnz.co.nz

Air Niugini Ltd
IATA Code: PX
Corporate website: www.airniugini.
  com.pg
Room 1901, 19/F.,
16 Harcourt Road
Admiralty
Hong Kong
Tel: +852 2527 7098

Alitalia
IATA Code: AZ
Corporate website: www.alitalia.com

Alitalia Beijing Office
Room 2602, CITIC Building
19, JianGuoMenwai Ave.
Chao Yang District
Beijing
Tel: +86 (0)10 8511 2958/2959
Fax: +86 (0)10 8526 2433

Alitalia Hong Kong Office
Room 1012, China Aerospace Tower
Concordia Plaza
1 Science Museum Road
Tsimshatsui East, Kowloon
Hong Kong
Tel: +852 2375 4001
Fax: +852 2375 3623

Alitalia Shanghai Office
Room 3607, The Centre
989 Chang Le Road,
Shanghai 200031
Tel: +86 (0)21 6103 1133
Fax: +86 (0)21 6103 1139

American Airlines
IATA Code: AA
Corporate website: www.aa.com

American Airlines Beijing Office
Hung & Kit Holdings,
Room 2112, Building 1 Yi,
KunTai International Mansion,

12, Chao Wai Street,
Chao Yang District,
Beijing 100020
Tel: 400-886-1001
Fax: +86 (0)10 5879 7400

American Airlines Guangzhou Office
Hung and Kit Holdings Limited
1213-15 Garden Tower
368 Huanski Dong Lu,
Guangzhou 510064, China
Tel: 400-886-1001 (within China)
Fax: +86 (0)20 8387 9055

American Airlines Hong Kong Office
The Walshe Group
Unit 3 - Mezzanine Level
New Henry House
10 Ice House Street
Central
Hong Kong
Tel: +852 3678 8500
Fax: +852 3678 8501

ANA
IATA Code: NH
China Website: http://www.
  anaskyweb.com/cn/c/ (Chinese)
Hong Kong Website: http://www.
  anaskyweb.com/hk/e/ (English)

ANA Beijing Office
1F Beijing Fortune Bldg.,
5 Dong San Huan Bei Lu
Chao Yang District
Beijing
TEL: +86 (0)10 6590 9191

ANA Guangzhou Office
2605 CITIC PLAZA
233 Tianhe North Road
Tianhe Ward
Guangzhou

ANA Hong Kong Office
Suite 501, 5th Fl. One
International Finance Center
1 Harbour View Street
Central
Hong Kong
Tel: +852 2810 7100

ANA Shanghai Office
Suite 208A East Shanghai Center,

1376 Nanjing Xi Lu
Shanghai
Tel: +86 (0)21 5696 2525

ANA Xiamen Office
Room 205, Crowne Plaza Harbourview
  Xiamen,
12-8 Zhen Hai Road
Xiamen
Tel: +86 (0)592 205 1888

Asiana Airlines
IATA Code: OZ
China corporate website: http://
  cn.flyasiana.com/Global/CN/
  en/index
China nationwide tel: 400-650-8000
  (Within China)

Asiana Airlines – Beijing Office
12th Floor A/F Tower GATEWAY
18 XiaGuangLi North Road East Ring
Chaoyang District
Beijing

Asiana Airlines – Guangzhou Office
Room 906, South Tower
World Trade Center
371-375, Huanshi East Road
Guangzhou

Asiana Airlines Hong Kong Office
Unit 3407-8, 34FL
Gloucester Tower Landmark
11 Pedder St
Central
Hong Kong
Tel: +852 2523 8585
Fax: +852 2524 6152

Asiana Airlines Shanghai Office
2F, Rainbow Hotel
2000 Yanan Road (West)
Shanghai 20005

Austrian Airlines
IATA Code: OS
Corporate website: www.aua.com

Austrian Airlines Beijing
Unit C604, Kempinski Hotel B.L.C.,
50 Liangmaqiao Road
Beijing 100016
Tel: +86 (0)10 6464 5999

Fax: +86 (0)10 6462 2166
www.austrian.com

Austrian Airlines Hong Kong
Rm.403, Mirror Tower
61 Mody Road
Tsimshatsui East,
Kowloon, Hong Kong
Tel: +852 2525 5221
Fax: +852 2868 5488

Azerbaijan Airlines
IATA Code: J2
Corporate website: www.azal.az
Room 413
Hotel "Silk Road"
Urumqi
Tel/Fax: +86 (0)991 258 14 13
E-mail: Ismail_safarov@mail.ru

Bangkok Airways
IATA Code: PG
Corporate website: www.bangkokair.
  com

Bangkok Airways Guilin Office
18 Binjiang Road
Guilin, Guangxi
541001
Tel: +86 (0)773 288 0835-6
Fax: +86 (0)773 288 0833

Bangkok Airways Hong Kong Office
Suite 1418
Jardin House
1 Connaught Place
Hong Kong
Tel: +852 2899 2597, +852 2899 2634
Fax: +852 2537 4567
E-mail: hkgrrpg@bangkokair.com

Bangkok Airways Hangzhou Office
19th Floor Biaoli Building
528 Yan'an Road
Hangzhou 310006
Tel: +86 (0)571 8577 4571-2
Fax: +86 (0)571 8577 4573
E-mail: hghrrpg@bangkokair.com

Bangkok Airways Jinghong
8 Jingdexi Rd
Jinghong
Xi Shuang Banna

Yunnan, 666100
Tel: +86 (0)691 212 1881-2
Fax: +86 (0)691 212 1880
E-mail: jhgrrpg@bangkokair.com

Bangkok Airways Shenzhen Office
10# Shop
Shangri-la Hotel
Renminnan Road
Luohu Distric
Shen Zhen
Tel: +86 (0)755 8232 1251, 8232 5252
Fax: +86 (0)755 8232 4345
E-mail: szxrrpg@bangkokair.com

Bangkok Airways Xian Office
B105 Pioneering Square
48 Keji Road
Xian Hi-Tech Zone
Xian, Shaanxi
710075
Tel: +86 (0)29 8835 0081-2
Fax: +86 (0)29 8835 0083
E-mail: xiykkpg@bangkokair.com

Bangkok Airways Zhengzhou Office
18th Floor
Weilai Building
69 Weilai Road
Zhengzhou
Henan, China
Tel: +86 (0)371 6562 8001-2
Fax: +86 (0)371 6562 8006

Bangladesh Biman Airlines
IATA Code: BG
Corporate website: www.bimanair.com
Huston Center Suite 216/217
63 Mody Road
Tshim-Sha-Tsui, Kowloon,
Hongkong
Tel: +852 2724 8600, 27241726
Fax: +852 2311 0884, 27246284
E-mail: bimanhkg@hutchcity.com

Batavia Airlines
IATA Code: 7P
Corporate wesbite: www. batavia-air.
  co.id
Batavia Airlines Guangzhou Office
Huanshi Dong Road
326 Room. 1109
Asia International Hotel

Guangzhou 510060
Tel: +86 (0)20 6120 6350
Fax: +86 (0)20 6120 6354

British Airways
IATA Code: BA
Corporate Website: www.ba.com
Tel: 400 650 0073 (Within China only)

BA Travel shop - Beijing
Room 2112, Building 1
Kun Tai International
Mansion Yi
12 Chao Yang
Men Wai Street
Beijing 100020
Tel: +86 (0)10 6459 0081
Tel: +86 (0)10 6459 0082
Tel: +86 (0)10 6459 0083

BA Travel Shop- Hong Kong
24 Floor
Jardine House
One Connaught Place
Central, Hong Kong
Tel: +852 2822 9000

BA Travel shop – Shanghai
Suite 703,
Central Plaza, 227 Huang Pi
North Road
Shanghai 200003
Tel: +86 (0)21 6835 5633

Cebu Pacific Air
IATA Code: 5J
Corporate website: www.cebupacificair.com
Unit 407 Mirror Tower
61 Mody Road, Tsimshatsui East
Kowloon, Hong Kong
Tel: +852 2722 1499/0609
E-mail: hkgofc@cebupacificair.com

China Airlines
IATA Code: CI
Corporate website: www.china-airlines.com

China Airlines Beijijng Office
Tower 1
Room 601
7 Jian Guo Men Nei Avenue
Beijing 100005
Tel: +86 (0)10 6510 2671

Fax: +86 (0)10 6510 2677

China Airlines Guangzhou Office
Room 3009
CITIC PLAZA
233 Tianhe N. Road
Guangzhoub PRC
Tel: +86 (0)20 38773370-2
Fax: +86 (0)20 38773385

China Airlines Hong Kong Office
Suites 901 – 907
9/F One Pacific Place
88 Queensway
Admiralty, Hong Kong
Tel: +852 2843 9800
Fax: +852 2845 0155

China Airlines Shanghai Office
HuaMin Empire Plaza Suite 22A
726 West Yanan Road
Shanghai 200050
Tel: +86 (0)21 52375269/70/71/72
Fax: +86 (0)21 52375322

China Airlines Shenzhen Office
Room 05 48/F
Office Tower
Shun Hing
Di Wang Commercial Center
5002 Shen Nan Dong Road
ShenZhen
Tel: +86 (0)755 82463560/61/62
Fax: +86 (0)755 82463877

Delta Airlines
IATA Code: DL
Corporate website: www.delta.com

Delta Airlines Beijing Ticketing Office
Excellent Services Consulting Co. Limited
Kung Tai International Center
25F, Suites 2503B
12, Chaowai Street
Chaoyang District
Beijing 100020
Tel: 86 (0)10 5879 7468
Fax: 86 (0)10 5879 7460
Email: service.bjs@escc.cc

Delta Airlines Guangzhou Ticketing
Office
Excellent Services Consulting Co. Limited
Bank of America Plaza, Suites 2515
555 Ren Min Zhong Road

Guangzhou 510145
Tel: +86 (0)20 8130 6292
Fax: +86 (0)20 8130 6252
Email: service.hkg@escc.cc

Delta Airlines Hong Kong Ticketing Office
Excellent Services Consulting Co. Limited
Unit 03 on 17th Floor Greenfield Tower
Conconrdia Plaza
1 Science Museum Road
Kowloon, Hong Kong
Tel: +852 2620 6678
Fax: +852 2620 6776
Email: service.hkg@escc.cc

Delta Airlines Shanghai Ticketing office
Excellent Services Consulting Co. Limited
Cloud Nine Plaza, Suites 609
1118 Yan An Xi Road
Shanghai 200051
Tel: +86 (0)21 6115 6996
Fax: +86 (0)21 6115 6990
Email: service.sha@escc.cc

EgyptAir
IATA Code: MS
**Corporate website: www.egyptair.
    com.eg**
Sunflower Tower Building
37 Maizidan Street
Beijing 100026
Tel: +86 (10) 85275000
Fax: +86 (10) 85275940

EL AL Israel Airlines
IATA Code: LY
Corporate website: www.elal.com

El Al Israel Airlines Beijing Office
Room 1812B, Kuntai International
    Mansion,
Yi No.12 Chaowai Street
Chao Yang District,
Beijing 100020
Tel: +86 (0)10 58797358
Fax: +86 (0)10 58797359
Email: lytktbjs@elal.com.cn

EL AL Israel Airlines Hong Kong
Room 2205 Tower One Lippo Center
89 Queensway
Hong Kong
Tel: +852 2380 3362
Fax: +852 2973 0720

Emirates Airlines
IATA Code: EK
Corporate website: www.emirates.com

Emirates Beijing Office
Room 1003, Tower A
Eagle Run Plaza
26, Xiao Yun Road
Chao Yang District
Beijing 100016
Tel: +86 (0)10 5108 8696
Fax: +86 (0)10 5108 8698

Emirates Hong Kong Office
11/F, Henley Building
5 Queen's Road Central
Hong Kong
Tel: +852 2801 8777
Fax: +852 2801 4802

Emirates Shanghai Office
Room 1905-1907, United Plaza
1468, Nan Jing Road West
Shanghai 200040
Tel: +86 (0)21 3222 9999
Fax: +86 (0)21 6289 9808

Ethiopian Airlines
IATA Code: ET
**Corporate website: www.
    ethiopianairlines.com**

Ethiopian Airlines Beijing Office
L203 China World Tower
2 China WTC
Beijing
Tel: +86 (0)10 6505 0314/5
Fax: +86 (0)10 6505 4120
E-mail: bjsam@ethiopianairlines.com

Ethiopian Airlines Guangzhou Office
Guangzhou WTC complex
South Tower, 13th floor
Room No. 1305
Huan Shi Dong Road No. 315-317
Tel: +86 (0)20 8762
    0836/87621101/876201102
Fax: +86 (0)20 8762 0837
E-mail: cansm@ethiopianairlines.com

Ethiopian Airlines Hong Kong Office
18 F Rm 183, Ruttonjee House
11 Duddell Street

Central, Hong Kong
Tel: + 852 2117 0233 / 2117 1863
Fax: +852 2117 1811

EVA Airways Corp.
IATA Code: BR
Corporate website: www.evaair.com

EVA Airways Beijing Office
22/F Block C
Central International Trade Center
6A Jianguomenwai Avenue
Chaoyang District,
Beijing, China
Tel: +86 (0)10 6563 5000
Fax: +86 (0)10 6563 0068

EVA Airways Hong Kong Office
Room 901, 9F
Jardine House
1 Connaught Place
Central
Hong Kong
Tel: +852-28109251
Fax: +852-25250025

FAT – Far East Air Transport
IATA Code: EF
Corporate Website: www.fat.com.tw
China Ticketing Office – Shanghai
Tel: +86 (0)215 112 5960

Finnair
IATA Code: AY
Corporate website: www.finnair.com

Finnair Beijing Office
Scitech Tower, Room 204
22 Jian Guo Men Wai Dajie
Beijing
Tel. +86 (0)10 6512 7180
Fax +86 (0)10 6512 7182

Finnair Guangzhou Office
Rm 3308-09A Citic Plaza
233 Tien He Bei Road
Guangzhou 510613 PRC
Tel: +86 (0)20 3877 3188
Fax: +86 (0)20 3877 3168

Finnair Hong Kong Office
Room 2312, 23/F, Cosco Tower
183 Queen's Road, Central

Tel: +852 2117 1238
Fax: +852 2117 1239
E-mail: finnair.hkg@finnair.com

Finnair Shanghai Office
Citic Square Room 2406, 24th floor
1168 Nan Jing West Road
Shanghai 200041
Tel: +86 (0)21 5292 9400
Fax: +86 (0)21 5292 9052
Email: finnair.shanghai@finnair.com

Garuda Indonesia
IATA Code: GA
Corporate Website: www.garuda-
indonesia.com/

Garuda – Beijing Office
RM 1902:19F: Kuntai
International Mansion Y112
Chaowei Avenue
Chaoyang District
Beijing
Tel: +86 (0)10 58790984
Fax: +86 (0)10 58790784

Garuda Guangzhou Office
Rm 1101-1102
Asia Int'l Hotel, 326 Section 1
Ghuangzhou, Guangdong
Tel: +86 (0)20 61206999
Fax: +86 (0)20 61206222

Garuda Hong Kong Office
Room 1501-1505
Dah Sing Financial Center,
108 Gloucester Road
Hong Kong
Tel: +852 25229140
Tel: +852 25229071
Fax: +852 28455021

Garuda Shanghai Office
Unit A 10 Fl East Ocean Center
West Wing, 618 Yanan Road East
Shanghai
Tel: +86 (0)21 53855398
Tel: +86 (0)21 53855399 Ext 199
Fax: +86 (0)21 53855337

JAL (Japan Airlines)
IATA Code: JL

Corporate website (China): http:// www.cn.jal.com/en/
Tel: 4008-88-0808 (within China)
Tel: +86 (0)21 5467 4530 (from overseas)

JAL Beijing Office
1st Floor, Chang Fu Gong Office
Jianguo Menwai Dajie 26, Chaoyang
Beijing 100022

JAL Guangzhou Office
Room 4601, 46th Floor
CITIC Plaza
233 Tianhe Bei Road
Guangzhou
Guangdong 510613

JAL Hong Kong Office
30th Floor, Tower 6
The Gateway, Harbour City
9 Canton Road
Tsim Sha Tsui, Kowloon
Hong Kong
JAL Shanghai Office
7th Floor, Huaihai Plaza
1045, Huaihai Zhong Road
Shanghai, 200031

Jet Airways
IATA Code: 9W
Corporate website: www.jetairways. com

Jet Airways Hong Kong GSA
Focus Air Ltd
Room 1802B, Regent Center
88 Queens Rd
Central
Hong Kong
Tel: +852 25237762 / +852 2533916
Fax: +852 2523 3547
E-mail: jetairhk@netvigator.com

Jet Airways Shanghai GSA
Bejing Beall GSA Business Consulting
 Services Ltd
Room 1907
World Trade Tower
500, Guangdong Road
Shanghai 200001
Tel: +86 (0)21 6362 0191 / 92

Fax: +86 (0)21 6362 0197
E-mail: 9w_sha@chinagsa.com

JETStar Airways
IATA Code: 3K
Corporate website: www.jetstar.com
Tel: + 852 2918 1771

Kenya Airways
IATA Code: KQ
Corporate website: www.kenya-airways.com

Kenya Airways Guangzhou Office
People's Republic of China
Room 605 6/F Dong Shan Plaza
69 Xian Lie Road
Guangzhou 510095
Tel: +86 (0) 20 8732 0042
Fax: +86 (0) 20 8732 1661

Kenya Airways Hong Kong Office
Pacific Aviation Marketing (Kenya) Ltd.
Room 2505A Caroline Centre
28 Yun Ping Road
Causeway Bay
Hong Kong
Tel: +852 3678 2000
Fax; +852 3579 0808
E-mail: restkt@kenya-airways.hk

KLM Royal Dutch Airlines
IATA Code: KL
For calls from China: 4008 808 222
For all other countries: +852 2808 2168
Corporate website: www.klm.com.cn

KLM Beijing Office
1609-1611, 16/F
Kuntai International Mansion Building
12, Chaoyangmenwai Avenue
Beijing

KLM Chengdu Office
1603B, Building A, Times Plaza
2 Zongfu Road
Chengdu 610016

KLM Hong Kong Office
18/F, Vicwood Plaza
199 Des Voeux Road, Central
Hong Kong
Website: www.klm.com.hk

KLM Shanghai Office
3901A, Ciro's Plaza
388 Nan Jing Xi Lu
Shanghai, CHINA

Korean Airlines
IATA Code: KL
Corporate Website: www.koreanair. com

KAL Beijing Office
901-3, Hyundai Motor Towers
38 Xiao Yun Road
Chao Yang District
Beijing, CHINA
Tel: +86 (0)10 8453 8421

KAL Guangzhou Office
Citic Plaza 5306
233 Tianhebei Road
Guangzhou, CHINA
+86 (0)20 3877 3878

KAL Hong Kong Office
11/F, Tower 2, South Seas Centre
75 Mody Road
Tsimshatsui East, Kowloon
Hong Kong
Tel: +852 2733 7110

KAL Shanghai Branch
3406 Maxdo Center 34F
8 Xing Yi Road
Shanghai
+86 (0)21 5208 2080

Lufthansa German Airlines (LH)
IATA Code: LH
Corporate website: www.lufthansa. com

Lufthansa Beijing Office
Beijing Lufthansa Center
50 Liangmaqiao Road
Unit S101
Beijing 100016
Tel: +86 (0)10 6468 8838
Fax: +86 (0)10 6465 3223

Lufthansa Guangzhou Office
C1557-1559 China Hotel
Liu Hua Road
Guangzhou, 510015
Tel: +86 (0)20 2832 6588
Fax: +86 (0)20 2832 6589

Lufthansa Hong Kong Office
Lufthansa City Center/Schenker Travel
Unit 2001-4
20/F The Broadway
54-62 Lockhart Road
Wanchai
Hong Kong
Tel: +852 2868 2313

Lufthansa Shanghai office
Unit 14-21
3rd Floor Building One
222 Corporate Avenue
Shanghai 200021
Tel: +86 (0)21 5352 4999
Fax: +86 (0)21 6340 6899

Malaysia Airlines
IATA Code: MH
Corporate Website: www. malaysiaairlines.com

MAS Beijing Office
Room 1005 10th Floor
China World Tower 2
1 Jianguomenwai Avenue
Beijing 100004
Tel: +86 (0)10 6505 0341
Fax: +86 (0)10 6505 2680

MAS Guangzhou Office
Shop M04-05 Garden Hotel
368 Huanshi Dong Lu Road
Guangzhou, 510064
Tel: +86 (0)20 833 58828/38
Tel: +86 (0)20 833 38989 EXT 3286
Fax: +86 (0)20 833 58898

MAS Hong Kong Office
23 Floor Central Tower
28 Queen's Road
Central, Hong Kong
Tel: +852 2916 0088
Fax: +852 2868 4080

MAS Shanghai Office
Suite 560, East Wing Shanghai Centre
1376 NanJing Road West
Shanghai, 200040
Tel: +86 (0)21 6279 8607/8629
Fax: +86 (0)21 6279 8657

Northwest Airlines
IATA Code: NW
Corporate website: www.nwa.com

Northwest Airlines Beijing Office
W501, 5/F West Wing
China World Trade Centre
1 Jian Guo Men Wai Ave
Beijing 100004
Tel: 40081-40081 (Within China)

Northwest Airlines Guangzhou Office
C509, China Hotel By Marriott
Liu Hua Lu
Guangzhou 510015
Tel: 40081-40081 (Within China)

Northwest Airlines Shanghai Office
East Podium
Shanghai Centre – Suite 207
1376 Nanjing Road West
Shanghai 200040
Tel: 40081-40081 (Within China)

MIAT Mongolian Airlines
IATA Code: OM
Corporate website: www.miat.com
Room 705, 7th floor
Sunjoy Mansion
Jianguomenwai
Ritan Lu 6
100020 Beijing
Tel: +86 (0)10 650 79297/61231
Fax: +86 (0)10 650 77397
E-mail: beijing@miat.com

Orient Thai Airways
IATA Code:
Corporate website: www.orient-thai.
  com
6th Floor
China Hongkong Center
122-126, Canton Rd
Kowloon, Hong Kong
Tel: +852 2366 5869
Fax: +852 2366 8646
Email: res-tktg@orient-thai.com.hk

Philippine Airlines
IATA Code: PR
Corporate website: www.
  philippineairlines.com

Philippine Airlines Beijing Office
Unit 603, Tower 1
Bright China Chang An Building
7 JianGuoMenNei Avenue
Dong Cheng District,

Beijing 100005
Tel: +86 (0)10 6510 2991 to 2993
Fax: +86 (0)10 6518 0882
E-mail: bjspr@bjspr.com

Philippine Airlines Shanghai Office
Shanghai Center
1376 Nanjing West Road
Suite 735A, East Wing
Shanghai 200040
Tel: +86 (0)21 627 98765
Fax: +86 (0)21 627 98762

Philippine Airlines Xiamen Office
Unit 7-8A, 3/F, The Bank Center
189 Xiahe Road
Xiamen 361003, Fujian Province
Tel: +86 (0)592 239 4729/4730/4765
Fax: +86 (0)592 239 4725
E-mail: xmnpr@xmnpr.com

PIA Pakistan Airlines
IATA Code: PK
Corporate website: www.piac.com.pk

PIA Beijing Office
617, Level 6
China World Tower
Beijing
Tel: +86 (0)10
   65051681/65051682/65051683
Fax: +86 (0)10 65052257

PIA Hong Kong Office
Room 1104A
East Ocean Center
98 Granville Road
Kowloon
Hong Kong
Tel: +852-2366 4770/+852 2366 4775
Fax: +852 2721 1739
E-mail: hkguupk@piac.com.pk

Qantas
IATA Code: QF
Corporate website: www.qantas.com

Qantas Beijing Office
Unit 7-8, 10/F West Tower, Twin Towers
B-12 Jianguomenwai Dajie
Chaoyang District
Tel: 800 819 0089 (within China only)
Tel: +86 (0)10 6567 9006

Qantas GSA Guangzhou
1213 Garden Tower
368 Huanshi Dong Lu
Guangzhou, 510064
Tel: +86 (0)20 8387 8389 / 9052
Fax: +86 (0)20 8387 9055

Qantas Hong Kong Office
24/F, Jardine House
One Connaught Place
Central, Hong Kong,
Tel: +852 2822 9000
Fax: +852 2822 9095

Qantas Shanghai Office
Room 3202, 32F
K Wah Centre
1010 Huai Hai Middle Road
Shanghai
Tel: 800 819 0089 (within China only)
Tel: +86 (0)21 6145 0188

Qatar Airways
IATA Code: QR
Corporate website: www.qatarairways.
  com

Qatar Airways Beijing Office
Unit A+F1, 16th Floor,
Building A,Gateway Plaza
18, Xiaguangli,
North Road East Third Ring
Chaoyang District
Beijing 100027
Tel: +86 (0)10 5923 5100
Fax: +86 (0)10 5923 5200
Email: bjsfeedback@cn.qatarairways.com

Qatar Airways Guangzhou Office
Room 1004, North Tower,
World Trade Center,
371-375 Huanshi Dong Road,
Guangzhou
Tel: +86 (0)20 8765 0795
Fax: +86 (0)20 8761 0276
Qatar Airways Hong Kong Office

Qatar Airways
Suite 4118-19,
Jardine House,
1 Connaught Place,
Central

Hong Kong
Tel: +852 2868 9833
Fax: 852 2868 9081

Qatar Airways Shanghai Office
Room 3703-04 Raffles City,
268 Xi Zang Road (M),
Shanghai, 200001
Tel: +86 (0)21 2320 7555
Fax: +86 (0)21 2320 7588/ 7566

Royal Brunei Airlines
IATA Code: BI
Corporate website: www.bruneiair.
  com
Room 305-306 Kerry Centre
1515 Nanjing Road West
Shanghai, 200040
Tel: +86 (0)21 5298 6688
Fax: +86 (0)21 5298 5241
E-mail: SHARES@rba.com.bn

Royal Nepal Airlines
IATA Code: RA
Corporate website: www.royalnepal-
airlines.com

Royal Nepal Airlines Hong Kong Office
Room No.704, Lippo Sun Plaza Building
28 Canton Road, Tsimshatsui
Kowloon, Hong Kong
Tel: +852 23 752180/756094
Fax: +852 23 757069

Royal Nepal Airlines Shanghai Office
Room B-405, Universal Mansion
1, Wan Hang Du Rd.
Shanghai 200040
Tel: +86 (0)21 3214 0717
Fax: +86 (0)21 3314 0715

SAS Scandinavian Airlines
IATA Code: SK
Corporate website: www.flysas.com

SAS Hong Kong Office
3607, China Resource Building
26 Harbour Road
Wanchai, Hong Kong
Tel: +852 2865 1370
Fax: +852 2865 1448
E-mail: sas@vikingtravel.com.hk

Silkair
IATA Code: MI
Corporate website: www.silkair.com

Silkair Chengdu Office
36C First City Plaza
308 Shuncheng Street
Chengdu, Sichuan 610017
Tel: +86 (0)28 8652 8626 / 8652 8636
Fax: +86 (0)28 8652 8656

Silkair Shenzhen Office
Rm 3007 Kerry Centre
2008 Ren Min Nan Road
Shenzhen 518001
Tel: +86 (0)755 8236 6106
Fax: +86 (0)755 8230 0032

Silkair Xiamen Office
International Plaza
11th floor unit G
8 Lujiang Road
Xiamen 361001
Tel: +86 (0)592 205 3257 /205 3280
Fax: +86 (0)592 205 3273
Email: xmnmi@public.xm.fj.cn

Singapore Airlines
IATA Code: SQ
Corporate website: www.singaporeair. com

Singapore Airlines Beijing Office
8th Floor China World Tower 2
1 Jian Guo Men Wai Avenue
Beijing 100004
Tel: +86 (0)10 65052233 (Reservations & Ticketing)
Fax: +86 (0)10 65051178 (Reservations & Ticketing)

Singapore Airlines Guangzhou office
Room 2701-04, Metro Plaza
183-187 Tian He Bei Road
Guangzhou 510620
Tel: +86 (0)20 87556300 (Reservations & Ticketing)
Fax: +86 (0)20 87555518 (Reservations & Ticketing)

Singapore Airlines Nanjing Office
Room 1761 World Trade Center
2 Hanzhong Road

Nanjing Jiangsu Provice
Tel: +86 (0)25 84719933
Fax: +86 (0)25 84713232

Singapore Airlines Shanghai Office
Rm 1106-1110
Plaza 66 Tower 1
1266 Nanjing Xilu
Shanghai 200040
Tel: +86 (0)21 6288 7999 (Reservations & Ticketing)
Fax: +86 (0)21 6288 7667 (Reservations & Ticketing)

South African Airways
IATA Code:
Corporate website: www.flysaa.com
General Office (Incl. Administration & Finance)
6th Floor
Club Lusitano
16 Ice House Street
Central
Hong Kong
Tel: +852 2722 5768
Fax: +852 2311 1174

Sri Lankan Airlines
IATA Code: UL
Corporate website: www.srilankan. aero

SriLankan Airlines Ltd Beijing Office
Unit S119, Lufthansa Center
50, Liangmaqiao Road,
Chaoyang District
Beijing 100016
Tel: +86 (0)10 6461 7208
Fax: +86 (0)10 6461 6081
E-mail:bjs.res@srilankan.aero

SriLankan Airlines Ltd Hong Kong office
Room 2703, 27th Floor
Tower 1, Lippo Centre,
89 Queensway
Admiralty
Hong Kong
Tel: +852 25210812 / 825 / 852 (Sales)
Fax: +852 28015600
E-mail: res_hkg@srilankan.aero

Swiss Air
IATA: LX

Corporate website: www.swiss.com

Swiss Air Beijing Office
S101, Beijing Lufthansa Center
50 Liangmaqiao Road
Beijing
Tel: +86 (0)10 8454 0180
Fax: +86 (0)10 6465 2997

Swiss Air Hong Kong Office
Airport Ticket Office
c/o Cathay Pacific Airways
Hong Kong Intl. Airport
Departure Level / Area E
Tel: +852 30 021330
Fax: +852 23 627513

Swiss Air Shanghai Office
314A Building One
Corporate Avenue
222 Hubin Road
Shanghai
+86 21 6340 6399
Fax: +86 21 6340 6355

Tajik Air
IATA Code: 7J
Corporate website: www.tajikair.tj
Tajik Air Urumqi Office
Tel/Fax: +86 (0)991 2552846
E-mail: tajikair-urq@mail.ru

Thai Airways
IATA Code: TH
Corporate Website: www.thaiair.com

Thai Airways Beijing Office
Units 303-4, Level 3 Office Tower W3
Oriental Plaza,
1 East Chang An Ave
Dong Cheng District
Beijing 100738
Tel: +86 (0)10 8515 0088
Fax: +86 (0)10 8515 1134

Thai Airways Guangzhou Branch
G3, West Wing
The Garden Hotel
368 Huanshi Dong Lu
Guangzhou 510064
Tel: +86 (0)20 8365 2333 Ext. 5
Fax: +86 (0)20 8365 2488

Thai Airways Hong Kong Office
Unit A24/F
United Centre
95 Queensway
Hong Kong
Tel: +852 2876 6899
Fax: +852 2735 8551

Thai Airways Shanghai Office
Unit 105 Shanghai Kerry Centre,
1515 Nan Jing Rd., (West)
Shanghai 200040, CHINA
Tel: +86 (0)21 5298 5555
Fax: +86 (0)21 5298 6166

Transaero
IATA Code: UN
Corporate website: www.transaero.ru
Rm 24, New Henry House
10 Ice House St
Central
Hong Kong
Tel: +852 25 22 46 89, 25 22 48 18
Fax: +852 25 22 48 18
E-mail: sales@transaero.com.hk

Turkish Airlines
IATA Code: TK
Corporate website: www.thy.com

Turkish Airlines Beijing Office
W103 Kempinski Center
50 Liang Ma Qiad Road
100016 Beijing
Tel: +86 (0)10 64 65 18 67
Fax: +86 (0)10 64 65 18 65
E-mail: thybjs@public.bta.net.cn

Turkish Airlines Hong Kong Office
Turkish Airlines Inc.
Room 1703
Jubilee Center
18 Fenwick Street
Wanchai
Hong Kong
Tel: +852 3101 0592
Fax: +852 3101 0596
E-mail: thyhkg@netvigator.com

United Airlines
IATA Code: UA
Corporate website: www.
unitedairlines.com

United Airlines Beijing Office
C/D1 Unit, 15th Floor,
Tower A, GATEWAY
18 Xiaguangli, North Road,
East Third Ring Chaoyang District
Beijing 100027
Tel: +86 (0)10 8468 6666 ext. 1

United Airlines Guangzhou Office
Shop G05, Garden Hotel
368 Huanshi Dong Lu
Guangzhou 610065
Tel: +86 (0)20 8365 2345

United Airlines Hong Kong Office
12/F, Tower 1, The Gateway
Harbour City
25 Canton Road
Kowloon
Hong Kong
Tel: +852 2810 4888
Fax: +852 3129-2433

United Airlines Shanghai Office
3301-3317, 33rd Floor
Shanghai Central Plaza
381 Huaihai Middle Road
Shanghai 200020
Tel: +86 (0)21 3311 4567

Uzbekistan Airways
IATA Code: HY
Corporate website: www.uzairways. com
Jian Guo Men Wai
19 Citic Building
2-01B, 100004
Beijing
Tel: +86 (0)10 6500 6442
Fax: +86 (0)10 6525 3867
E-mail: bjs@uzairways.com

Vietnam Airlines
IATA Code: VN
Corporate Website: www. vietnamairlines.com

Vietnam Airlines Beijing Office
S121, Kempinski Hotel
Beijing Lufthansa Center
50 Liangmaqiao Road
Chaoyang District
Beijing 100016

Tel: +86 (0)10 84541196 / 84541289
Fax: +86 (0)10 84541287

Vietnam Airlines Guangzhou Office
Room 954 - 955 Garden Hotel
368 Huanshi Dong Lu
Guangzhou 510064
Tel: +86 (0)20 83867093 / 83338999
Fax: +86 (0)20 83827187

Vietnam Airlines Hong Kong Office
Suite 3012, 30th floor
One International Finance Center
1 Harbour View Street
Central
Hongkong
Tel: +852 28106680
Fax: +852 28698856

Vietnam Airlines Shanghai Office
1376 Nanjing Rd (W) - Jing An district
200040 Shanghai
Tel: +86 21 6279 7777
Fax: +86 21 6279 7788

Virgin Atlantic Airways
IATA Code: VS
Corporate website: www.virgin-atlantic.com

Virgin Atlantic Hong Kong Office
8th Floor, Alexandra House
18 Chater Road
Central
Hong Kong
Tel: +852 2532 3081
Fax: +852 2537 4544
Email: customer.relations.hk@fly.virgin. com

Virgin Atlantic Shanghai Office
Suite 217, Second Floor
12, The Bund
Zhong Shan Dong Yi Road
Shanghai 200002
Tel: +86 (0)21 5353 4600
Fax: +86 (0)21 5353 4601

Vladivostok Air
IATA Code: XF
Corporate website: http://www. vladavia.ru
Diwangdasha building

26, office #1303
Ganshuilu 150090
Harbin, China
Tel: +86 (0)451 82289590, 82269590,
   82269591
Fax: +86 (0)451 8228 9593

Cargo Operators in China

Air Bridge Cargo
IATA Code: RU
**Corporate website: www.
   airbridgecargo.com**

Air Bridge Cargo Beijing Office
Room 2108, Air China Plaza
36 Xiaoyun Road
Chaoyang District
Beijing 100027
Tel: + 86 (0)10 8447 5936/37/38
Fax: + 86 (0)10 8447 5935
E-mail: service.pek@airbridgecargo.com

Air Bridge Cargo Hong Kong Office
Room 536A, 5/F
South Office Block
Super Terminal One,
Chek lap Kok, HK Intl Airport
Tel: + 852 2215 3928
Fax: + 852 2215 3878
E-mail: service.hkg@airbridgecargo.com

Air Bridge Cargo Shanghai Office
Room 3104-3105
Shanghai Maxdo Center
8 Xingyi Road
Shanghai 200336
Tel: + 86 21 52080011
Fax: + 86 21 52080508
E-mail: service.sha@airbridgecargo.com

Air China Cargo
IATA Code: CA
**Corporate website: www.airchina.com.
   cn**
Corporate HQ (Beijing)
BeiJing international post office
PO BOX: 100600-6606
Beijing 100600
Global Sales Hotline: +86 4008 100 999
Tel: +86 (0)10 6459 5912
Fax: +86 (0)10 8479 8686

AHK Air Hong Kong Limited
IATA Code: LD
**Corporate website: www.airhongkong.
   com.hk**
Cathay Pacific Airways Cargo is appointed
as the worldwide general sales agent of

Air Hong Kong for general cargo, please see details for Cathay Pacific Airways local sales offices for any cargo enquiry.

Atlas Air
IATA Code: 5Y
Corporate website: www.atlasair.com
Asia Pacific Office
Hong Kong
Tel: +852 3403 1822
Fax: +852 3403 1810
E-mail: gperkins@atlasair.com

Cargolux Airlines
IATA Code: CV
Corporate website: www.cargolux.com

Cargolux Airlines International S.A.
Room 341 BGS Cargo Terminal
Beijing Capital International Airport
Chao Yang District
Beijing 100621
Tel: +86 (0) 10 6459 0572
Fax: +86 (0) 10 6459 0571
E-mail: asiapacific@cargolux.com

Carogolux Airlines Hong Kong Office
Units 615-616, North Tower, Concordia
  Plaza
1 Science Museum Road
Tsimshatsui East
Kowloon
Hong Kong
Tel: +852 2736 7832
Fax: +852 2730 5137
E-mail: hkg@cargolux.com

Cargolux Airlines International S.A.
Room 3704, Bund Center
222 Yan An road (E)
Shanghai 200002
Tel: +86 (0)21 63350012/13/14/15
Fax: +86 (0)21 63350016
E-mail: sha@cargolux.com

China Cargo Airlines
IATA Code: CK
Corporate website: www.cc-air.com
Domestic Space Control (SHA)
Shanghai Pudong Int. Airport
Shanghai
Tel: +86 (0)21 62682821/ 68331005
Fax: +86 (0)21 62687141

China Postal Airlines
IATA Code: 8Y
Corporate website: www.cnpostair. com
Unit 11-14
Beijing Capital International Airport
Beijing 100037
Tel: +86 (0)10 6845 8899
Fax: +86 (0)10 6847 7555
E-mail: cpa@cnpostair.com

DHL CHINA
Corporate website: www.cn.dhl.com
DHL-Sinotrans Ltd. (Joint Venture)
45 Xinyuan St.
Chaoyang District
Beijing 100027
Tel: +86 (0)10 6466 5566

Focus Air Cargo
Corporate website: www. focusaircargo.com
750 SW 34th Street
Fort Lauderdale, Florida 33315
United States of America
Tel: +1 954 332 0545
Fax: +1 954 359 4385
E-mail: info@focusaircargo.com

Great Wall Airlines
IATA Code: IJ
Corporate website: www.gwairlines. com

Great Wall Airlines Beijing Office
Room 201-203
BGS Cargo Terminal
HuoYun Road
Capital International Airport
Beijing 100621
Tel: +86 (0)10 6459 1433
FaX: +86 (0)10 6459 1449

Great Wall Airlines Shanghai HQ
17F POS Plaza
1600 Century Avenue
Pudong New District
Shanghai 200122
Tel: +86 (0)21 6876 5256
Fax: +86 (0)21 6876 8588
E-mail: sales@gwairlines.com

Jade Cargo International
IATA Code: JI
Corporate website: www.jadecargo.
com
Jade Cargo International Company
Limited
Shenzhen Airlines Flight Operations
Building, 6/F
Baoan International Airport
518128 Shenzhen
Guangdong
Tel: +86 (0)755 2991 0267
Fax: +86 (0)755 2991 0309

KUZU Air Cargo
IATA Code: GO
Corporate website: www.kuzuairlines.
com
317 Xian Xia Lu.
Far East International Plaza B Building
Room 1901
Shanghai 200051
Tel: +86 (0)21 6235 0690
Fax: +86 (0)21 6295 1509
E-mail: info@kuxzuairlines.com

Polar Air Cargo
IATA Code: PO
Corporate website: www.
polaraircargo.com
Polar Air Cargo Beijing Office
311 BGS Cargo Terminal
Beijing Capital International Alrport
Shunyi District
Beijing 100621
Tel: +86 (0)10 6459 6489
Fax: +86 (0)10 6459 2087

Polar Air Cargo Hong Kong Office
Suite 605-607, One Citygate
20 Tat Tung Road
Tung Chung, Lantau
Hong Kong
Tel: +852 2769 6110
Fax: +852 2756 4085

Polar Air Cargo Shanghai (PVG) Office
Room 4331-4333
Jin Jiang Hotel
59 Mao Ming Rd
Luwan District

Shanghai 200020
Tel: +86 (0)21 5111 9548
Fax: +86 (0)21 5466 3063

**Sinotrans Air Transportation
Development Co., Ltd.**
Corporate website: www.sinoair.com
17-18th/F, Jiuling Building
21 Xisanhuan Beilu
Beijing 100089
Tel: +86 (0)10 6840 5628/29
Fax: +86 (0)10 6840 5628/68405629
E-mail: hq@sinoair.com

Trade Winds Cargo Airlines
Corporate website: www.tradewinds-
airlines.com
Tradewinds Airlines Inc
243A Burgess Rd
Greensboro, NC 27409
United States of America
Tel: +1 336 665 7149
Fax: +1 336 665 7145
E-mail us: info@tradewinds-airlines.com

Transglobal Airways
Corporate website: www.tgairways.
com
1st Floor
Airport Material Supplying Building,
Xiamen Gaoqi International Airport,
Xiamen
Fujian
Tel: + 86 (0)592 573 5900
Fax: + 86 (0)592 570 7080

Transmile Air Services
IATA Code: TH
Corporate website: www.transmile.
com
Transmile Hong Kong Office
Room 207, 10, Chun Ping Road,
Hong Kong International Airport, Lantau
Hong Kong
Tel: +852 2215 3718
Fax: +852 2215 3719
Email: bhgan@cenworld.com

Transmile Shenzhen Office
Room 301B
Air Cargo Terminal

Shenzhen BaoAn International Airport
Shenzhen
Tel: +86 (0)755 2777 0951
Fax: +86 (0)755 2777 0952
Email: bhgan@cenworld.com

UPS CHINA
IATA Code: 5X
Corporate website: www.ups.com
UPS Customer Service Center (Call
   Center)
People's Republic of China
Nationwide Toll Free No: 800-820-8388 /
   400-820-8388 (For cell phone users)
Overseas Dial-In: +86 (0)21 3896 5555
Fax: +86 (0)21 5831 0314

UPS Beijing
Room 1818, China World Tower 1
1, Jianguomenwai Avenue
Chaoyang District
Beijing 100004

UPS Guangzhou
Room 1801-1805/2705, Jianlibao Tower
410-412 Dongfeng Road Central
Guangzhou 510030

UPS Shanghai
23/F, China Insurance Building
166 Lujiazui East Road, Pudong District
Shanghai 200120

Volga Dnepr Airlines
IATA Code: VI
**Corporate website: www.volga-dnepr.
   com**
Volga-Dnepr China
2108 Air China Building
36 Xiaoyun Road
Chaoyang District 100027
Tel: +86 (0)10 8447 5502
Fax: +86 (0)10 8447 5501
E-mail: az.sales@vdachina.net

Corporate Executive Travel

Deer Jet Executive/Charter Services
Corporate website: www.deerjet.com
Beijing Headquarters
24-hour Customer Service Center
6F Macrolink Building
18 Daojiayuan
Dongsihuan
Chaoyang District
Beijing 100025
Tel: +86 (0)10 6506 8300
Fax: +86 (0)10 6506 8221
E-mail: sale1@deerjet.com

Heliservices
**Corporate website: www.heliservices.
   com**
The Peninsula Hong Kong
Salisbury Road
Kowloon
Hong Kong
Tel: +852 2802 0200
Fax: +852 2824 2033
Contact form: http://www.heliservices.
   com.hk/contact.php?dept=cs

MetroJet Executive Travel
Hong Kong Aviation Group
Corporate website: www.metrojet.com
Suite 608
One Citygate
20 Tat Tung Road
Tung Chung
Hong Kong
Tel: +852 2525 4747
Fax: +852 2525 4342

Useful Websites and Addresses for Expats in China

www.chinatoday.com – General Information about China

www.made-in-china.com – A decent website for those in the trade business who want to snatch that golden bargain for bulk buying!

http://english.peopledaily.com.cn/ – China People's Daily online newspaper

www.gov.cn – The Chinese Central Government Web Portal

www.china.org.cn – China's official gateway to news and information.

www.elong.net – Travel website

www.ctrip.com – Travel website

www.alibaba.com – Trade directory for import/export of goods fro China

www.enjoychina.net – News and Discussion portal for Chinese and expats.

www.asiaexpat.com – Expat website for major cities in Asia

www.chinamaze.com – Discussion website for expats in China

www.yp.com.cn/english – Mainland China Yellow Pages Website

www.britishexpat.com – Expat website for Brits around the world

www.fmprc.gov.cn/eng – Ministry of Foreign Affairs of the People's Republic of China

www.chinaview.cn – Xinhua News Agency- Yhe official news agency in China

www.xianzai.com – Website for expats with links to major cities in China

www.chinaeconomicreview.com – Website for up-to-date economic information on China

www.travelchinaguide.com – Travel website in China

www.chinats.com – China Travel Service website

Ministry of Education for the People's Republic of China
37 Damucang Hutong
Xidan
Beijing 100816
Tel: +86 (0)10 6609 6114
Website: www.moe.edu.cn/english/index.htm

The Office of Chinese Language Council International
17th Floor
Fangyuan Mansion
B56
Zhongguancun South Street
Beijing 100044
Tel: +86 (0)10 88026121
E-mail: zonghe@hanban.edu.cn
Website: http://english.hanban.edu.cn

ACKNOWLEDGMENTS

With thanks to the following for their great support and advice:

Staff members at the British Embassy in Beijing
Staff members of the British Consulate-General in Guangzhou
Staff members at the European Chambers of Commerce, Beijing
Staff members at the American Consulate General in Shanghai
Staff members at the Chinese Embassy in London, UK
Staff members at the Canadian Embassy in Beijing
Staff members at the American Embassy in Beijing
Staff members at the British Chamber of Commerce in Guangzhou
Mr James A.C. Sinclair – Senior Consultant at Interchina Consulting in Shanghai
Mr. Richard Barnard – Dulwich College Management, Shanghai, China
Mr. Roger Houghton, Hong Kong
Mr. Ben Chan, London
Mr. Chen Qiang, Loughborough, UK
Mr. Qiao Chang, Shanghai, China
Ms. Lingjia "Sabrina" Ying, Loughborough, UK

INDEX

ABOUT THE AUTHOR

Navjot Singh is a British-Indian who relocated to Hong Kong and mainland China in 2002, where he has since had the privilege of living and working. Navjot has had first-hand experience of witnessing the benefits and challenges of being an expatriate in China. Navjot has also taught English in the cities of Shenzhen, Beijing, and Guangzhou.

Navjot was educated at Dulwich College (UK) and Loughborough University (UK). Navjot enjoys sharing his time between Hong Kong, Guangzhou (China), and London.

"I would like to dedicate this book to all my friends, with whom I shared many great and unforgettable memories during my time in China. Life is a wonderful and amazing gift from God, so enjoy every moment of it. Navjot."

Breinigsville, PA USA
01 February 2010
231727BV00003B/44/P